HOCKEY TOWNS

Stories of Small Town Hockey in Canada

BILL BOYD

Seal Books

Seal Books and colophon are trademarks
of Random House of Canada Limited.

HOCKEY TOWNS

Seal Books/published by arrangement with Doubleday Canada

Doubleday Canada hardcover edition published 1998

Doubleday Canada trade paperback edition published 1999
Seal Books edition published December 2000

ISBN 0-7704-2859-2

Seal Books are published by Doubleday Canada,
a division of Random House of Canada Limited.
"Seal Books" and the portrayal of a seal, are the property
of Random House of Canada Limited.

Cover photograph courtesy Comstock © Bill Wittman
Cover design by Susan Thomas/Digital Zone

Visit Random House of Canada Limited's website:
www.randomhouse.ca

PRINTED AND BOUND IN CANADA

TRANS 10 9 8 7 6 5 4 3 2 1

For my children,
Adam and Pippa,

and with thanks to friends
Brian Vallée, Terry Clark
and Tony Hillman.

I would like to acknowledge the encouragement and help of Don Sedgwick, formerly of Doubleday Canada, and Kathryn Exner, associate editor at Doubleday.

Contents

Preface

I MET GEORGE SAYLISS playing oldtimers hockey in Peterborough, Ontario. He is sixty-six, was born in Montreal, grew up in Toronto, and played junior hockey with the Toronto Marlboros and in Stratford. He belonged to the New York Rangers and went to two Ranger camps at Saranac Lake, N.Y. Following junior he played for the Renfrew Millionaires in a league with Thurso, Hull, and Pembroke that was dotted with ex-NHLers, including Johnny Quilty, who had won a Calder Trophy in Montreal.

Later, Sayliss was an assistant captain of the East York (Toronto) Lyndhursts. They were a Senior B team sponsored by a car dealership, Lyndhurst Motors, and played in a league with Markham, Stouffville, and some other places around Toronto. In 1954 the Lyndhursts won Canadian hockey immortality when the Soviet Union — "the Russians" — beat them in Stockholm at the world championships. Until then, apart from being upset at the 1936 Olympics by Britain (a team liberally salted with Canadians), Canada had never lost abroad. "We went over on the *Queen Mary* and came back on something called the *Liberty*," Sayliss says. "It was a helluva long trip home."

George Sayliss is a big man with a broad face, a crew cut, and a chipped front tooth. He has a jumbled scrapbook with the reports of that 1954 world championship. He points out that in the six games before meeting the Soviet Union, the Lyndhursts had outscored their opponents 57–5 and had handily beaten Sweden, whom the Soviet Union could only tie. "We were really up for the game, but we just couldn't do anything right," he says. "A Swedish kid wanted to buy my second pair of skates. He'd ask me every day. Finally, after we'd lost, I said to the woman at the hotel desk that if a kid came by looking for me, to send him to my room. The kid showed up and I gave him the skates, a good pair of Tacks; gave them to him, that's how bad I felt."

That losing game was on a Sunday, March 7. It was grey and overcast in Ottawa. I was returning home from an afternoon's skiing with friends in the Gatineau Hills when we heard about it on the car radio. We were surprised, but we saw it as a fluke, something that would soon be remedied — and it was, the next year, by the Penticton Vees. But after that Canada began to lose more than it won.

In the fall of 1972, more than eighteen years after the Lyndhursts' loss, I was back in Ottawa. I was directing a scene for a CBC-TV documentary on the excitement being generated by the final game, being played in Moscow, of the series between the Soviet Union and the NHL's best. We were filming several members of the Soviet embassy staff around a TV set. I don't know what these staffers felt, but for me they gave new meaning to Soviet stoicism: they didn't show a thing, no matter who scored, even when Paul Henderson won it for Canada with his late goal. Maybe they'd been told that to react would be unseemly, un-Soviet — win, lose, or draw. Then again, maybe they weren't even hockey fans and didn't give a damn but had been ordered to appear as a goodwill gesture, in spite of the Cold War. Or maybe they felt that because of the closeness of the series, which Canada was expected to win easily, it was a Soviet victory of sorts, regardless of who won that last game. Anyway, they weren't saying.

When I met Sayliss in the autumn of 1996, I hadn't covered any hockey for more than thirty years, since the 1964 Olympics in Innsbruck. (That was the first year of Father David Bauer's national teams, and Canada finished fourth.) However, thinking about the Lyndhursts and the changes in hockey since then, I became curious about whether hockey, away from the big cities, is as important as it was when I was young. So I hit the road, from Glace Bay, Nova Scotia, to Powell River, British Columbia.

This is not a serious study. It's not meant to be a definitive account of small town hockey. There are all kinds of great hockey towns I didn't get to. But I wasn't looking for the town that has produced the most players or the best players or won the most championships. And I'm not interested in hockey as a metaphor for Canadian life or whether it's our wintry religion or a frozen chunk of our soul. I'll leave that to the poets and sociologists. I just wanted to go to a few towns, see a few games, and talk with some players and ex-players and coaches and scouts and owners and fans. And I did, scores of them, gracious, generous, amusing, forthright people who have been shaped by hockey, or have helped to shape it, or simply love it — or used to. None of what follows is scientific, or probably important, but doing it was great fun.

Lakefield, Ontario
September 1998

I

On the Road to Peterborough

December 1996

IT'S GETTING ON FOR ELEVEN O'CLOCK on a moonless Saturday night. A hundred miles east of Toronto, snow as hard as gravel is sweeping in from Lake Ontario, over bleak and frozen farmland. On the Trans-Canada Highway, Don Barrie pulls out to pass a tractor-trailer, but the blowing snow and the slush thrown up from the truck's huge tires force him to drop back.

"Just like tonight's game, we're not going anywhere," he says. "The guys I went to see didn't show me anything."

But in spite of the poor weather, and the poor game, Barrie seems surprisingly relaxed. That's because he's used to both. He drives a lot in winter and long ago lost count of the hockey games he's seen — the good and the bad. He fiddles with the radio, trying to get a Buffalo station through the static. He wants to hear how the Buffalo Sabres did. "I can usually pick up WGR," he says. He turns the radio off, saying that the reception will be better in a while.

For an instant there's a break in the snow. The highway glistens like a black silk ribbon on a white sheet. Barrie pulls out again. He gets by the truck. A few miles along, at Port Hope, he turns north onto Highway 28. As Lake Ontario falls behind, the wind drops and the snow eases off. There's a sliver of a moon now, and not much traffic. Barrie switches the radio back on and he's right, the reception is clearer. After a few minutes he learns that the Sabres not only won, they got five goals. "That's god," he says. "We haven't been scoring much." He's pleased because when the Sabres do a good job, it's a sign that he's doing one, too. He's one of their chief scouts.

From October to May, Don Barrie and dozens of other men search hockey arenas from Summerside, on Prince Edward Island, to Prince George, in northern British Columbia, as well as in the United States and Europe, trying to spot that youngster who could become the next Ray Bourque or Wayne Gretzky or Jaromir Jagr. But, until that one comes along, they'd be thrilled with another Marty McSorley or Vincent Damphousse or Adam Graves.

Barrie is fifty-seven. His first game was lacrosse. He played and coached it professionally and recently was elected to the Canadian Lacrosse Hall of Fame. In hockey, he didn't even reach Junior B. "But I played a lot and I went to every game I could, and I made a study of them, and I read all the hockey books." He joined the Sabres after one of their executives heard him analysing junior games on radio. He began to scout full-time when he retired from teaching high school two years ago.

Tonight he's on his way home to Peterborough from an Ontario Hockey League game in Belleville where the Bulls played the Sault Ste. Marie

Greyhounds. The Soo meant Joe Thornton, the OHL's reigning superstar. Unfortunately, Thornton, suffering from a bad leg, hardly played at all. "He's already been drafted by Boston," Barrie says. "But it was too bad. I still like seeing him play." Yesterday afternoon Barrie was at a tournament in Aurora, forty minutes north of Toronto, and last night he was at a game in Hamilton. Tomorrow he goes to Oshawa and he'll spend next week in Quebec. After that he'll stay home for a couple of days, then he will be on the road again.

"That's why when you're right about a kid, when he makes it, you feel so good. It makes up for all the crap you got to go through sometimes," Barrie says.

Belleville's Daniel Cleary, a Newfoundlander, and highly thought of, disappointed Barrie and the other scouts tonight. "They say he came to camp fat and out of shape," Barrie says, "and he still shows it and we're more than two months into the season. I can't understand a kid doing that. I wonder if they realize it's such a fine line between making the NHL and not. You won't always have your best game, but you've got to work hard out there, work hard every night. If not, you'll spend your career, if you have one at all, in the minors."

Nikos Tselios, an American, is a defenceman with Belleville. He's a cousin of NHL defenceman Chris Chelios. (Chris's family smoothed out the spelling of their name.) "He's a wide-track skater, skates with his legs well apart," Barrie says. "This makes him steady, but it also means he doesn't have much jump if he has to get quickly into the play." He points out that a year ago Tselios was playing midget in Chicago and probably had only ten tough games all season. Now he's playing eighty-plus games, half of them on Belleville's Olympic-sized rink. "I'll bet that's a real attention-getter for him," Barrie says.

Don Barrie notes that one of the problems in assessing talent is that on the whole, the kids are all so good. They each offer something; and it doesn't end when a player is drafted. He may still have two years of junior, so the pro scouts continue to watch him to see if he's worth signing. "But even if the kid doesn't play a position we need filled, we'll take him if he's the best still available. There's no point passing up a front-line forward for a barely adequate defenceman. We can always make a good trade if we have to."

Passing through the farming hamlet of Fraserville, in the light from a barn window, a man can be seen clearing snow from a small outdoor rink. "Almost home," Barrie says, and then begins to talk about two of his favourites, ex-Peterborough Petes Jamie Langenbrunner, with the Dallas Stars this season, and Mike Ricci, who has played for four NHL teams, including the Colorado Avalanche when they won the Stanley Cup in 1996. "All the way through junior, Ricci gave it all he had. And he still does. It shows every time you see him play," Barrie says. Then he tells a story of Ricci risking injury by crashing into his own net to save a goal. "Maybe not the smartest play in the world," Barrie says, "but it's the only way he can play: all out."

Before he retired from teaching, Barrie, who was the Petes academic counsellor, got to know Ricci well at Thomas A. Stewart Secondary School. "I think I take more than a scout's interest in him," he says. "The same with Jamie and also Rob Ray. Robbie always plays hard. He doesn't score much, but he'll take on anyone in the league. There's eight or ten teams that would take him in a minute. He's a great kid."

Barrie pulls into his driveway. It's stopped snowing and the stars are out. He gets out of his car, stretches and looks around. "You know," he says, "if you like hockey, I can't imagine living anywhere else."

About seventy thousand people live in Peterborough. It's on the Otonabee River, part of the Trent-Severn waterway, eighty miles northeast of Toronto. Beyond its housing subdivisions, and its factory belt with its doughnut shops and car lots and carpet outlets, are the rolling, rock-strewn fields of livestock farms, dotted with thick groves of maple and birch and cedar and criss-crossed by wooden snake fences. Thirty miles to the south is Lake Ontario. Northwards are the Kawartha Lakes and their summer cottages.

The city sprang from rough-and-tumble pioneering communities of Scots, Irish, and English where, according to temperance advocates, there were more places selling rum at twenty-five cents a gallon than there were private homes. By the mid-nineteenth century things had quieted down and Peterborough was getting rich shipping lumber across Lake Ontario to New York state. The railway linked the town to Toronto and Ottawa. The first bank — a branch of the Bank of Montreal — opened in 1843. There were grist mills and tanneries, and then came newspapers and libraries and fine homes with lawns and English gardens, and soon sherry was outselling rum. Tennis and cricket were the games of summer; in winter, on ponds and creeks, there was skating and curling.

Peterborough is still a formidable redbrick city, its downtown marked by its old clock tower. It has wide, tree-lined streets and graceful parks and big churches. There's a symphony orchestra, an active live theatre, and an art gallery. There are also a few cracks: Canadian General Electric and Quaker Oats have cut their workforces drastically; Westclox, the clock maker, has about twenty workers now, down from nearly five hundred; and the Peterborough Canoe Company, which once made the world's best wooden canoes, has since sunk under aluminum and fibre glass. But smaller manufacturers have taken up some of the slack. Trent University opened in the '60s, and the region's quiet conservatism is pulling in a lot of retirees.

True to the city's Victorian roots, City Hall flies the Union Jack. (It was taken down a couple of years ago, but there was such a fuss it was immediately hoisted back up.) And a huge portrait of the Queen hangs at the Memorial Centre. That's the home of rock concerts, wrestling, tractor pulls, and lacrosse, which is another Peterborough passion. But nothing rivals the Peterborough Petes, one of the premier franchises in major junior hockey.

Legend has it that hockey was first played by British soldiers garrisoned at Kingston. If so, it didn't take long to move up the Trent Valley. By 1870 Peterborough had its first arena. It was natural ice and it doubled as a curling rink. In 1891 an indoor arena solely for hockey was built and three years later Peterborough won its first hockey championship, thrashing a Toronto team called the Granites 14–0 in what was called the Ontario Hockey Association Junior Series.

As Peterborough's working-class base grew, so did team sports. For forty years, senior and intermediate hockey created exciting rivalries between Peterborough, Kingston, Belleville, and Oshawa. But by the 1970s, people were spending winter evenings watching television instead of sitting in cold rinks. The popularity of these leagues waned and the players went off to minor professional leagues in the United States and other parts of Canada.

Art Heal, who is now eighty, played on two intermediate championship teams in Peterborough. The first, in 1939, was called the Petes. The other was put together during the Second World War by the army training centre in Peterborough, although Heal wasn't in the army because he was nearly blind in one eye. "One year we each got a pocket watch and another year we got a fifty-dollar war bond. You got any idea what fifty dollars was in 1940? A helluva lot of money."

In the living room of his bungalow just north of Peterborough, from where he can see snowmobiles zooming about on Chemong Lake, he leafs through a scrapbook four inches thick with yellowed newspaper clippings. "This is the first time I've had this out in years," he says. "It took me a while to find it." He reads aloud that more than five hundred Peterborough fans chartered a train to follow their team to Hamilton. He looks up. "Yeah, it was really something. And here, we'd always fill the old Brock Street arena, maybe thirteen or fourteen hundred. If we made the Ontario playoffs in Maple Leaf Gardens we'd draw three or four thousand."

Heal says that he played at 130 pounds. "I don't think there was a hockey player in Ontario got knocked on his ass as much as I did, but I'd bounce right back up. My nickname was 'Rubber.' We played all over the place." He laughs. "Nothing like standing in a shower after a game in St. Catharines at eleven at night knowing you had to be at work at GE in the morning."

Heal has lost his hair, but he looks in good shape and he still weighs 130 pounds. He laughs, and says,

"I remember one night in Belleville. It was hot and the sweat was running into my eyes, really stinging them. The referee blows his whistle and points at me and I yelled, 'What the hell am I getting a penalty for?' And he said, 'You're not. You're bleeding to death.' It turns out I'd been clipped in the head and it was blood, not sweat. I got stitched up and played the rest of the game."

Heal says that early in the war he played against a team from the Royal Canadian Air Force base at nearby Trenton. "Nearly all those fellows were aircrew and they went overseas shortly afterwards," he says. "I used to wonder how many made it back."

He puts the scrapbook aside. "My last game was in 1947 when we lost an intermediate final. I took off my equipment, threw my hoc-key underwear into the corner of the dressing room, and said, that's it, and it was. I wanted to get married and settle down. Hockey was fun, and Peterborough was the best place to play, but I don't reminisce much. Those days were over a long time ago."

The current Peterborough Petes were born in 1956, when NHL teams had extensive farm systems, and belonged to the Montreal Canadiens. Their first coach was an ex-Canadien, Calum "Baldy" MacKay. (Among his successors have been Scotty Bowman, Mike Keenan, and Roger Neilson.) The Petes' first game was before 5,400 people at Maple Leaf Gardens — the Memorial Centre wasn't ready — and the Toronto Marlboros beat them 4–1.

By 1996 the Petes had been in the league uninterruptedly longer than any other team. Bob Gainey, Steve Larmer, and Cory Stillman are all Peterborough natives. Mickey and Dick Redmond were born in Kirkland Lake but they grew up in

Peterborough. Their father, Ed, moved down to play senior hockey in the early '50s. Bill and Barclay Plager, two more former Petes, were also born in Kirkland Lake. Among other NHLers who came to town to play for the Petes are Steve Yzerman, Ron Tugnutt, Craig Ramsay and Chris Pronger. In all, nearly two hundred former Petes have either played in the NHL or at least been drafted. That's more than from any other junior team, but it still works out to an average of about only four players a season over the Petes' first forty years, an indication of just how hard it is to crack the NHL, even from a first-rate franchise. The Petes won the Memorial Cup in 1979 and have twice been runners-up. They have the most playoff appearances — seven — since the round-robin system began in 1972.

In his office at the Memorial Centre, Jeff Twohey, the Petes general manager, is getting ready to go on one of his rare road trips with the team. Because of the annual Christmas tree festival there's no ice for a week, so the Petes will be away for three games. "I don't go usually because there's too much to do here," he says. "But this is a long one so I like to be along."

Twohey, sitting behind his desk in his shirtsleeves, is thirty-six, a lean, dark-haired, serious man with heavy glasses who's living his dream. He grew up in Lindsay, twenty-five miles west of Peterborough. He played a bit of hockey but had to quit because of a concussion. So, while he was still in high school, he wrote to every Junior B team in Ontario, offering to scout. Aurora was the only team that replied so, at age fifteen, he went to work for them, unpaid. Later, studying commerce at Laurentian University in Sudbury, he began to scout the north, still unpaid, for the Petes.

"I got my degree," he says, "so I guess I could be working for Procter and Gamble or a bank or whatever, but hockey is all I've ever wanted."

When Dick Todd became the Petes coach and asked Twohey if he wanted to be team trainer, Twohey jumped at the chance. "I wasn't even sure what a trainer did," he says. One thing he had to learn in a hurry was how to sharpen skates. "I've done everything here from washing underwear to selling ads." And he still scouts: "Last Sunday I drove to Cornwall for an afternoon game and then to Nepean, near Ottawa, for a night game," he says. "More than 550 miles in one day."

While NHL scouts check out the Petes and the other junior teams, the juniors are checking out midget players (aged sixteen and under) and lower levels of junior for their annual draft. One criticism of the system is that it can be too hard on youngsters, often uprooting them from home and school, sending them to the care of strangers.

"We look after our boys really well," Twohey says. "Look, I've two daughters of my own. I wouldn't want my young players having a bad time any more than I would my own family." Today he's angry over the news that two junior coaches had sexually molested teenage players, calling the coaches "rotten sons of bitches." Swivelling around in his chair, he stops suddenly and says, "But Christ, they haven't shut down the Scout movement, or the priesthood. And they've sure as hell had their share of perverts."

He turns back to his desk and holds up a three-inch file of papers. "These are scouting reports I haven't looked at yet." Next he holds up a paper with coloured graphs. "I try to track as many players as I can," he explains. The Petes have five scouts, four in Ontario and one in P.E.I. "We don't bring in

Americans' kids," he says, "because we'd have to pay for them to go to school here — seven to nine thousand dollars, and we can't afford it. We have one German kid and a Russian but they're through school. We're a small market, just like the old Winnipeg Jets. We're stable, but we have to find ways of staying stable."

He mentions the new and bigger arenas in Barrie and Detroit that have substantially more seats than Peterborough's 3,900, as well as bigger populations to draw from.

"But to me junior hockey *is* small town," he says. "That's why Ottawa got me so goddamn mad last year when we both bid for the Memorial Cup and they kept putting us down, making fun of us, saying our rink was too small. So what if our rink is smaller than theirs? That doesn't mean hockey is more important to them than it is to us."

"BJ" Ketcheson joined the Peterborough Petes as a sixteen-year-old last fall. He's from Napanee, just east along the Trans-Canada between Peterborough and Kingston. It's not far away, but he's homesick at times, even though the family he boards with treats him like a son. He's a defenceman, six foot four, and 185 pounds, but stripped of his helmet and equipment, he looks like any gangly teenage schoolboy. He's in the rec room, where he lives, with Kevin Bolibruck, a Petes veteran, who also lives there. The Maple Leafs and the Pittsburgh Penguins are playing silently on TV; the volume is turned way down. Ketcheson says that he doesn't like hockey on TV. "It's kind of boring," he says. "I hardly ever watch it." He sounds almost ashamed to admit it.

Ketcheson is in grade eleven and must work hard at school because of all the games and travel. And after school each day there's practice. He's a good skater, "but Kevin pointed out that I was turning into my check awkwardly so I'm working on that."

The Petes' program calls Bolibruck "the heart and soul of the team." He's a fourth-round pick of the Ottawa Senators and has taken the younger Ketcheson under his wing. When Bolibruck isn't playing, he's at Trent University. When he is playing, he patterns himself after Sylvain Lefebvre, the stay-at-home defenceman who's played with Montreal, Toronto, and Colorado. "Anyone can improve if they work hard," Bolibruck says. "And you better, because you need every edge you can get if you're going to make the next level." He is one of the Petes' tough guys. Besides that, his strengths, according to him, are "a good sense of the game. I know what's going on."

Bolibruck and Ketcheson say they haven't given much thought to a future that doesn't include the NHL. But for players who don't turn pro, there's major junior hockey's scholarship program. It pays any player who doesn't turn pro three thousand dollars for each year he was with the Petes if he chooses to go to university. By the fall of 1996 the Petes had paid out around eighty thousand dollars.

2

Peterborough, Ontario

January–February 1997

RON KEAST GREW UP IN South Porcupine, in northern Ontario. As a young teenager he was on a team there with Dean Prentice, who later spent twenty-two years in the NHL, and Murray Costello, who was there for four. Keast moved to Peterborough in 1962. He says that there was a time when he'd spend nearly every winter evening at a rink, but now his shift has changed at Quaker Oats so he doesn't get out as much. "My sons played hockey," Keast says. "One of them went to university in the states, Brown, but he played lacrosse there, not hockey."

Keast is walking, head down against the blowing snow, across the parking lot of the new Evinrude Centre. It's a bright, clean, shiny building with wide corridors and spotless concession stands. Debate over whether Peterborough needed another hockey arena — it already had four indoor surfaces — lasted a year. Quite a few people figured that too much money was already being spent on sports, particularly hockey. And even Herb Warr, a member of the Peterborough Petes executive, says he'd rather have seen a multi-purpose facility. But hockey and skating won out and in the fall of 1996 the arena, with two ice surfaces, opened. It's home to the Junior A Trentway-Wagar Bees (a level down from the Petes), who wear the maroon and white of the Petes and most other Peterborough teams. One of their coaches is Bill Plager, back home after parts of nine seasons in the NHL.

The Bees are on a hot streak. They've won ten and tied one of their last eleven games. Among the other teams in the league are Orillia, Cobourg and Newmarket. The Lindsay Muskies are in town tonight and six hundred or so fans are sitting and standing. The Bees president is "Bubs" McCarthy. He's a short, peppy man in his fifties who has been involved in hockey and baseball in Peterborough all his life. He's leaning against the glass at ice level behind the Bees goal, looking around. He likes what he sees. "We played in the Memorial Centre last year. In there this crowd would be lost. Here they pack the place," he says. "More important, they've all paid, at least I figure 90 percent have. Hell, it's so easy to get in a side door at the Memorial Centre that when we played there probably less than half the crowd paid."

It's a friendly crowd — youngsters, who've been practising at the adjacent rink, teenage boys and girls, parents and grandparents. One man has his three-month-old granddaughter bundled up in a carry cot. "Her mother is working and her father's playing in an oldtimers game, so I brought her along," he says. "She'll sleep through anything."

McCarthy says the Bees' budget runs at $52,000–$55,000. It comes from the gate and raffles and bingos and volunteer fundraising. The bus company Trentway-Wagar provides transportation, and there are individual sponsorships.

"Three hundred dollars gets a company's name on the home-game sweater and five hundred for home and away," McCarthy says. Just then, the kid wearing the sweater of "Jim's Pizzeria" scores. "McIntyre's Auto-Wreckers" draws an assist. "Hell of a nice goal," McCarthy says, then returns to the issue of money. "We still have four or five sweaters with nothing on them. That's more than a grand."

Talks turns to Peterborough's Atom tournament beginning the coming weekend, one of the biggest hockey tournaments in North America. More than 120 teams are entered, so lots of volunteers are needed. A man says that two teenagers just told him they would help out but insisted that they'd only work certain hours. "I told them to hell with it, to bugger off," the man says. "If they want the hours on their record then they work what we need, not what they want. Jesus, you'd think they were doing me a favour!" He walks away shaking his head.

McCarthy explains that the man was referring to kids ordered by the court to do community service. "He's right. The kids don't call the hours, we do. It's not a holiday." This time he laughs. "The court has asked me over the years and I use them sometimes at tournaments I run. Mostly they're not bad kids. Just a little wild, maybe. Mind you, I don't let them too close to the money."

Another man comes and stands by McCarthy. He looks down the rink to where there's a picture of the Queen. "How come the Queen is here, too?" he asks.

"I don't know," McCarthy replies, without looking away from the game. "We just play here, we don't own it."

"Jesus," the man says, "and there's the big one at the Memorial Centre." He walks away mumbling, "Too many goddamn Brits."

• • •

It's about seven o'clock on a wet, slushy Thursday evening a couple of weeks later and the Memorial Centre is beginning to fill up. The Belleville Bulls are in town. The big portrait of the Queen hangs high up on the south wall, flanked by Canada's Maple Leaf and the Union Jack. The Major George Bennett chapter of the I.O.D.E. commissioned it. "We used to be the Imperial Order of the Daughters of the Empire but it has been officially shortened to I.O.D.E.," Ruth Standish explains. Major Bennett, she says, was the first area man to be killed in the First World War. The portrait was done in the early 1970s by David Bierk, who happens to be the father of the Petes' goalie, and the I.O.D.E. paid him $2,500. Standish says that the I.O.D.E., although much smaller than it was before the decline of the British Empire, still does good works and has "put up a lot of pictures of the Queen around the city." She says that because the Memorial Centre commemorates the war dead, and because many Canadians fought under the Union Jack, it seemed appropriate to put up a picture of the monarch.

Ironically, Bierk was an American citizen when he did the painting. He'd come to Peterborough from the United States a couple of years before to teach high school. "It was more than twenty years ago," he says. "I was just getting started and I needed the money, so it was great, even if it was sort of odd to be asked to paint the Queen."

Bierk's son, Zac, joined the Petes in 1993 and has signed with the Tampa Bay Lightning. He says that at a Memorial Cup game in the spring of 1996, he'd stood looking up at the picture his father painted, while his brother, Sebastian Bach, of the New York-based heavy metal group Skid Row, sang O Canada.

"I felt really proud," he says. "All three of us there, giving something."

In the dressing room that's turned over to scouts and the media for Petes games, a young woman is serving coffee, soup, and bagels. Eight or ten scouts sit in ones and twos on the benches that run around the room, including ex-Red Wing defenceman Thommie Bergman, a Swede, who works for Anaheim, and Dennis Patterson, a Peterborough native, who scouts for the Philadelphia Flyers.

Patterson used to work out of Peterborough, but the Flyers wanted him closer to the action. They looked at a map and decided on Detroit. "I can see a game every night," he says. "NHL, international league, junior, U.S. college. I see around 180 games a year either around there or on the road."

Nick Beverley, former Toronto Maple Leaf general manager and, briefly, interim coach, is sitting by himself, checking his notebook in sober resignation. The Leafs will likely finish near or at the bottom of the league this year. Normally that would mean a high draft pick. But they've traded away their first two so unless they get something back in another trade, they won't pick until the third round. By then, the best players will have long gone.

Don Barrie says that there's a camaraderie between scouts because they see so much of each other. "Everyone is watching out for what they want but our wants are often different. We don't pump each other, but we don't keep secrets. For example, if a number of us want to see a particular guy say tomorrow night, and another scout finds out that he's not playing because he's hurt, he'll tell us. We spend enough time on the road and in rinks that we don't need any wasted trips."

Gary Dalliday, the sports director for CHEX-TV,

Peterborough's television station, comes into the room. He and his son broadcast the games on the CHEX-owned KRUZ radio. Dalliday's humour softens his pugnacious Irish face. He stands in an alcove off the room, out of sight of the door, and lights a cigarette. Smoking is banned in the arena. "Hey, Gary," someone calls, "Scotty phoned yet?"

"Could be any day now," Dalliday answers. He tries to wave away a cloud of smoke.

Scotty Bowman coached the 1960–61 Petes — a team that included the late Barclay Plager, Bryan Watson, and Claude Larose, all three who went on to have long NHL careers. Dalliday was on that team for two games before Bowman sent him down to Junior B in St. Thomas. "He told me not to worry, that he'd be bringing me back up, that he'd phone me," Dalliday says. "I'm still waiting. Maybe he hasn't got my new number."

Before the game Cameron Mann, the Petes' best player and the property of the Boston Bruins, is to be honoured for being on Canada's junior team which has just won the world championship in Switzerland. He's to pose at centre ice with his Team Canada sweater; but there's no sweater. The man in charge has forgotten it in his office.

A handful of fans begin to shout, "Crispy, Crispy," and soon the shouting has spread to a whole section. "Crispy" is Jeff Crisp, in charge of marketing. He runs off to get the sweater. Crisp is twenty-five, stocky, with reddish blond hair, like his father, Terry, ex-player and former coach of the Tampa Bay Lightning and Calgary Flames. Jeff has been with the Petes since graduating from the University of Calgary two years ago. He reappears with the sweater. The crowd cheers, he waves, and the pictures are taken.

• • •

For game nights Jeff Twohey wears a white shirt, dark tie, navy blue blazer, and grey flannels. As he moves up through the stands to his plywood box over centre ice, beside a huge banner proclaiming that Peterborough is "The Major Junior Hockey Capital of the World", he recognizes a scout. "Jesus Christ, every time you're here we stink the joint out," he says shaking his hand.

A PA announcement says that the referee comes from Minnesota. The crowd boos. "That's one of the problems," Twohey says. "The NHL dumps its trainee refs on us and they don't know the kids or the league."

During the singing of O *Canada* tonight, Mike Davies, who covers the Petes for the Peterborough *Examiner*, points out that most of the men not only are standing straight, they've taken off their caps and hats, which is rare these days, and many are turned towards the flags and David Bierk's picture of the Queen. "It's usually like that," Davies says. "Peterborough is a conservative city and this is the 'Memorial' Centre, and 'Memorial' means something here." Years ago, when the *Examiner* was published by the novelist, playwright, and wit Robertson Davies (no relation to Mike), it was seen as one of the best small newspapers in Canada. The Davies family sold it to the Thomson group; it's now owned by Conrad Black.

Sitting together on the aisle in the unreserved seats at the north end of the Memorial Centre, opposite the Queen, high up so they can see the whole ice surface, are two former NHL goalies, Charlie Hodge and Les Binkley. Hodge spent most of his career with the Canadiens; Binkley played for Pittsburgh. They're both scouting for Pittsburgh, doing what's called a "crossover." "It's like going to another doctor for a second opinion," Hodge says. "We check out each other's picks."

A passerby, heading up the stairs, says to Hodge, "Considering you two guys and Johnston, isn't Pittsburgh a little top-heavy with goalies?" He's referring to Eddie Johnston, the Penguins coach, who was also a goalie. Hodge looks up from his note book and grins. "Only way we can have an intelligent conversation," he says. In a dark overcoat, sports jacket, white shirt and tie, Hodge sticks out among the parkas, windbreakers and duffel coats. He comes from Lachine, Quebec, but now lives in B.C. Grey-haired and round, he's sixty-three, and except for a couple of years selling real estate he's been in hockey full-time since he began in junior at fifteen. "Getting on for fifty years," he says.

"We all look for the standard things: size, speed, puck-handling, and heart," he says of scouting. "It goes in cycles. This looks like a good year for Ontario juniors." His dream, "hell, probably every scout's dream," is to find another Dickie Moore. Moore was a long-time teammate of his in Montreal. "He could do everything," Hodge says, "and he was tough as hell." Hodge has a reputation for being a thorough note-taker and he's still writing up a Petes goal when Belleville scores. He turns to Binkley. "Goddamnit, I missed that."

"That's okay," Binkley says. "The goalie missed it, too."

Jeff Twohey watches games standing up. He says he's too hyper to sit. He points to a large dent in the plywood wall of his box. "I put my fist through there during the Memorial Cup. We were playing Granby. Anyway, we scored the first goal and it was disallowed. You know how important the first goal is."

Robert Francz, a big forward from Germany,

plays the point on Peterborough power plays because of his heavy shot. During a Belleville penalty he moves well in off the blue line and lets go a slapshot. The puck flies over the net. "That kid has all the skills but one," Twohey says dryly. "He can't score."

Shawn Thornton, who leads the team in penalties, but can also score a bit, gets the Petes' first goal. He's back in the lineup after sitting out a couple of games. A fight in a game with the Oshawa Generals left his nose broken and his face so swollen that he couldn't see properly. Away from the rink he's taking a computer course at Sir Sandford Fleming, the local community college. He's a nice-looking, quiet, polite young man, not unlike many hockey tough guys. The Colorado Avalanche drafted him and he was at their camp in the fall. He says his future depends on this year. That's the main reason he hated being hurt.

Up in the stands, a scowling eldery man, neatly dressed in a dark overcoat and a tweed cap, is pacing behind the last row of seats. He yells, "Jesus, get with it." He stamps his feet and grits his teeth. "Get organized, for Christ's sake." His name is Bob Huffman. He grew up in Napanee, the hometown of the Petes' young defenceman Ketcheson. "I played ball with his grandfather," he says, "but I always liked hockey best. I played a lot, damn nearly lived at the rink, but I was too small to get beyond intermediate." He stands about five foot six. "Jesus Christ, thank God for Bierk," he says, not taking his eyes from the game. He's disgusted with the way the Petes are playing in the third period. "They get their lead and they just sit back, disorganized as hell." He's particularly upset by the Petes' defence. "They're not completing enough passes," he says. "Even when there's no one on top of them, no one bothering them, they're missing their goddamn passes. They got to start carrying the puck out of their own end, thinking a bit. There's no point just firing it out if the other team is going to get it and send it right back in."

The coach, Brian Drumm, bothers him. "He's not playing the rookies. Christ, where are they going to learn? Practice isn't playing. They've got to play more. He depends too much on the veterans, and they get tired."

Huffman says that he sees every home game and occasionally goes on the road. Including playoffs, that can mean fifty games a year. He says he gets so excited that at times he's almost sick to his stomach. "Hockey is our game, Canada's game. It's the best goddamn game in the world," he says. He pauses, then he adds, without the hint of a smile, "I guess you can see that I take it very seriously."

Jason MacMillan, who should be drafted fairly high, scores near the midway mark of the third period and the Petes win 3–2. "I'm happy we won," Twohey says, "but I'm never satisfied."

After the game Mike Davies and a reporter from CHEX-TV wait in the hallway for one of the Belleville players, Ryan Ready, before he boards the team bus for the drive home. "We usually try to get something from him because he's from Peterborough," Davies says. "And we're lucky tonight because he scored a goal."

Ryan Ready finally appears. His hair is wet from the shower. His face is pale and he looks tired. He sets himself in front of the TV camera. Then he swears softly, patting his windbreaker pockets. He finds his bridge with its three front teeth and puts it in his mouth, pushing it into place with his tongue. The camera clicks on and Ready tells the TV reporter that it was a tough game that could have gone either way, sounding like the rookie in the movie *Bull Durham* after being schooled in what to say to reporters. But he's affable and smiling. When the camera is switched off he takes his teeth out again — "It's more comfortable," he says — and repeats to Mike Davies pretty much what he said on TV.

The Carousel, a restaurant and favourite meeting place in the east end of Peterborough, not far from Highway 7, the road to Ottawa, is big, with lots of windows. It's usually busy for lunch and today, a Friday, it's even busier. The Petes, who won last night, are eating before getting on their bus for a game tonight in Ottawa against the 67's. Ottawa have lost only four of thirty-eight games so far this year and they'll likely end up in first place after the sixty-six-game regular season, as they did last year. But it was the Petes then, not the 67's, who went on to the Memorial Cup final, so the Petes know that Ottawa can be had. After the game the Petes will turn around and come straight back, getting home around 2 a.m. Tomorrow they'll go to Kingston for another game. "That's three games in three nights. It happens now and then," shrugs Jeff Twohey. "We got to live with it."

A bantam team from Brockville, in Peterborough for a tournament, are also having lunch at the Carousel. They've just lost 3–2 to a Kitchener team. The youngsters are hitting the buffet hard, but they're somewhat subdued. "We gave up all three goals in the first period," one of the players explains. He's slight, with carrot-red hair. "We almost came back, though. We'll be better tomorrow." He and his teammates didn't like the ice. Another player says, "It was slow, sticky, we couldn't get going. Our ice at home is hard and fast. We'll do better tomorrow."

Steve Larmer, a former Chicago Blackhawk and New York Ranger and one of the best scorers of his time, is sitting by a window a few feet away drinking coffee. He wears a white cotton T-shirt and a navy blue baseball cap. Larmer is thirty-five. His face has a few scars, noticeably one that looks like a question mark running up from his right eyebrow. Apart from them he has that open, youthful, Huck Finn look that writers pinned on Tom Watson, the golfer, when he was younger.

"Maybe I could have played another year or two, I don't know, but my back was bad and there was the chance I might do it permanent damage," Larmer says. "You know, I played thirteen, fourteen years without being seriously hurt. A few cuts, lost a few teeth, that was all. I'm very thankful for that."

Larmer comes from Peterborough. He joined the Blackhawks in 1982 after four years of junior and one in the American league. He'd been Chicago's eleventh choice in the 1980 draft, the 120th player chosen overall, pretty well down the list. His first year he scored forty-three goals and won the NHL's rookie award. By the time he retired from the New York Rangers after the 1994–95 season, and after helping them win the Stanley Cup the year before, he'd scored 441 goals, one year scoring fifty-nine.

"But numbers were never why I played," he says. "That was never what it was about for me. I loved playing. I just loved playing hockey." He pauses for a second and then mentions Glenn Hall, the great goalie who played more than a thousand games in the 1950s and '60s. "Glenn used to say he'd play hockey for nothing, he loved it so much. If they wanted to pay him to play, he'd say that was okay, too, but he'd play for nothing," Larmer says. "I'm like that. Hockey is demanding, but it's a game, it's fun. It's not like football with every play set and pro-grammed, and it's not like baseball, man against man, pitcher against batter. You need teamwork, but you've got to think on your own, too. When you have the puck you have to make plays, be imagina-tive. And when you're playing defence, you have to have a lot of discipline. To me it's the greatest game in the world."

Larmer is back in Peterborough now, coaching in the minor hockey system and studying business at Sir Sandford Fleming, the community college. He doesn't know what he'll do with the rest of his life, but for the time-being it doesn't include a full-time job in hockey. "I'm busy and enjoying every bit, including going to school," he says. "Skiing, snowmobiling, just being with my family in winter for a change, things I've never been able to do."

The young red-headed hockey player gets up from the nearby table and comes over. "You were an *ex-cep-tion-al* hockey player," he says, leaning into each syllable. Larmer says thanks and smiles. He signs the piece of paper the kid holds out and the kid smiles back and returns to his table.

3

Lakefield, Ontario

March–April 1997

ABOUT TWENTY MINUTES NORTH OF Peterborough on old Highway 28, past Trent University, is the village of Lakefield. The towering smokestack of its long-abandoned cement factory can be seen for miles. About two thousand people live in Lakefield year-round and many more in the summer. The village, at the south end of Lake Katchewanooka, is the last stop for cottagers en route north to the Kawartha Lakes. It's also a favourite mooring spot for the hundreds of boats that travel up and down the Trent-Severn Waterway from May, when the locks are opened, until Thanksgiving, when they're closed for the winter.

Lakefield's first writers of note, Catharine Parr Traill and Susanna Moodie, chronicled pioneer times in the mid-1800s from the delicate, English middle-class perspective. A century and a half later, Margaret Laurence spent her last troubled years in Lakefield. Awash in booze and suffering from cancer, she was hurt and bewildered as local zealots sought, in vain as it turned out, to have her earthy prose banned from schools and libraries. A modest plaque marks the house where she lived, and died, opposite one of Lakefield's five churches. An annual literary gathering is held in Laurence's memory. Prince Andrew attended Lakefield College School, one of Canada's oldest private schools, for less than a year. A bakery and general store, a condominium development, and a small island are named after him.

Two blocks from the Laurence house is the Lakefield arena. Inside, hanging from its roof, are pennants celebrating championships won by the Lakefield Junior C Chiefs and by Lakefield College School. The school team is coached by Ian Armstrong, thirty-one, a history teacher, who played defence for the Peterborough Petes and was drafted by the Boston Bruins. He has the team working on a breakout play. One defenceman passes the puck behind the net to the other, who dumps a short pass softly off the boards inside the blue line to a forward cutting across. It's easy in practice. Armstrong, moving gracefully on skates, yells, "Keep it moving, c'mon, keep it moving, you won't have that much time in a game. Move it!" He is well over six feet tall and weighs more than two hundred pounds. In just a windbreaker and sweatpants, he still looks far bigger than most of the players do in full equipment, but not much older.

Bob Armstrong, Ian's father, played twelve years for Boston and later taught and coached at Lakefield; he died in 1990. For a while, under him, Lakefield was one of the top high school teams in Ontario. But things are changing. The school plays in the private-school league and is not having a good year. It is a much smaller school than Upper Canada College in Toronto or Trinity College School in nearby Port Hope. Ian Armstrong says his team has five or six top players, but little depth.

"We don't have the money for scholarships the way the bigger schools do. They're spending lots, more each year," he says.

Later, sitting in a doughnut shop across from the arena, Armstrong says, "I wanted like hell to play in the NHL. It doesn't matter now why I didn't make it. Maybe I wasn't strong enough, maybe too much golf in the summer and not enough work on the weights. Dad kept trying to get me on the weights. I always knew it would be hard, but I did think I had a good chance."

When Boston didn't exercise its option and sign him, the Philadelphia Flyers did and sent him to the AHL. One afternoon in the summer that he was twenty-three, after two seasons with Hershey and one with Baltimore — and not one game in the NHL — Armstrong went to see Roger Neilson, a friend of his and his dad's who has a cottage near Lakefield.

"I said, 'Roger, am I ever going to make it?' He didn't say anything for a minute, then he said very quietly, 'Maybe, if there's more expansion, with luck you might end up as the seventh or eighth defence-man.' It was devastating, but it was what I needed to hear." Armstrong laughs and says, "Roger hates giving bad news." He puts down his coffee cup and tells a story that Marc Crawford, the former coach of the Colorado Avalanche, told him. "Marc was playing for Roger in Vancouver and Roger called him into his office and, head down, mumbled that he had to cut him. Marc said, 'Roger, you've told my shoes, now tell me.'"

Ian Armstrong had been going to Trent in the summers so when he quit pro hockey he already had some university credits. His father had got to know Jack Drover, the athletics director at Mount Allison University, because he'd sent him some Lakefield graduates to play hockey. Ian Armstrong talked with Drover and liked what he heard, so off he went to Sackville, New Brunswick. He had to sit out one year because he'd played pro; then he played for three for the university.

Armstrong says he is very happy and has no regrets about the turn his hockey life has taken. His wife is pregnant with their second child, and he loves his job. "But, God, it was fun. I loved playing," he says. "And it taught me a lot. I had to fight for my job every day. It didn't come easily. I had to compete every day, just like the real world." He pauses. "But, yeah, looking back, I'd have loved to have played in the NHL. Yeah, I would have and I guess I always will."

The Petes got by Kingston easily in the first playoff round. In the second round they met the Oshawa Generals, their neighbours and bitter rivals. It was a rough, sometimes dirty series and it ended on a cold, dreary Tuesday night in early April that was more like late February. The Generals had finished ahead of the Petes in the regular season and they won the first three games of the best-of-seven series. The Petes came back to win the next two. The sixth game was played in Peterborough before a sellout crowd of 3,929. Peterborough scored first, and after Oshawa tied it, a young Russian, Evgeny Korolev, put the Petes ahead again with a short-handed goal. But that was it. Oshawa scored four times in a row and won 5–3 to take the series four games to two.

Bob Huffman, the emotional man who seldom misses a game, was remarkably sanguine afterwards. Looking down over the empty ice surface as people filed out around him, he said that things might have been different if three regulars had not been out with injuries — Dave Duerden, the team's leading scorer, and a Florida Panther draft who had a broken wrist, and two defencemen, Andy Johnson, a Blackhawk draft getting over a concussion, and Ryan Schmidt, eligible for this year's draft, who'd had knee surgery.

"I'm sorry to see it over, but maybe we just weren't meant to be there this year," he said. What rankled Huffman, and others, was the Oshawa players' refusal to stay on the ice after the final game for the traditional handshake. "I've never seen anything like it," he said. "That's one of the things that makes hockey different. You play hard as hell, you hurt each other maybe, but you shake hands when it's over."

The Petes coach, Brian Drumm, who played his junior hockey for Oshawa, said, "Win, lose, or draw, you shake your opponents' hand after a game. It's got nothing to do with friendship, it's a question of respect; they showed no class."

Zac Bierk, the goalie, said, "I've played against a guy like Ryan Lindsay a hundred times in my life. It would have been nice to shake his hand and wish him luck. I might never see him again."

Twohey, the Petes GM, was also upset. "It's always disappointing to lose, but it's also bad the way it ended," he said.

But Bill Stewart, the ex-NHLer in his first year as the Generals coach, was unperturbed. "I don't believe in shaking hands," he said. "I never have. In all the years I played I never shook hands after a playoff series."

The village of Douro, a few miles northeast of Peterborough, is not more than four corners — a school on one, a general store on another, and a cemetery on a third. On the fourth is a huge, grey stone Roman Catholic church, St. Joseph's, that makes Douro look more like a village in Quebec than one in loyalist Ontario. It was built in 1893 for the hundreds of Irish immigrants who settled here — some of the thousands who fled to North America during Ireland's potato famine. George "Red" Sullivan, the former NHL player and coach, goes to St. Joseph's every morning. He's got a lot to be thankful for.

Gary Dalliday, the CHEX-TV hockey broadcaster, has said it was because of Sullivan that he learned as a kid what hockey means to Peterborough. "I was at St. Peter's school and the nuns called us together. They said something awful had happened to Red and told us to pray for him because he might die. And I really prayed. He was one of my heroes."

Reminded of this while sitting over coffee in his living room, Sullivan nods. "Well, they gave me the last rites," he says. "It was that close." He says it began on a Saturday night in Montreal, towards the end of a game when he was playing for the Rangers. "I went into the corner with Doug Harvey and I kicked the skates out from under him and he went down hard. Now that's something players don't do, kick another player's skates. It's too dangerous. A guy could fall and hit his head and be seriously hurt, hell, maybe even kill himself. Remember, this was before helmets, too. I can't remember why I did it, whether it was an accident or I was mad at him or what, but I do know that he said, 'I'll get you tomorrow night, Sullivan.'

"That was when, in the old six-team league, we'd often play back-to-back games. So we're in New York and I'm carrying the puck across the Canadiens' blue line. Harvey's skating back with me. All of a sudden he stops and lets me have it with his stick, spears me. I had to leave the ice, I couldn't breathe. Between periods it didn't get any better so I was put in a cab and sent to the hospital. I'm at the hospital forty minutes and they operate. I had a ruptured spleen and damn nearly didn't make it. Later I'm telling a Montreal sportswriter that I didn't think Harvey meant to hurt me that bad and the sportswriter says he's not so sure. He says that Harvey told him, 'I don't care if the son of a bitch dies.' But, ah hell, I never figured he really meant it, even meant to hurt me the way he did. I've never thought that. He wanted to get me, sure, but not hurt me. I think we played differently then."

Sullivan's ranch-style home is a few miles from St. Joseph's, on a small hill surrounded by fields and clumps of evergreen. It was built for him and his wife, Miriam, nine years ago. A creek runs below it. "This is a great part of the country, full of woods and lakes," Sullivan says. "All kinds of guys who played for the Petes, whether they came from Peterborough or not, come back and settle around here."

Sullivan is sixty-seven. He was born and grew up in Peterborough. His hair is still red and he still looks slim and hard, the way he looked playing junior hockey in St. Catharines and later during eleven years in the NHL with Boston, Chicago, and the Rangers. He also coached the Rangers, Washington, and Pittsburgh, and he scouted until two years ago.

"I loved everything about hockey so much that I never considered it work," he says, "so in a way, I guess, I can say that I've never worked a day in my life."

Sullivan begins to twist the large ring with the New York Rangers crest that's on his left hand. "I'll tell you a story," he says. "One autumn a friend, Arnie Dugan, and I hitchhiked to Detroit to go to the

Red Wings camp. We were to play Junior B in Peterborough that season, so I guess we were fifteen, Jesus, just kids. Anyway, Arnie had an uncle in Detroit where we could stay. We got to the old Detroit Olympia and I bet there's a hundred guys already there, sleeping on cots in the corridors. I'm not exaggerating. I've never seen so many hockey players in one place at the same time. We go to Jack Adams — he's general manager — and we say, 'Mr. Adams, we'd like to try out.'

"'You got your skates?'

"'Yessir.'

"'You got a place to stay?'

"'Yessir.'

"'Okay, then.'

"So away we go. They gave us equipment and we worked out for five days, maybe six. Remember, we were fifteen, for God's sake, working out with the pros. Then Adams calls us into his office. He said, 'Thanks, boys, for coming,' told us to go home and work on our skating. He gave us each twenty-five dollars. Jesus, we were so happy. There were a lot of good hockey players there Adams had to look at. Besides the Red Wings themselves there were the two main farm teams, Indianapolis in the AHL and Omaha of the old United States Hockey League, and all the juniors, too."

Sullivan laughs and twists some more at his Rangers ring. "Another thing I remember about that trip is that hitchhiking home Arnie and I got as far as Hamilton and we got stuck. We couldn't get a ride. So after a while, we're tired and hungry I guess, he says something to me and I say something back and before you know, we're in a fight, right there on the road." He laughs some more. "Aahh, those days were fun.

"Anyway, the next year I'm playing an exhibition game at Varsity Arena in Toronto and Baldy Cotton, the old Leaf who scouted for the Bruins, puts me on their negotiation list. Now and then after I'd made the Bruins I'd run into Jack Adams and he'd laugh and clap me on the back and say, 'Well, Red, you were one guy I missed.'"

Sullivan remembers how unsophisticated he was when Boston first called him up. "I took the train from Toronto," he says. "I'd been on trains before but never for long trips. Thank God there was a referee on board I knew from junior. He took me under his wing. Hell, I didn't even know trains had dining cars." He pauses for a moment. Then he says, "That was another great thing about hockey. Here I am, a kid from a small town, and before I know it I'm a regular in Boston, New York, Chicago, Montreal, staying in the best hotels, eating in the best restaurants. It was a hell of a good life, believe me."

Sullivan has reservations about the game today. "When I played," he says, "and someone got cut around the face, it was usually, maybe not all the time, but usually an accident." He says that one night in Boston he lost his balance and hit Boom-Boom Geoffrion in the mouth with his stick. "I knocked out most of his front teeth. I felt really bad about that. Now, they wear all that stuff and they think they can do anything they want. They don't respect each other. It hurts the game. You might not like the other guy, but he's another player. You got to respect him for that. We did."

Bobcaygeon has a winter population of 2,500 that swells to more than three times that in summer. It's thirty miles north of Peterborough, built around the lock where Pigeon Lake meets Sturgeon Lake, on the edge of Haliburton County, in one of the most beautiful parts of Ontario. The hills are covered with maples and birches, the water is cold and clear, and the fishing is wonderful.

When Percy Nichols got back home to Bobcaygeon after his hockey days were over, he worked at the liquor store for more than twenty years. "When I was playing I'd do some guiding in the summer to tide me over between seasons; lots of tourists want to fish," he says. "But once I quit I needed a real job. Hockey hadn't given me much."

Nichols, eighty and a widower, lives alone in the house where he's lived most of his life. Trophies for golf and pitching horseshoes are on his shelves beside fishing lures and full-size wooden ducks which he carved. On a wall of his living room is a photograph of him all dressed up in a dark suit and white shirt and wearing a bowler. It was taken when he was Bobcaygeon's reeve. "In those days we'd get dressed for council meetings," Nichols says. "We always tried to look good."

On another wall is a picture of the pre-NHL Vancouver Canucks, the 1947–48 champions of the Pacific Coast Hockey League. It shows a group of clean-cut young men in topcoats, shirts, and ties, some in fedoras, smiling and waving as they board a plane. "That's when we're going down to San Diego to play the Skyhawks. They're the ones we beat in the final," Nichols says. "Our playing coach was Mac Colville, the old New York Ranger. Billy Carse was on the team. He played with Detroit and Chicago."

Nichols was a big defenceman. He still is big, without being fat. He wears glasses, has most of his hair, and most of his teeth. "Just lucky," he says. He played minor hockey around Peterborough and then he played two seasons in the American Hockey

League, one with Baltimore and one with a team named the New Jersey Skeeters. "I was Ranger property and I might have made them, but the war came along and before I knew it I was in the army. I would have given it a good shot, anyway."

Nichols played for army teams in Peterborough and Kingston — one which beat the Ottawa RCAF that Boston greats Milt Schmidt, Bobby Bauer, and Woody Dumart played for. Then he was sent to Debert, the army base in Nova Scotia that was usually the last stop before being shipped overseas. "I got off the train and an officer comes up and says, 'You Percy Nichols?' and I says, 'Yeah.' And he says, 'Jesus, I'm glad to see you. We're playing Truro in the finals.' I told him I didn't join the army to play goddamn hockey. Besides, I didn't have any equipment."

He shakes his head and laughs. "It was the same goddamn thing when I got to England. I'm hardly there and Hub Macey, a guy I knew who used to be with the Rangers and Canadiens, says he wants me to play for an army team in Brighton. I told him the same thing, and I didn't play again until I got home."

When he did come back there were offers from three teams, "Vancouver, the Sydney Millionaires, and another team somewhere in the Maritimes, Saint John, maybe. I took Vancouver because I'd never been west." Nichols opens a scrapbook and produces his air ticket: Toronto–Vancouver, Trans-Canada Airlines — $167.70. "That wasn't cheap then," he says. "And it took me fourteen hours. It seemed like forever. We put down everywhere, and I'm thinking, 'Where the hell is Vancouver? Am I ever going to get there?' It was a great year, though, we won it all, and when it was over I came back east. I was thirty-three. It was time to slow down a bit."

Back at home the next season, he and his brother,

Ernie, six years younger, were playing one night in Orillia. "Yank Boyd is there. He had played in the NHL and now was scouting for the Bruins. I knew Yank and after the game he tells me that he likes Ernie. They gave him three hundred bucks to put him on their negotiation list. That was fifty years ago. Three hundred dollars was okay, don't forget.

"So autumn comes and so does a letter from Boston telling Ernie to report to Providence, the Bruins' American league farm club. Ernie reads the letter, says the hell with it. He uses it to light the stove, for Christ's sake. He tells me he doesn't want to leave home. Jesus Christ, I was mad. He gives it all up because he didn't want to leave home."

In his house a few streets away, Ernie says, "That's right. I was just back from the army and I didn't feel like leaving again. But they must have really wanted me because around Christmas I get a call from them. They tell me to take the train to Ottawa and someone would meet me there and take me to Providence." He laughs. "Maybe they thought I'd get lost. Anyway, I still didn't go. I said the same thing, I didn't want to leave home."

Ernie Nichols wasn't the only young man from the Bobcaygeon area who was afraid of getting homesick. Percy Nichols says that he recommended a kid to Bill Cook, who was working for the New York Rangers. "This kid was a marvellous skater, puck-handler. Big and strong, too. He goes off to camp and two weeks later I hear that he's back home, so the next time I saw Cook I asked him. He said the kid had every-thing. The trouble was that after practice he'd head straight for the tavern. It wasn't a question of him being a drunk, Cook said, but to the Rangers it looked like he didn't want to play hockey very badly. When I heard this I asked the kid straight out and he said yeah, that was true. He didn't want to play in New York, he wanted to stay at home. Jesus Christ, I didn't understand it then and I still don't."

In the early 1950s Percy and Ernie managed the rink in Lakefield and played for Lakefield in the old Trent Valley Hockey League, and they made a few dollars betting on games. Percy begins to laugh. "When things were quiet on the crime-fighting front the police chief would come by the rink and we'd play euchre. He figured he knew a lot about hockey, and I guess he did, but not as much as we did, and he liked to bet."

Nichols says the betting was usually over how many goals Lakefield would win by. "We hardly ever lost so there wasn't much point betting against us. One night there's maybe a couple of minutes to go and we're ahead by two goals, and Ernie and I are sitting on the bench. Suddenly I look at him and he looks at me and we're thinking the same thing: Jesus Christ, the bet was we'd win by three goals, not two! So we're over the boards and there's a faceoff in their end — Norwood, Campbellford, whoever, I can't remember. Anyways, Ernie played centre and he wins the draw and the puck gets to me and we score. I remember skating off the ice and I says, 'Jesus Christ, Ernie, that was a close one? We got to start paying more attention.'" He laughs some more. "I don't want to sound boastful, but Ernie and I were pretty good. We could usually control the game. Yeah, we were that good."

Percy Nichols still likes hockey, but he gets angry at the checking from behind that the NHL keeps insisting that it's cracking down on. "They keep saying they'll do something about it but they never goddamn well do," he says. "Anyone who'd hit someone from behind is nothing but a coward. Nothing but a goddamn coward."

4

Yorkton, Saskatchewan

July 1997

METRO PRYSTAI WAS BORN IN Yorkton, a farming town on the Saskatchewan prairie east of Regina, and except when he was away playing hockey he has lived there all his life. At seventy, he's not much heavier than he was during eleven NHL seasons as a centre with the Chicago Blackhawks and the Detroit Red Wings, about 175 pounds, and he still has a brush cut, although his hair is now grey. He plays golf around Yorkton in the summer, and spends a month or so in Victoria in the winter. He received $35,000 this year when the NHL Players' Association won its fight over pensions. "Not a hell of a lot," he says, "but not bad when you're not expecting it." Sitting on his back patio on a sunny day, he seems a very contented man.

Prystai's parents were Ukrainian, but they met and were married in Canada. His father farmed and then went to the CNR as a section man — working on the tracks. "The first time my dad came to Detroit to see me play he didn't know about heated arenas, so he's dressed for a prairie winter," Prystai says.

"My seats were beside Alex Delvecchio's and Benny Woit's, so Julie Woit gets to talking with him. All the time my dad's getting hotter and hotter in his big wool coat, sweating like hell. Suddenly he says in his heavy accent, 'Hey, somebody musta turned up the sshh-team.' Julie was laughing when she told me. I'll bet if she walked in here now she'd say, 'Hey, Metro, somebody musta turned up the sshh-team.' She was very nice to him."

Until he was three or four, Prystai spoke only Ukrainian. He says, thinking back, "I started to skate before I was old enough for school. After my brothers left in the morning, I'd pull on a pair of their skates over my shoes — that's how small I was — and skate on the road." He says that his older twin brothers, Bill and Harry, might have made the NHL if it hadn't been for the Second World War. (Bill isn't sure. "I got my share of goals in senior," he says, "but I don't think I was that good.")

When Metro Prystai was a youngster, the Terriers, a senior team, were Yorkton's hockey elite. The players had come up through junior hockey in the west, some had played professionally, one or two had even reached the NHL. "If I didn't have a nickel to get in to watch them, I'd try to get in by carrying a player's skates. Sometimes I'd have to wait until the third period, when I could get in for nothing." Prystai played junior for the Moose Jaw Canucks: "I got room and board and fifty dollars a month. I was happy as hell. I was getting paid to play hockey." It was there that he got his first new skates. Ross Thatcher, later Saskatchewan's premier, was part owner of the team. "One night he said, 'Hey kid, those your best skates?' I said they were my only skates. He told me to come down to his hardware store the next day and he'd give me a new pair."

Prystai's first professional camp was with the Cleveland Barons. It was in Detroit and he was still a junior. "We practised in the morning and the Red Wings practised in the afternoon. Then we'd go to a place called the Red Wing Bar. I think it was on Grand River. They'd be drinking beer and I'd be drinking 7-Up. I was proud as hell to be there. Adam Brown played for Detroit and he was nice to me. Then, a few years later, I'm playing with him in Chicago. He could throw more punches in half a minute than anyone I ever saw."

Prystai says another tough one was Elmer Lach, the great Canadiens centre, who came from Nokomis, not far from Yorkton. "He'd played senior in Moose Jaw so when I came up that first year and we'd be facing off he'd say, 'Hi, kid, how are things in Moose Jaw?' and then let me have it with the stick. God, he was a hell of a hockey player, a beautiful skater. One year he's fighting for the scoring championship with Buddy O'Connor when O'Connor was with the Rangers. We didn't want a Canadien winning so we're almost giving O'Connor the puck, but that night he couldn't have put it in the ocean." (In 1947–48 Lach outscored O'Connor 61 to 60 in a sixty-game schedule to win the scoring. O'Connor, how-ever, was awarded the Hart Trophy as the league's most valuable player.)

Prystai went directly from Moose Jaw to Chicago in the fall of 1947. "Johnny Gottselig was coach, and then Charlie Conacher. Gottselig wasn't much but Charlie was okay. He loved hockey, but it was hard on him. He was trying to build a team and Bill Tobin, the general manager kept trading away players. Bert Olmstead went to Montreal. I went to Detroit. I always figured Chicago management didn't know what the hell they were doing. That's why we were at the bottom all the goddamn time."

In Chicago, Prystai and some other players stayed at the Mid-West Athletic Club, owned by the Norris family, which also owned a piece of the Blackhawks. "It was meant to be a hotel, but it was more of a hangout," Prystai says. "And there's one guy who's always asking me about the team, this and that, and I'm telling him. He seemed nice, and I'm a kid from Yorkton; what the hell do I know? I didn't think anything about it. I just thought he was being friendly. Turns out it's Al Capone's kid brother, Maddy. Jesus . . ."

That winter, 1948, the NHL president, Clarence Campbell, suspended Billy Taylor, a veteran, and Don Gallinger, a youngster, from the NHL for life. He ruled that they'd been giving inside information to gamblers about their team, Boston. It was only then, Prystai says, that he realized what was going on. He tried to discourage Capone, but it was difficult. "He was around all the time, but I stopped telling him about the team. I'd give him autographed hockey sticks, though. I sure as hell didn't want to get on his bad side." Capone offered him a job. "He said I was making peanuts playing hockey and he'd give me big bucks. I asked him what I'd do and he said, 'Carry a gun.'"

Prystai says it was a relief when he was traded to Detroit, in spite of the general manager, Jack Adams. "I was making ten thousand dollars and I'd had a pretty good year so I asked Jack for five hundred dollars more. He says, 'Jesus, Metro, I got guys lined up ready to take your place for a helluva lot less.' So I ended up signing the same contract. I didn't want to be sent to the minors. In the old days they could send you down and nobody would ever see you again. They all did it then." Prystai says that's why he has so much respect for Ted Lindsay, one of his Detroit teammates. "He took the owners on when no one else would. He started it all."

He pauses for a couple of seconds. Then he says, "But I always loved hockey, the game and the guys I played with. We travelled by train and we were very, very close. I'd come back here in the summer and by August I could hardly wait for training camp to start. The money wasn't anything like now, but it was a lot more than most guys were getting outside hockey. I think I might have scored a few more goals, but I broke my leg twice and that buggered me up. But I was up there for eleven years, so that was good."

In Regina, Bill Prystai is in his rec room. It's Sunday afternoon and the neighbourhood is quiet. He has a New York Mets game on TV, but the sound is off. Shelves around the room are laden with hockey photos and awards. Bill Prystai was involved in hockey for years as a player, coach, and official. He's seventy-four, bald, slight, and wears glasses, but when he talks about hockey he's a kid again. "In 1940–41 my brother Harry and I made Yorkton juveniles, just below junior, and we never lost a game," he says. "We played Regina, Moose Jaw, North Battleford, you name it. Oh God, what a thrill for a kid from Yorkton! And the Yorkton newspaper put on a hell of a spread for us and they bought us jackets. It was fantastic, I tell you."

During the war he was on an air force team with two other Saskatchewan natives, Harry Watson and Garth Boesch, both of whom went on to solid careers with the Maple Leafs. "We played all over the west and every time we went anywhere I was on the same plane with Boesch — he was a pilot — and Watson. I guess that's because I was on a line with Harry. Some damn good professional players were around. One was a big defenceman who played for Detroit. He knocked me on my ass a few times. Jesus, I've forgotten his name, but remember, that's more than fifty years ago. He could hit, though, I remember that much."

One of Bill Prystai's most vivid memories involves his younger brother. "In 1954, when Montreal won the sixth game of the Stanley Cup final, four of us decided over a cup of coffee in Yorkton to go to Detroit for the seventh game. I sent a telegram to Metro. In those days you could send a telegram to a train. He got it when he was on the train from Montreal to Detroit. He booked the tickets. We drove for two days and got there three hours before the game. The game went into overtime. I tell you, it was like a dream come true — watching your brother in a seventh game of a Stanley Cup final that goes into overtime. And Tony Leswick scored, and Detroit won, 2–1. Leswick's from Saskatchewan, you know."

5

Back in Yorkton

July 1997

BACK IN YORKTON, THE HOT July weather has made
the air in the Parkland Agriplex arena clammy and
there's a light mist on the ice. Thirty-four boys, the
youngest only seven years old but most of them in
their teens, are finishing up goalie school. The
International Goaltenders School was started in the
early '80s by Reg Kachanoski, an old goalie. It's
based in Yorkton but is on the move all summer,
from Thunder Bay to Kamloops, with a dip into
Wisconsin. It's on its way to Redcliff, near Calgary,
this evening, so two puck machines and a tennis ball
machine — "for off-ice hand-to-eye training" — and
trampolines — "to help the kids' agility" — and
video cameras and cassettes and dozens of pucks and
tennis balls and sticks must be packed into a cube
van for the trip. The school also carries a pro shop of
pads and gloves and sweaters but Kachanoski is
phasing out that end of his operation. He says it's too
much work to keep the inventory up to date.

The school has five regular instructors, and a five-
day session costs about four hundred dollars. "We

don't try to change a goaltender's style," Kachanoski says. "That's one of the worst things you can do. Some goaltenders can't do the butterfly, for example, they're stand-up goalies. A lot depends on their builds. But one thing we're trying to teach is to cover the bottom part of the net, because most goals are scored low. Some do this with the butterfly, others will crouch."

Kachanoski is sixty-seven. He comes from Souris, Manitoba, not far from Brandon. "Per capita, more goalies probably come out of Brandon than almost anywhere," he says, and he lists Turk Broda and Ron Hextall, Bill Ranford and Glen Hanlon. Kachanoski played senior hockey in Dauphin and then for the Yorkton Terriers. "I'm one of those guys who's been in hockey all his life and doesn't want to get out of it until he has to," he says. "Hockey people are great people."

Unlike many ex-players his age, Kachanoski feels that hockey is as good now as it was in the past; and he thinks it's tougher to play goal than ever before. "For one thing, the defenceman used to be a defenceman and he'd turn the guy to the outside and if he scored from that angle it'd be your fault. Now, the defence are in the rush and if they're caught up ice goalies are facing two- and three-on-ones coming the other way. And they must have great lateral movement because players are shooting from everywhere and they're shooting harder."

While the goalie school is packing up inside the arena, outside, on the edge of the Yorkton fairgrounds, two men and a woman are unpacking a small truck and, in an old tent, setting up chairs and hooking up a sound system. A bumper sticker on the truck says, "Your marriage doesn't need a divorce, it needs Jesus." Over the entrance to the tent is a big banner, "Expect a Miracle, Jesus is Here!" Another banner says, "Repent or Perish." One of the men setting up the chairs says to come back that evening and Jesus will cure whatever needs curing. He's about seventy and most of his lower teeth are missing.

The fairgrounds and the arena are on Broadway, Yorkton's main street, near the turn west to Melville, the hometown of Sid Abel, the great old Detroit Red Wing. Across the street and down a bit is Pockets, a sports bar. Paul Josephson, nursing a beer, says that he went to the tent revival meeting a year ago when it came through town. "My golf swing was off," he says, "but they couldn't do a damn thing about it." He almost has to shout to be heard over the music. Josephson, stocky and fair-haired, is a teacher. Following junior hockey with the Prince Albert Mintos he went to the University of Denver. Among his teammates was Bill Masterton, later a Minnesota North Star, who died in a freak hockey accident. Josephson also played with Omaha, and then came home to Saskatchewan.

He's sitting with three more ex-players: Merv Kuryluk, briefly a Chicago Blackhawk and a long-time minor leaguer — Calgary, Buffalo, St. Louis and Los Angeles, before they entered the NHL, and Sault Ste. Marie; Barry Sharpe, a retired teacher, who played with the University of Saskatchewan Huskies; and Vern Pachal. Pachal once played for Eddie Shore, the Saskatchewan boy who had been an All-Star defenceman with the Boston Bruins and became an all-star eccentric as a minor league coach and owner. After leaving Shore, Pachal went to the University of Alberta. He retired from teaching a few years ago. The four men, in their fifties and sixties now, all played together with the Yorkton Terriers, and they meet here once a week.

"One of my objectives in life was to make the NHL, and I fulfilled it," says Kuryluk, who worked for Labatt's for twenty-five years. "It was something I set out to do, and I did it. If I have any regrets it's that I didn't go to university. But college players then weren't recognized the way they are now. So you played junior. That's the way everybody went."

Barry Sharpe played junior in Saskatoon and Weyburn, before moving on to the Terriers and the Huskies. He is on the small side, talks quickly, and laughs easily. He came back to Yorkton as a new teacher with a young family. He says he was uncertain about playing serious hockey when he got a call. "The guys said they really needed me for a game in Saskatoon, so I left school early, jumped on the bus, and went down," he says.

"Anyway, we're playing and I had the puck in my skates and I looked down and the next thing I know I hit the boards face first. I could see my teeth coming out. Someone had cross-checked me from behind. When I came to he was lying beside me on the ice. One of my defencemen had got him and he ended up with a detached retina and never played again. God knows how many stitches I took. And I lost all those teeth. I remember the next day sitting in the bathroom at home shaking my head in terrible, terrible pain. And I decided, well that's it for me. But you know, after a couple of years I missed hockey. Senior hockey had gone, but I played intermediate."

Vern Pachal, a slim and introspective man, grew up in poverty. His father had lost the family farm when the bank foreclosed during the Depression. "My mother died about then," he says. "The shock was too much for her, I guess. She'd had a rough life. We moved into Yorkton, my father and five kids. We had nothing. He did odd jobs just to feed us. I remember going to school covered in bedbug bites."

Pachal played minor hockey in Yorkton and hoped to play junior in Moose Jaw. Not only was that his pal Metro Prystai's old team, but another friend, Larry Popein — who later played for, and coached, the New York Rangers — was there. But at sixteen Pachal had signed a "C" form with Eddie Shore which meant, in those days, that an owner could do pretty well what he wanted with a player for as long as he played pro hockey. After a training camp in Kitchener, Shore put Pachal on a train for southwestern Alberta and the Bellevue Lions, a team Shore helped sponsor. Instead of playing for the Moose Jaw Canucks, Pachal would be playing against them.

Bellevue is one in a string of coal-mining towns in the Crowsnest Pass. The pass cuts through the Rocky Mountains from Alberta to British Columbia near the U.S. border. It has a sad and violent history. In 1903 a landslide buried part of the community of Frank under ninety million tons of granite, killing at least seventy people. Five years later 128 miners died in a mine explosion. And six years after that an explosion killed 189 miners — the worst mine disaster in Canadian history. Thirty more were killed in another explosion in 1926. Angry over working conditions and threats of pay cuts, fourteen hundred miners went on strike in 1932, shutting down all the mines in the pass. The companies, appealing to the prejudices of the day, accused the union leaders of being communists and the RCMP moved in. They crushed the demonstrations but the strike lasted eight months.

When Pachal arrived in 1948 the mines were still operating near their Second World War capacity. Shore had said that the Bellevue Lions would pay Pachal sixty dollars a week. "But that came from working in the mines, when we weren't playing, for eleven dollars a day," Pachal says. "At least I knew I had my grade twelve to fall back on if I had to, and that meant more then than it does now. Anyway, in my third year I was able to quit the mines because the team was paying me ninety dollars a week. I was the highest paid junior in western Canada. My first year there I finished tenth, I think, in the scoring. The second year, 1948–49, I won it with fifty-nine goals and forty-seven assists in forty games. The next year, my third and last year in junior, I came second to Guyle Fielder."

Pachal says support for the team came from the nearly dozen towns in the pass. "But most of it was from Crowsnest itself so we changed our name from the Bellevue Lions to the Crowsnest Lions. The Bellevue arena could hold only two thousand but we filled it. We outdrew the Regina Pats. On the road we travelled by U-drives or bus except when we went to Regina and Moose Jaw. We'd go by train, play doubleheaders in both towns, and stay aboard. They'd pull our car aside and we'd sleep in the berths."

The Crowsnest Pass mines are closed now because of the shrinking market for coal. What's left of the timbered entrances to their shafts jut out of the hills like curiously blackened, broken teeth, in jagged contrast to the green and graceful hills around them. Six or seven hundred men from the pass work mines on the B.C. side, and there are a couple of sawmills, but unemployment is high — about 12 to 15 percent — its list made up of miners who can't find work, and unskilled youth. And when the mines went, so did the heady days of the Pass being home to some of Canada's best juniors.

Following junior Pachal played for the Springfield Indians and the Syracuse Warriors, both owned by

Shore, in the AHL, the Quebec senior league, and the eastern league. And, like anyone who played for Shore, he has his stories. "One year at training camp in Niagara Falls he caught the guys rooming with me out after curfew," he says. "It didn't matter that I hadn't been out; he kept us on the ice from six-thirty that morning until half past twelve — six hours. He had coaches working in two-hour shifts."

Pachal leans forward. "I got another story. We're scrimmaging. I'm playing centre and George Ford is one of my wingers. Shore wants us to forecheck hard, as if we were in a game. George is to nail the opposing player coming out of the corner with the puck. George was a miserable little bugger but even he wasn't going to cream one of his own players in practice. I mean, we all had to make a living. So Shore blows his whistle. He yells, 'George, you bring the puck out and I'll show how to do it.' Shore's in his standard dress, the blue suit, brown fedora, and the skates barely laced up — the way he always wore them — and he's about fifty years old. George starts out, Shore starts in. At the last second George throws an elbow, catches Shore right under the chin, lifts him about six inches off the ice. His fedora goes one way, his stick another, and he comes down flat on his back. We're all watching. Not a sound in the rink. Shore gets up, brushes himself off, puts on his hat, and says, 'Okay, let's face off. That was a hell of a check.' He dished it out, but he could take it, too."

However, after four years, even Pachal had had enough. When Shore tried to send him to the Glace Bay Miners, on Nova Scotia's Cape Breton Island, for two defencemen, Pachal said he wouldn't go, he'd quit first. "Shore said he'd bring me back next year but that right now he had five centres and he needed the defencemen. But I didn't see much of a future for me. He gave me a week to think it over. After a week he asked me what I was going to do and I said I was going home. He said, 'Okay, pack up your car and go,' and I did. When I got home I got married and that fall instead of going to training camp, for the first time since I was fifteen, I went to the University of Alberta and studied to become a teacher. I never saw Shore again."

Pachal has, surprisingly perhaps, few resentments over his years with Shore. "There were a lot of negatives about him, but there were a lot of positives, too. He was certainly the best coach I ever had. He was the only one who ever taught me to skate properly, and pass. He was the best hockey man I ever knew. As far as keeping me in the minors, spoiling any chance I'd have of making the NHL, I don't know. Being a very good junior in the west made me think I might make it. I wonder sometimes. And there'd be rumours that he was going to sell me, but I guess he couldn't get what he wanted. Bars and taverns are full of guys who would have made it if it hadn't been for this or that. But as I said, I just don't know. I'm not going to squawk about Shore the way Don Cherry does." After a moment he adds, "I took hockey very seriously. I didn't want anything to jeopardize the living I was making. I knew what it was like to be poor, really poor. I loved hockey, but I never thought it was fun, not as a pro. When I played pro it was hard work, it was my job, and I didn't want to screw up my job."

6

Indian Head, Saskatchewan

July 1997

INDIAN HEAD, BETWEEN YORKTON AND Regina, has fewer than two thousand people, but its main street is called Grand Avenue and it is wider than the nearby Trans-Canada Highway. Along the street there's Bigway Foods, a Stedman's, two drug stores, the Sportsman's Pub, and the office of the Economic Development and Tourism Committee. The opera house, built in the late 1800s, is now the Nite Hawk cinema but it has just changed hands and the new owners may renovate it for live entertainment. It's almost de rigueur for prairie towns to have at least one Chinese restaurant, testimony to the indentured Chinese who built the railways, and Indian Head's is the China Garden. On the streets off Grand Avenue are big, stone houses, built by the Scots and English who came to farm a hundred years ago.

The *Indian Head-Wolseley News* comes out each Tuesday. According to its masthead it also covers the news in Qu'Appelle, Montmartre, Odessa, and Carry the Kettle. "I try to be positive," says Ken McCabe, the publisher. "I don't go looking for a fight."

McCabe, sixty years old, has spent most of his life in Indian Head. He left school after grade ten, worked eventually as the town's recreation director, and wrote sports for the newspaper. When local business-men bought it to keep it out of the hands of out-of-towners, they asked McCabe to run it. "If we have bad weather and bad crops, I report it," he says. "But you can't go poor-mouthing everything and expect people to move here and do business. Agriculture is still the big thing here. We have the government experimental farm and a tree nursery. Not many small towns in Saskatchewan have as many trees as we have. This year alone we planted 3,200 at the golf course and we have new grass greens, a new swim-ming pool, and the rink's fairly new."

McCabe, with his glasses, greying moustache, and greying hair, might pass for Jacques Demers, the coach of the Tampa Bay Lightning. McCabe played goal for years for the Indian Head Chiefs, a senior hockey team. Depending on which teams were oper-ating, the Chiefs were in the Mainline League or the Triangle League or the Qu'Appelle Valley League. He was fourteen or fifteen when he played his first senior game. "I hitchhiked to Qu'Appelle, nine or ten miles down the road, to see a game and one of the goalies didn't show up. I played for the Wolseley Mustangs against the Fort Qu'Appelle Sioux Indians and we lost, 10–6. They paid me five bucks. Hockey was a big attraction back then and we got big crowds, six, seven hundred, not just Indian Head, but other towns, too. Winter was hockey or curling. That was it.

"Over the years we had some good hockey players, guys maybe just a couple of steps short of making it up there. But the best we ever had was a fellow named Gerry Walker. He was a big scorer for the

Regina Pats, and remember, they were one of the best junior teams in whole goddamn country. The New York Rangers wanted him but instead he went to university in the States. He came here to work for the Royal Bank. I never played with anyone who could dominate a game the way he could."

The office of the *Indian Head-Wolseley News* is between a convenience store and the liquor store in the Arrowhead Mall, at the bottom of Grand Avenue, near the CPR line and the grain elevators. McCabe puts out the paper with the help of three women; two of them are his daughters. Sharing his office space is the Rural Sports Hall of Fame and Museum, which he created. There are Grey Cup programs from way back and baseball uniforms and football and hockey sweaters, and footballs and baseballs and bats, hockey sticks and curling brooms. There are golf clubs and boxing gloves and piles and piles of photos, some recent, some from before the First World War. McCabe is also one of those responsible for bringing athletes to town for sports dinners and such. "Henri Richard has been to Indian Head, and Guy Lafleur, Norm Ullman, and Gilbert Perreault," McCabe says. "George Chuvalo, too, talking about drug abuse." He waves a finger for emphasis. "And I've done it without any government help. It's not worth having to do all kinds of goddamn paperwork just to satisfy some bureaucrats."

On the wall, there's a photo of Murray Westgate, the actor who for years did the Esso commercials for TV's *Hockey Night in Canada*. "He went to school here," McCabe says. There's also one of Eric Petersen, of TV's *Street Legal*. "He was born here. He comes back to see his mother." And there's a picture of Johnny Esaw, the long-time CTV sportscaster.

McCabe says Esaw once broadcast baseball games from Indian Head.

He picks up a photograph album. "Look at these. In the '40s and '50s we hosted the biggest baseball tournaments in western Canada. We'd draw fifteen, twenty thousand. The pictures are right here." And they are, showing thousands of people in the stands and ringing the field. McCabe goes on, "A lot of hockey players played ball here," and he goes to a stack of handwritten lineups that include the names Doug and Max Bentley, Billy Mosienko, Gordie Howe, Metro Prystai, Emile Francis, Bert Olmstead, Jackie McLeod, Nick and Don Metz, and Bill and Gus Kyle. Rollie Miles, the great Edmonton Eskimo, is there, too. "And look here." McCabe holds up two more photos. They're of Pumpsie Greene, the first black to play for the Boston Red Sox, and Tom Alston, another black, who played parts of four seasons with the St. Louis Cardinals. "Lots of black kids played here in the summer. A team, the Jacksonville Eagles, used to come up from Florida and be the Indian Head Rockets for the season. When the Eagles stopped coming their place was taken by the Florida Cubans."

McCabe's father walked out on the family when McCabe was three. "My mother and my sister and I lived in an apartment. My mother worked in a grocery store. She was very good, but if it hadn't been for the RCMP and my coaches and my teachers, and for sports, I don't know what would have happened to me. That's why I went ahead with the sports hall of fame, to give something back."

He goes on, "Maybe kids with single parents got special attention, but if we did, I needed it. We had a cop as football coach and he'd say, 'I know you were out drinking beer last night so if you want to be on this team do twenty-five push-ups,' things like that. Another time a baseball coach made me run all the way home for my baseball cap because he'd said practice was in full uniform and I'd forgotten it. I told him it wasn't important. He said if I wanted to play ball, it goddamn well was. And one night I came home late and the RCMP constable is parked in front of the Windsor Apartments where we lived, right beside the livery barn. He said, 'You come home late again and we're going into that barn and only one of us is coming out.' Can you imagine telling a kid that today? But it was what I needed."

Ken McCabe is quiet for a moment, sipping his Diet Coke. Then he says, "None of that seems very far back. I can still see a kid coming to the football field on horseback and tying the horse to a tree while he practised. And I'll never forget that before we had artificial ice around here the rinks were so goddamn cold that being a goalie you nearly froze."

Not far from Indian Head, by the Qu'Appelle River, which keeps the Qu'Appelle Valley green in the summer and where generations of youngsters learned to skate in winter, Fred Brown has 2,500 acres under seed, and eighty head of cattle. Brown is sixty-two, short, soft-spoken, with a farmer's hands and face. He played senior hockey with the Indian Head Chiefs from the age of eighteen until he suffered a heart attack at forty-two. "It was the first game of the season and I got a butt end right here," he says, tapping the middle of his chest. "It hurt like hell but I figured I was just winded and I finished the game." The next morning, however, he nearly collapsed doing the milking. "Milking by hand," he says. "I went inside and told my wife that she better finish it for me and I went and lay down, and Jesus, I began to vomit and it hurt even worse so I figured then it was more than a butt end. She took me to the hospital."

Brown's playing days were finished, but that autumn he took over as coach, until his doctor read about it in the newspaper. "He gave me hell. He said there was far more stress coaching than playing so I quit and started to play oldtimers, and I still do."

Brown says that as a child he was a weak skater and the other kids made fun of him, so he quit. "When I was about ten I started again and I skated until I learned how and I became a good skater. And it didn't matter whether it was twenty or thirty below, we cleaned the ice and played. There wasn't anything else to do then, no TV, no dope to smoke. I think it's harder on the kids today, there's so much going on."

The Regina Pats, a force in junior hockey, invited Brown to their training camp. "But it was September and we were still harvesting so I stayed on the farm. I've wondered sometimes if I should have gone, but I didn't so that's that. I played senior here for twenty-four years and I was captain for eighteen. How many people can say that? I'm really proud of it."

In his garage he has a seat from the old Montreal Forum. It cost him $340. He sits in it every day to pull his workboots on and off. "I've always been a Canadien fan, which is rare around here. There's lots of Toronto and some Rangers and now Philadelphia. But the Canadiens, they're the great skaters and they know how to pass the puck and play position." He moves around in the old forum seat, getting comfortable, and smiles. "Maybe my wife will let me bring it into the house when I watch them win their next Stanley Cup." Then he adds, "You know what I'd really like some day? I'd like to meet Jean Béliveau."

7

Estevan, Saskatchewan

August 1997

ESTEVAN CLAIMS MORE HOURS OF sunlight than any other point in Canada, which is easy to believe on a day like today. In the glare of the afternoon sun, everything looks white and shimmers because the low prairie buildings offer little shade and there are few trees. It's a Saturday afternoon, but it's so hot that the streets and sidewalks are nearly deserted. What traffic there is runs to and from the baseball parks because there's a kids' baseball tournament on and teams have come from across the west. The motels and hotels are packed and at the Houston Pizza Family Restaurant on Souris Avenue a waiter named Frank got a real workout serving lunch. He says to a late customer, "At least it's cool in here. I could be working for Prairie Coal."

About twelve thousand people live in Estevan, which is two and a half hours southeast of Regina. A hundred years ago, as settlers flocked in to farm, important coal deposits were discovered beneath the prairie. The mines now fuel two thermal generating plants that supply more than half of Saskatchewan's electrical power. And since the 1950s there has been commercial production of crude oil and natural gas. Like Crowsnest Pass and other mining communities from Nova Scotia to British Columbia, Estevan has had labour strife. But it's a quiet, comfortable, and prosperous place now and, besides the baseball tournament, there's a reunion marking the fortieth anniversary of the Estevan Bruins, the junior hockey club. Two hundred former players and their wives are in town. There was a pancake breakfast at the curling rink, beside the arena, and there's to be a banquet there tonight.

Gail Rasmussen works in the Bruins front office. She's a young fortyish, bustling with energy. She says it took about a year to get the reunion organized. On top of that, she and her husband billet Estevan players. Because of cuts and trades, twenty-two players went through their home last season. "I just called them all 'Bud'. I couldn't keep their names straight," she says. "I was really glad when the season was over. But I like them and I like hockey. We've never had any trouble in the six years we've been taking them in."

Across the railway tracks from the curling rink, just off the main street, which is 4th Street, some ex-Bruins are relaxing in the cool gloom of the Planet Billiards Sports Bar with its sixteen pool tables. Joe Watson, who played fourteen years in the NHL and won two Stanley Cups with the Philadelphia Flyers, and whose brother Glen coaches Estevan, is sitting with Dave Paderski and Jack Norris. They were teammates in Estevan thirty-five years ago. Watson, with a few scars on his face, is outgoing, direct, and intense, hardly surprising for someone who played for Fred Shero. He works for the Flyers in marketing and he came all the way from Philadelphia for the

reunion. Dave Paderski, Watson's old defence partner with Estevan, didn't play professional hockey. He
went to the University of Denver on a hockey scholarship. He still lives in Denver, where he owns a
string of dry cleaners. He's tall with a deep voice and
a nose that's been broken at least once. He was born
in Flin Flon, in northwestern Manitoba, Bobby
Clarke's hometown. He came south to Notre Dame,
in Wilcox, not far from Estevan, the spartan school
founded by Father Athol Murray where hockey is
very important, and he moved up to play in Estevan
when he was seventeen. He says he doesn't mean to
put easterners down, but that it was probably harder
growing up in small northern and western towns
than it was in southern Ontario. "Farming, mining,
out here was pretty tough," he says. "Hockey was a
way out of it."

Jack Norris, big and fair-haired, was a goalie with
Boston, Chicago, and Los Angeles in the NHL and
Edmonton and Phoenix of the old World Hockey
Association. He's a grain farmer near Delisle, an
hour or so south of Saskatoon. Delisle is the home of
the Bentley family, which, as hockey families go,
ranks up there with the Conachers and the Patricks
and the Bouchers and the Hextalls — just behind the
Sutters. Norris's wife, Deanna, is there, too.

"I didn't marry a hockey player," she says. "I married a farmer. I don't even like hockey, even though
my best friend is Doug Bentley's daughter, Pat. I
don't know why I don't like it, but I never have. It
may be because when Jack began, goalies didn't wear
masks and I was frightened, or that goal is the hardest position to play, the last line of defence.

"It's funny, though, what a lot of wives don't like
about hockey I liked. I enjoyed moving around, the
travelling. Jack played on seven teams in thirteen

years. You meet interesting people. And I made good friends and they are still friends after twenty-five years. But it certainly isn't glamorous." On this hot Saturday in Estevan, however, what's on her mind besides hockey are the reports that the Nike shoe company is exploiting its workers in its factories in the Far East. "Our church wrote a letter to Nike," she says. "It's not right to make money that way. If enough people make a fuss maybe Nike will do something. I hope and pray something will be done."

The Estevan Bruins were originally the Humboldt Indians. They moved south in 1957 when Humboldt couldn't support them any more because it was too small. The Estevan *Mercury* ran a contest to name the new team. According to the official team history, the winning name, Bruins, was chosen by a C. H. Hook of Toronto, who happened to be passing through town, because the team was sponsored by Boston. (Although Estevan now plays in the Tier II Saskatchewan junior league, it still wears the black, white, and gold of the Boston Bruins.) Losing names for the team included Boomers, Gushers, and Soo Liners — the last for the railway line running up from North Dakota.

The team was first owned by the brash, combat-ive Scotty Munro. He was only about five feet five inches tall, but with his loud voice and nearly ungovernable temper he scared the hell out of men much bigger. Munro had been coaching for fourteen years before he got to Estevan and he'd already sent a lot of players to the NHL, among them Al Rollins, Jack Evans, Bert Olmstead, Metro Prystai, Glenn Hall, and Bill Gadsby. Munro drove his teams hard and wouldn't hesitate to be outrageous. Once, when an opposing player had a breakaway, he threw a bucket of pucks on the ice. Another time, after being suspended for several games for shoving a referee, he put his wife, Rose, behind the bench.

The more Munro screamed and yelled, the more the fans loved him, or hated him, and they crowded into the rinks to watch his teams. In Regina someone threw a steel bolt, hitting him on the head and knocking him out. Bruin players clambered into the stands swinging their sticks. Police finally forced them into their dressing room and Jack Norris says Munro was lying there on a stretcher, a big gash on his forehead. "Suddenly he comes to, opens his eyes, and, still on the stretcher, says, 'Wait till we get those sons of bitches back in our rink. The place'll be packed.' He was right," Norris says, "and we beat the hell out of them."

Dave Paderski, who studied marketing at university in Denver, says, "I was sitting in the lecture hall one day and it struck me. Jesus, I just spent three years with a guy who could market anything, hockey or detergents. He was a hell of a psychologist."

Joe Watson says of Munro, "I'll always remember first meeting him. I'd just got here and I was in a hotel room and the door opens and I see this short, stubby guy in a fedora with a cigarette and clouds of smoke and I thought, who the hell is that? I was only sixteen and our coach had been death on smoking. And the guy says, 'I'm Scotty Munro,' and I thought, Jesus Christ, that's the guy I'll be playing for?"

"We're in Prince Albert," Jack Norris says, "and we're losing after the second period and Scotty's giving us hell. He hated being interrupted but I said, 'Scotty, I smell smoke.' And he says something like, 'For Christ's sake, I'm smoking, that's why, now shut up, I'm trying to tell you something.' A couple of minutes later I said that I really smelled smoke and he tells me again to shut up. But I'm sitting by the door and I open it and all I can see is smoke. 'Jesus Christ,' Scotty yells, 'you're right.' The goddamn rink was burning down. We grabbed our clothes and ran outside in our skates and equipment. Jesus, it had to be about thirty below."

Joe Watson came to play in Estevan from Smithers, in British Columbia, a town of twelve hundred about five hundred miles north of Vancouver. "Joe Tennant, an engineer with the CNR in Smithers, was the juvenile coach," Watson says. "He had me scouted at the B.C. juvenile final in Prince George and the scout recommended me to Munro. Tennant was a great man and great with us kids. He lived kitty corner from the rink. When it was thirty or forty below, the pipes at the rink would freeze and we couldn't flood, so Joe would fill a barrel with water from his house and drag it over the ice himself. Joe gave me that first push to be a better athlete and a better person.

"I remember in 1957 or '58, when I was fourteen, the teacher asked us to write about what we wanted to do in life, and all I wrote was that I wanted to play in the NHL. Mine was the only one he read out in class. And the class laughed and he smirked. I can still see the smirk. But I got the last laugh. They're still there." As for Munro, Watson says, "I always had the desire to play, but Scotty gave me the discipline. If it hadn't been for him I'd still be in Smithers."

Jack Norris says, "One night we lost here to Regina, 3–1 or something, and Scotty's mad as hell, particularly at me, because I was one of his main guys. He came into the dressing room and tells us to leave on our stuff. 'You're not finished yet,' he said. So we sit there for half an hour and he comes back and gives us a pep talk. Next he made us skate — no pucks, just skate. He said we weren't in shape. And after an hour and a half of this he tells us to be back by six in the morning for more. Then he chews my ass out and says I'm no longer needed, I'm finished, no good, to clear out and go back to Delisle. I went to our boarding house. I felt awful. Joe and a couple of us sat and talked the rest of the night. At six I went to Scotty's office for my final cheque. He said, 'Well, things aren't as bad as I thought and you're one of the guys I'm counting on, so go out and have a good practice.' After practice he said he'd decided to keep me. That story may seem funny now but to an eighteen-year-old kid, to be told that he's useless, no good to anybody, is hard to take. But, you know, I liked him."

Dave Paderski adds, "I'm not saying Scotty Munro's style would work with the kids today, but for our era it was perfect."

"I do hockey schools in North America and Europe," Joe Watson says, "and I still teach some of the things Scotty taught me thirty-seven years ago. Scotty would say the less time you spend in your own zone the better, and years later with the Flyers Freddy Shero said the same thing. So most of our practices were spent getting the puck out of our zone. We had three or four systems in Philly, really basic, but Freddy used to say we'd win as long as we didn't let the other team break them down. Direct passes; we seldom used the boards. Give it to the offside defenceman, up the wing, up centre, or reverse the play — but always direct passes. Always very basic in our zone."

Watson goes on, "I remember we're playing Boston in the sixth game of the Stanley Cup final in '74 and Freddy said, 'Win today and you walk together forever.' We did win and it's so goddamn true. Twenty-six old Flyers still live around Philadelphia and when we have alumni functions others come from all over. Fred made us all believe in ourselves."

Watson says he went to the hospital when Shero was dying of cancer. "He was so thin, all shrivelled up, only his head looked normal. And you know, all he wanted to talk about was hockey. That's all, hockey. So we talked about hockey and the next day he died."

At the Beefeater Inn, Estevan's biggest motel, while the lobby bustles with youngsters in baseball uniforms and the ice machine hums loudly, Lorne Henning, in a room just off the lobby, talks quietly about hockey.

The former New York Islander is another ex-Estevan Bruin back for the reunion. In spite of the heat he's been playing golf with some of his old teammates. He's just showered and is waiting to go to the reunion dinner. With his bald head and glasses and his light grey summer suit, shirt, and tie, Henning looks more like an upwardly mobile banker or broker or lawyer than a man who retired in 1981 after nine years in the NHL and has been coaching since.

Henning was brought up first on a farm and later in the community of Resource, northeast of Saskatoon. Fifty people used to live in Resource, he says. Now there are three. "My mother and my father and my grandmother. There's no railway any more and the general store is gone. And the grain elevators are gone. They sort of kept the place together." Gone, too, is the curling rink. It was natural ice and as a child Henning skated there after the curling season ended for as long as the ice lasted. And his father built a rink on the farm where the two of them skated. When Lorne was ten, Robert Henning got a job at the federal agricultural research station in Resource. "So we moved and I built a rink there," Henning senior says. "We had to haul him off it for bed. He wouldn't come in on his own."

Robert Henning played intermediate hockey for Melfort, which is near Resource, and one year they won the Saskatchewan championship. "He was a very good hockey player so I guess I got the bug early," Lorne says. "He'd skate with me every day after he'd finished work. I could hardly wait."

Lorne Henning was first scouted at the provincial midget championships at Notre Dame, in Wilcox, by Scotty Munro and Ernie "Punch" McLean. Munro had left the Estevan Bruins and was running a junior team in Calgary. McLean had succeeded him at Estevan. "They flipped a coin for him and Ernie won," Robert Henning says, "so he went to Estevan."

But Lorne's first stop was with the North Battleford Beaver-Bruins, a farm team for McLean's Estevan Bruins, two hundred miles from home, where he was boarded with a family. He was fifteen. "It was a junior team in a senior league, mostly just boys against men," his father says. "They were in with Turtleford, Meadow Lake, and I think Unity. He came second in the scoring. He learned a lot of hockey that year." The following year he joined McLean in Estevan. A program note from that time says, "The Bruins' top three scorers last season, Greg Polis, Lorne Henning, and Brent Taylor, accounted for 128 of the Bruins' 237 goals."

Lorne Henning smiles and shakes his head. "We'd go by bus to Flin Flon. It seemed to take hours and hours. Flin Flon was a helluva tough town to play in. Bobby Clarke was playing for them. He was vicious even then, slashing, spearing, and the crowd would scream and throw stuff at us. We'd have two games, back to back, and you could guarantee that if we won the first game, it was automatic that the gloves would be off by the first shift of the second one.

"One night in Flin Flon we're in the dressing room between periods and we hear a commotion. It turns out Ernie's up in the stands taking on some Flin Flon fans. He's all by himself, for God's sake, so we all piled out to help him." He pauses, then he says, "And you know, the crazy bugger still had the glass chips in his eye from the accident," referring to McLean's crash in a small plane the previous spring.

"Another time we went on a week's trip and played five or six games," he says. "We started in Bismarck, North Dakota, with an exhibition game and then went to Flin Flon for two games. I can't remember for certain how long it took but seventeen hours sticks in my mind. Then it was to Kinisto for another exhibition game. But the bus broke down and they sent a school bus for us. We were running late so we had to change into our hockey stuff on the bus. The fans waited and the game didn't start until nine-thirty." He pauses and frowns. "You know, Prince Albert was in there somewhere, too. Anyway, finally, we're on our way home and the bus breaks down again. The club's executive had to drive their cars out to bring us home to Estevan. It was a horrendous trip. Things like that you'll never forget."

Henning says hockey demands so much. "In basketball or football, when a player gets hurt it's sometimes a joke," he says. "Hockey players often have to play through so much pain. It takes courage. It teaches you a lot about handling life."

His one regret is that he missed university. "Education wasn't much of a factor when I played junior. Kids now can get an education and play hockey. I spent a lot of years in high school but because we practised every afternoon I could only go for half the day. I eventually got it, and a couple of years of university, but it took a long time."

Robert Henning is very close to Lorne. "His mother and I have always tried to be a good influence on him. Because he's an only son we were together a lot. Besides hockey, we had a ball team in summer and we went fishing together. He gave me his first Stanley Cup ring."

8

Viking, Alberta

August 1997

DUANE SUTTER IS ON HIS farm for the summer, but
soon he'll be off to Florida and his job as an assistant
coach with the Panthers. Sutter, along with Lorne
Henning, was on those great New York Islander
teams of the early '80s that won four Stanley Cups.
"Nineteen consecutive playoff series without a loss,"
he says. "That's a record that'll never be broken."

About twelve hundred people live in Viking, the
Sutters' hometown, on the prairies east of
Edmonton. Early in the 1900s the Viking *Gazette*
promoted it as a railway town, "The Hub of the
Grand Trunk Pacific", and young families flooded
in. In the museum is a photograph of the "19th
Alberta Dragoons", taken in 1912. It shows seventeen young men, boys really, and an officer, in tunics
and wide-brimmed hats, some holding rifles, squinting into the sun, trying to look grown up. Matching
the names under the photograph, some of which are
difficult to read, against those on Viking's small
cenotaph, it seems that three of the seventeen didn't
return from the First World War.

Viking is no longer the "Hub" of anything, but it's still a robust farming community. Its official guide calls it the "Home of the Sutters". But long before Duane and his brothers came along there was Eddie Wenstob, who, for a while in the '30s, was the third-ranked light-heavyweight in the world. He fought before a huge crowd at London's Wembley Stadium. Murray Murdoch, hockey's original "Ironman" when he played for the New York Rangers, also in the '30s, and who later coached Yale, lived in Viking in the off-season. Viking had its own symphony orchestra in the 1930s. In 1952 Foster Hewitt officially opened Viking's rink. It's named the "Carena" because it was built with money raised by raffling off cars, and it's still being used. When they weren't outside on the ponds and sloughs, that's where the Sutters learned to skate.

"Mom and Dad were always an example for us, the way they worked, the way they lived," Sutter says. He's in the cool of his house with his young son on this sunny, hot afternoon. His wife has driven to the Edmonton airport with their daughter and a friend who is returning to Florida. Sutter is in jeans and a flannel workshirt, looking like the farmer he is, part-time. The house is big and comfortable. He's in the kitchen, which overlooks the fields between his farm and his father's.

"On a farm you have to work your rear end off from sunrise to sunset. It's the same with hockey," he says. "You can have all the talent in the world, but if you don't have the drive you'll never make it. We'd come home from school and three or four of us would go to the field to help Dad and the others would help Mom in the garden. And then there was homework.

"We had a big dairy barn and after chores we'd play hockey with a tennis ball in the hayloft. In the fall when the sloughs froze we'd skate. On Saturdays we'd be in town playing from eight in the morning until evening. We'd come home, do the chores, and try to catch the last couple of periods of *Hockey Night in Canada*.

"On Sunday we'd start playing on a pond near the barn, and there are always yard lights around a farm so between them and the light from the moon we'd keep playing long after dark.

"When we got older we'd play in Viking and down the line towards Wainwright. Mom was the one who'd rub our cold feet after a game, our older brothers would tell us to get back out there and quit crying, and Dad would supply discipline. If you spent too much time in the penalty box or took a misconduct he'd say, 'You do that again and next time you're not coming.'"

Duane followed his brothers Brian and Darryl from minor hockey in Viking to Red Deer and then to major junior hockey in Lethbridge. "When you're younger than your brothers a lot of people say you rode on their coattails, but I think that's baloney. You get a look maybe before another kid but that's all. After that you're on your own. Nobody is going to do you any favours."

Getting back to his mother and father, he says, "They instilled things in us and I think a coach and management can do the same thing. Al Arbour and Bill Torrey could, anyway. When I went to the Islanders I was nineteen and Al was like a second father to me, gave me a good kick when I needed it. We called him 'Radar'. He thought it was because his glasses made him look like Radar in *M*A*S*H**. It was really because he seemed to have the knack of knowing if you'd been out for a couple of beers or where you'd been."

Sutter says one reason for the Islanders' success was that the players respected each other. "You didn't have to be a Mike Bossy and score fifty goals or a Denis Potvin and be the best defenceman in the league. We all had our roles. There were no egos. Al used to say the minute we stepped into that dressing room, we'd better be ready to play together."

Driving over to his father's, Duane's half-ton throws up a plume of dust as white as a cloud against the high blue sky. This has been one of the driest summers in years. Louis Sutter is sixty-six. His house is a few minutes from Duane's and like Duane's is big and comfortable and very neat. There's a barn and a spacious farmyard, with heavy farm machinery in sheds. In spite of his sons' success, Louis Sutter is still a working farmer, and looks like one, browned by wind and sun, in jeans and a denim jacket. He's sitting in the rec room, surrounded by evidence of his boys' hockey careers from the time they were children. Louis Sutter looks a bit like Will Rogers, the American cowboy philosopher of the '30s, and he even has Rogers' slow, soft way of speaking. When he's asked for a favourite memory of his sons' achievements, his reply is thoughtful and understated, eschewing winning goals or Stanley Cup triumphs.

"One of the biggest thrills was watching their skating improve," he says. "Around here they'd seem to be on their ankles, then suddenly they'd be better. One winter I didn't see the twins, Rich and Ron, play for about a month. Then I went to a game and I was amazed by their skating. And it was all because they worked so hard at it."

He continues, "You know, Brent never played a game of midget. He went straight from bantam to the Red Deer Rustlers in the Alberta junior league and it was a tough league. Each team was allowed a couple of twenty-year-olds. There's a big difference between fifteen and twenty. I remember coming out of that Red Deer arena and it seemed every night was fifty below. Jesus, it's a cold arena, right down by the river."

Duane misses playing. "The toughest time is the playoffs," he says. "Specially when you see someone not playing, sitting out because of a little bruise or something and you think, 'Hell, he should be playing. I know I would be.'"

9

Trail, British Columbia

August 1997

THE OLD WESTERN INTERNATIONAL Hockey League was rough and entertaining, made up of ex-NHLers on their way down and those who had never made it up and felt that they had something to prove. The "International" came from two American entries — Spokane, Washington, and the Los Angeles Ramblers. A 1946 Ramblers program gushed that the WIHL had brought "the king of winter sports to southern California for the first time." The WIHL champions, besides getting a few extra dollars in their pay packet, were presented with the Shore Cup — put up by Dinah, the singer, not Eddie, the hockey man.

The Ramblers didn't last any longer than many Hollywood marriages, but for as long as they did they played in an arena named for Sonja Henie, cinema's figure-skating sweetheart. The WIHL's other teams were just the opposite of glittery L.A. Coming from the mining and lumber towns of British Columbia's East Kootenays, they were the Nelson Maple Leafs, Rossland Warriors, Kimberley Dynamiters, and Trail Smoke Eaters.

The city of Trail is on the Columbia River, about halfway between Calgary and Vancouver. It's a company town with a capital *C* — the *C* standing for Cominco, the lead-zinc mining and smelting giant. Cominco's huge, misshapen smelter broods possessively over the city and the river, looking like a medieval monastery or castle. About 25,000 people live in the region. Modernization has cut the Cominco workforce to nineteen hundred from nearly six thousand. Lumber mills have taken up some of the slack but according to the publisher of the *Trail Times*, Ray Picco, nothing has replaced Cominco, and in 1997 unemployment was a couple of points above the national average. However, with the modernization, Cominco has cleaned up its act, so at least Trail is no longer an industrial wasteland. The air is clear and clean, the surrounding mountains are green with trees, and the water sparkles in the nearby lakes and streams.

In spite of Trail's temperate climate — it's like coastal B.C.'s only without the rain — hockey has always been the major sport, and when an artificial ice arena was built in 1927, it was the only one at the time between Winnipeg and Vancouver. Beginning in the late '20s, until they folded in the mid-'80s, the Smoke Eaters won a handful of provincial championships, two Allan Cups, and two world titles. And Trail is not modest about it all. At city hall the phone is answered with "Trail, home of champions". A woman on the phone explains that the champions include Olympic-winning skiiers Nancy Greene and Kerrin Lee-Gartner, who are from Rossland, seven miles away, up Red Mountain. Robert Hampden Gray also came from Trail. He was a pilot attached to Britain's Royal Navy when he was killed attacking a Japanese destroyer. He was the last Canadian to be awarded the Victoria Cross in the Second World War.

In the Smoke Eaters' glory days — a provincial junior team now carries on the name — Cominco was very good to hockey players, giving them jobs and time off to play. This kept a lot of local players not destined for the NHL at home and it attracted others, especially from the wintry prairies. One of these was Dave Rusnell, who played centre. He was with the Yorkton Terriers when he agreed to join the Smoke Eaters for the world championships in 1961, and he's been in Trail ever since. He says the 1961 Smoke Eaters, who won the world title against all odds, were a close-knit group. "We had to be, we were all against Kromm, the little Hitler. He worked us so damn hard." Bobby Kromm, who had arrived ten years earlier from Calgary to play for Trail, had taken over the team in 1959.

Cal Hockley was the Smoke Eaters' captain. "Bobby wasn't very big, but he was a hard little bugger," he says. "One night we were in Spokane and he got in a fight with a fan. Four cops came into the dressing room and picked him up. His skates were shooting sparks on the concrete when they dragged him off to jail. He'd never quit."

The Chatham Maroons beat Trail in four straight games to win the Allan Cup in 1960. (Cesare Maniago, who starred in goal for Chatham, came from Trail.) In those days the Allan Cup winners would automatically be asked to represent Canada at the world championships the following spring. But when the Maroons couldn't afford the trip, it fell to the Smoke Eaters as runners-up. The city and its citizens raised the money to send them, but they were not a popular choice. Sportswriters, largely from the east, and even Jack Roxburgh, president of the

Canadian Amateur Hockey Association, called Trail the weakest team to leave Canada in years. Nevertheless, on March 12, 1961, in Geneva, before a capacity crowd of more than twelve thousand, including hundreds of Canadian servicemen who'd come in from their NATO bases in France and Germany, Canada defeated the Soviet Union 5–1 to win the world championship. When the Smoke Eaters returned home, even the Nelson Maple Leafs, arch league rivals, joined the celebrants, parading with a mock coffin to represent the funeral of the critics who'd kept saying Trail wasn't good enough.

According to James Cameron, the team's president, what these critics hadn't taken into account, besides the resolve of the players, was Kromm; he coached like a man on a life mission. In a book he wrote on the team, Cameron said that on the month-long, nineteen-game tour that preceded the world championships, Kromm ordered that no one keep track of goals and assists. He didn't want any star system to threaten his hard-work philosophy. Neither did he go along with hockey's convention of a few beers after a game. He recognized the significance of the bigger European ice surfaces, thus fitness was more important than ever. And because the puck had to travel farther, passes had to be quicker and harder.

"Before we went to Europe he had us on the ice two or three hours a day, seven days a week," says George Ferguson, who, like Rusnell, comes from the prairies. "You got off work at Cominco and you got on the ice. When we got to Europe for the exhibition games he never let up on us. On days we didn't play, we practised twice."

Dave Rusnell says, "At one point we flew from Stockholm to Helsinki and then had a five-hour bus ride to Tampere for a game. The plane was late but Bobby phoned ahead to tell the rink we were going directly to practice. Hell, we're looking at nine-thirty at night. That's the only time we rebelled. We said, 'Bobby, we aren't going anywhere until we eat.' He sulked about that for quite a while. But it was because of him we won."

Rusnell is sixty-four. He has retired from Cominco and lives with his wife in Warfield, on the outskirts of Trail. He's a family man with children and grandchildren. After he quit competitive hockey he played old-timers for a bit. "But I guess I didn't have the right temperament," he says. "I mean, I found guys forty and fifty years old still trying to make a reputation for themselves and I couldn't be bothered with that." In the winter Rusnell skis. In the summer he sails and swims. "It's important to keep in shape," he says. "After fifty, it's payback time."

He was born in Wadena, in central Saskatchewan, where his father ran a restaurant. He gestures towards a coffee table where the weekly TV magazine has broadcaster Pamela Wallin on the cover. "She's from Wadena," he says. He returns to hockey. "When I was fifteen I joined Humboldt juveniles for the provincial playdowns and I signed what they said was a proof-of-age card. The next year the Regina Pats, under Murray Armstrong, wanted me. I was on a line with Eddie Litzenberger in the pre-season. We would have a helluva team. The night before the first regular game I get a call from Murray. 'Dave,' he says, 'we got a problem. You can't play with us.'"

It seems the card Rusnell had signed had bound him to Humboldt and Humboldt had dealt him to the Moose Jaw Canucks. "I'd have loved to have stayed with the Pats," he says. "That was a hell of a disappointment. My dad was so upset, but in those days you couldn't do anything.

"They had a strict system in Regina. Murray had contacts with every high school teacher in town and if you didn't show up for school or were fooling around, he'd know about it. And if you didn't smarten up, you didn't play. The people who ran the Canucks were very nice, but they weren't like that."

Following junior Rusnell played for the Milwaukee Chiefs in what was then the International Hockey League. "Most of the guys were on the way down, not up, and had left their families behind in Ontario," he says. "They spent all the time partying and boozing and here I am, a kid, trying to make the NHL. It totally disillusioned me. Even the coach would disappear for a couple of days at a time. We'd go on road trips and there wouldn't be enough money to eat. I guess I didn't have the balls to hang in. Anyway, I came back and played for Yorkton."

Later he spent two years in Britain, one of them in Nottingham with Chick Zamuck, the Winnipegger who was the first Canadian to make a career in British hockey. "He'd have been good wherever he played," Rusnell says. "And he made me a better hockey player." Zamuck was the first player Rusnell saw with a curved blade, long before Chicago's Bobby Hull and Stan Mikita came along. He says that Northland, the hockey stick manufacturers, had a branch outside London and made the sticks specially for Zamuck.

Zamuck also taught Rusnell the importance of body strength. "When I came home I got a job as a travelling salesman for a patent drug company. I used to carry weights in my car and work out in my hotel room at night. I also got a punching bag and learned how to scrap."

Rusnell says that he returned to Canada to build

security for his family because he didn't have much education. "I'd seen a lot of Canadians over in Europe getting fairly well paid with soft jobs in the summer, holidays on Majorca, all that; then, suddenly they're thirty-five and past it and they have nothing. Mind you, Yorkton didn't pay. We worked out a split of the gate. One year it was twenty-one dollars. But I was making myself known in hockey again so when Trail was looking for a centre, they wanted me. I moved my family out in October 1960; we had two children, and we had to live in an apartment over the beer parlour for the first three weeks. My wife's an organist and she was asked to play at the Baptist church. She noticed people around her looking at her and sniffing and she realized that all our clothes smelled of beer and tobacco.

"But we liked it right away. Cominco hired me as a research technician. I had a grade eleven education and they taught me on the job, working on the re-greening of land around mines. And this was a red-hot hockey town. There were lots of prairie people and they'd stop you in the street to talk. It was a small town then and it's tough to play in a small town. You have to go to work the next day and at work they sure as hell will let you know how you did." Rusnell smiles and looks across his garden. It's very quiet. "I love it here," he says. "The Kootenays are the best-kept secret in Canada."

Seth Martin, the goalie, was the only Smoke Eater who went on to play in the NHL, backing up Glenn Hall with the St. Louis Blues for a season. Like the others, he gives a lot of the credit to Kromm. "He wasn't the easiest guy to get along with," Martin says. "He was really strict, maybe at the time we thought too strict. Between that and the travel things might get a bit tense and the guys would start bitching at each other, but he sorted it all out. No matter what happened, the bad press from home or the bad press over there, Bobby kept us focused."

Martin has retired from the Trail fire department and lives in Glenmerry, a suburb across the Columbia River from Trail. He was born in Rossland, where the main attractions are skiing and hiking. "That came later," he says. "Back then hockey was the game." He laughs. "One year we're in a midget championship against Nelson. It's a Friday-Saturday, two-game, total-goal series. Our team spent most of Friday shovelling the snow off our outdoor rink for the game that night so I guess we were pretty tired. Anyway, Nelson beat us 10–1. The next night we played in Nelson, the big civic arena, artificial ice of course. It was a helluva thrill but also pretty scary for a kid from Rossland who'd never been around. We lost again. This time 16–0. . . ."

Martin says another hockey memory stands out, this one from the world championships. "It was against Czechoslovakia and it was 1–1 towards the end of the third period. The puck was shot and it hit the toe of my skate, bounced off one goal post, then across and bounced off the other post, but it stayed out. If we'd lost that game to Czechoslovakia, we wouldn't have made it to the finals to play the Soviet Union." (Cal Hockley was back-checking on the play. "I saw the whole thing. Perfect view. I might as well have been watching a slow-motion movie of my own execution.")

In the mid-'60s, Martin played three years for Canada's national team, the team built by Father David Bauer to take part in world championships. "It was a real honour, even if we didn't win a thing," he says. "I'd get letters calling us a bunch of useless

prima donnas, giving us hell, saying we had no business representing Canada. They didn't realize what
Father Bauer was trying to do, that he was only a
couple of players away from a really good team. And
he sure as hell wasn't getting much help from back
home. Teams didn't want to release players to him."

George Ferguson, a teammate of Rusnell's with the
Moose Jaw Canucks as a junior, and with the Smoke
Eaters, lives in a small house just off the main street
in Rossland with his wife, Maxine, and four cats.
He's sixty-three and he's still built like the proverbial
fire hydrant he was when he played. He was born
and grew up in Moose Jaw and, like many prairie
boys, when he hit the Kootenays he got a job with
Cominco, and stayed. Hockey was his life. "I always
worked real hard at it. I mean I was twenty-one
before I ever drank a beer," he says. "When I was a
kid I lived at the rink. I'd finish one game and someone would say, 'Hey, we're short a guy,' and I'd play
another and another. Age didn't matter. I didn't have
a father so my mother would have to send the cops
down to bring me home, but at least she knew where
I was all the time."

The Chicago Blackhawks signed Ferguson out of
juvenile. "They said that they couldn't give me any
money because I was only fourteen," he says. "But
they looked after my mom pretty good with school
expenses and hockey sticks and stuff for me." After
Moose Jaw, Chicago sent him to Galt, Ontario, for
his final year of junior.

That summer, aged twenty, Ferguson got married.
Shortly afterwards he went to the Blackhawks'
camp. "I played two exhibition games, one in
Toronto and one in Calgary, and it looked like they
might keep me. But when I said that I wanted my

wife to move down they were mad as hell. They didn't know I'd got married. They said that I was too young." Ferguson said the Blackhawks wanted him to leave his wife back home. "But I wouldn't do that, so they suspended me and I went to work for her dad. He was a contractor in Flin Flon."

In spite of this, Ferguson says he's not bitter over Chicago, and on his living room wall there's a big picture of him in a Blackhawk uniform, in that classic sideways pose, the stick raised, the ice chips flying.

Chicago lifted his suspension after a month and Ferguson joined Calgary in the old western league, akin to today's AHL. "I was the fifth defenceman, just sitting there. They were starting a senior team in Rossland in the WIHL. I'd never heard of Rossland, or Trail for that matter. I just wanted to play. So I said I'd come for one year and here I am, still here more than forty years later."

Ferguson hasn't been to a hockey game in three years and he doesn't watch them on TV until the playoffs. "They shoot pretty good, but you don't see good plays, all that goddamn grabbing and holding," he says. "And no direct passes. Everything's off the boards, eh? And all that money they're paid. Jesus . . ." He says the most he ever made was five hundred dollars and a team jacket. "But I played on a world championship team and that makes up for it all."

Cal Hockley worked at Cominco and now is in real estate in Trail with Coldwell Banker. Sitting in his office two blocks from the Cominco arena, where he played for so many years, he's a happy man, and hockey is the major reason. "I played four years for Kimberley, until the roof of the arena caved in," he says. "So I came to Trail. It was 1956. First, I made a deal for a job at Cominco, and then I made a deal with the hockey club. We've a nice home. We raised our family here. It's a great place to live."

He says that at one time Cominco hired a lot of athletes. "Baseball players and hockey players. I think the theory was that men who were team players would be good employees. And they usually had motivation and drive. A lot of guys they brought in got up quite high in the company, and stayed around and made a real contribution to the community."

At six feet and 190 pounds Hockley was the biggest man on the Smoke Eaters. Today, he's a bit bigger. He was born in Fernie, B.C., towards the Alberta border from Trail. "One season I played for four teams: high school, midget, juvenile, and intermediate." Like several other Smoke Eaters, including his friend Don Fletcher, he played junior with the Lethbridge Native Sons.

"He and I were laughing the other day about the time in Edmonton the team got a real deal on sticks," Hockley says. "Four dozen of them, nearly worth their goddamn weight in gold to us. We travelled in four big cars in those days, so we lashed the sticks in a stick bag to one of the back bumpers, the car I'm in, and took off for Lethbridge. We're whipping along and suddenly cars behind start honking. We can't see a goddamn thing out the rear window because of the frost. We figure they wanted to race so the guy driving steps on it. Christ, they stay right behind us, still honking like hell. It turns out our exhaust pipe had set the sticks on fire. We must have looked like a goddamn rocket flying down that highway streaming flames."

After junior Hockley signed with the New York Rovers. They played in the old eastern league and were owned by Madison Square Garden, which also owned the Rangers. "Gaye Stewart was with the Rangers and he'd skate with us sometimes," Hockley says. "He was great to me, a really nice man. I'll never forget that. It meant a lot when you're a kid and that far from home." There's another thing he'll never forget: "That year in New York showed me that I wasn't good enough for the NHL. I went to a few minor pro camps after that, but I figured for me senior hockey and a job was the way to go, and I don't regret it, not for one goddamn minute."

As for the world championships, he says, "For a bunch of hicks from a little town like this to go over and represent Canada, and win, was a real thrill. You can't beat that."

10

Timmins, Ontario

October 1997

IT'S A COLD AND DARK night, a harbinger in northern Ontario of colder and darker nights to come. The wind is whipping through the trees up on the old mine property behind the McIntyre Arena and down below, dry leaves make a scratching sound as they're blown across the arena's parking lot. A teenage boy lugs a bulky hockey bag and two sticks to his car. He opens the trunk and suddenly a gust of wind slams the trunk closed again, nearly knocking him over. "Jesus Christ!" he exclaims. He braces himself against the car's bumper while he puts his bag and his sticks in the trunk with one hand and holds the lid with the other.

Inside the arena, after the dark outside, the white ice and the white boards are dazzling under the banks of white lights. A handful of fathers, drinking coffee from Styrofoam cups, are waiting to take their sons home once they've finished practising. Tomorrow is a school day. One father says, "He likes the outdoors so maybe he can get something in Minnesota or Michigan." He's talking about hockey scholarships.

Another father points towards one of the coaches on the ice. "He doesn't let them fool around, which is good because if they fool around in practice, they might in a game and it could cost them."

Denis Robichaud says that his son, André, wants a career in hockey. "But he's good in school, too, so we'll have to see what happens." He says whether his son goes after a scholarship to an American school or tries to play junior in Canada, "We'll live with it. It's his life. We just feel lucky to be part of it."

Denis is a small, slim man. His son, at only sixteen, is six foot one and 177 pounds and is lifting weights to try to get bigger and stronger. He's in grade eleven and says he has an 80 percent average. He plays defence. "I know the game, I'm a smart player, I play my position well," he says. "How good I am as far as the OHL goes, never mind the NHL, remains to be seen. I'd like to make a life in hockey, though. It's the best game there is. It just blows you away. That's all you can think about up here in the winter."

His father says, "Damn right. Hockey is a big part of our life. There's not too many guys around Timmins and South Porcupine who didn't play hockey. It's always been hockey up here. Player after player has come from here."

Another man says, "Yeah, and if you want to know anything about the old days, ask Carlo, Carlo Cattarello, he'll know."

"Yeah," another man agrees, "ask Carlo."

"They say that, do they?" Carlo Cattarello, eighty-four years old, sounds pleased. "But I forget some names now. There's been so many of them."

It's a glorious afternoon. Last night's storm has passed and Carlo is in his garden checking on some grapevines. He and his wife, Mary, live in the same small, yellow clapboard house in South Porcupine that they moved into when they were married in 1936. Carlo is a slight, white-haired, gentle man. He smiles a lot in spite of a bum knee that stopped him from playing tennis the past summer. Back in the house, in the living room's clutter of books, magazines, newspapers, and Mary's sewing machine and clothes, Carlo comes up with a photograph of himself with the late Roland Michener, the Governor-General, taken at a seniors' tennis tournament in Toronto; and there's one of Carlo with Jean Béliveau.

Carlo Cattarello was born in Cobalt, on the Quebec border, about three hours south of Timmins. His father, an immigrant, took the family back to his native village, near Turin in northern Italy, when Carlo was six. "The first year we toured around," Carlo says. "Just about every hill in Italy has a church and my aunts were very religious so we probably climbed every hill and went to every church. After that we settled down. I had an old pair of skates with me. Not often, but now and then, the river would freeze along the shore and I could skate a little." After four years, in 1923, the family returned to northern Ontario and Carlo's father opened a pool hall and a bowling alley in Timmins.

Carlo was a good hockey player in the league made up of teams from the mines that dot the area. During the Second World War, before he went overseas with the artillery, his teammates at the military base at Petawawa included Turk Broda, the great Maple Leaf goalie, and Detroit's Connie Brown. Back at home after the war, he became friendly with Frank Boucher, the old New York Ranger and later Rangers coach and general manager. Carlo scouted for the Rangers for years, and also began to coach.

Maurice Switzer, who has been publisher of both the Sudbury *Star* and the Timmins *Press*, knows the north. He also knows Carlo well. "I've never heard him speak a malicious word about another human being," Switzer says. "So it's probably no accident that I've never heard anyone say an unkind word about him."

Carlo shrugs. "I don't know about that, but if so it's probably because I never yelled at my players. I never wanted to discourage them from hockey because up here hockey means everything, and they were kids and I've never been sure what good it does to yell at kids."

Watching some youngsters practise at the South Porcupine arena, a few minutes from his home, Carlo says, "I think when I coached we played more like the Russians. Puck control was very important. We didn't dump it in the way they do now."

Nearly fifty thousand people live in the city of Timmins, which since 1973 includes Schumacher, Porcupine, and South Porcupine. For the first half-century the area's fortune was dependent on the mines — largely Hollinger, Dome, and McIntyre. "We began because of mining and we're still here because of it," says Paul Caron, who runs the Timmins self-help office. "Almost everything is a spinoff." Fewer mines are operating today, though, and, as in many northern communities, the trains don't stop here any more. "But there's a good airport," Caron says. "Timmins is a hub, a distribution centre."

From the '30s to the '60s, Timmins and the other mining towns in northeastern Ontario and north-western Quebec — Cochrane, Kirkland Lake, Rouyn-Noranda, and, to the south, Sudbury and North Bay — probably produced as many good hockey players per capita as any other part of

Canada: Toe Blake, Bill Durnan, Tim Horton, Ted Lindsay, Dick Duff, Dave Keon, Bob Nevin, Gus Mortson, the Mahovlichs, the Hillmans, the Hannigans, the Costellos, Johnny McLellan, Pete Babando, Allan Stanley, Dean Prentice, Larry Regan, Jim Pappin, Willie Marshall, Kent Douglas, Tom Webster, Leo Labine, Real Chevrefils, Pete Palangio, Al Arbour, Ed Giacomin, Dale Rolfe, Bep Guidolin, Walt Tkazchuk, Ron Duguay, Don Lever . . .

"In the '40s and '50s it was as if there was a pipeline right to Toronto and the OHA, particularly St. Mike's, and down it our players would go," Carlo says. "Ted Lindsay was going to play for a junior team I coached but he ended up at St. Mike's. The kids around here had an advantage then; they could really skate because of the long winters. But now, in the south, with all their artificial rinks, they've caught up."

In 1974, Carlo and Mary went to the Soviet Union with a party of Canadians that included Fred Shero, then the coach of the Philadelphia Flyers. "The Russians loved Fred because of hockey," Mary says. Then she adds, forthrightly, "He was a very nice man but he didn't eat properly, he didn't look after himself. He didn't seem well." Mary was able to help with interpreting. Her family came from Russia and her maiden name was Barilko. Bill Barilko, who scored the dramatic overtime goal against Montreal in 1951 that gave the Maple Leafs the Stanley Cup, was her first cousin. Among the Cattarellos' mounds of newspaper clippings are the reports of the plane crash that killed Barilko on a fishing trip to James Bay in August 1951.

Barilko was the stick-boy and backup goalie on one of the most successful teams Carlo Cattarello coached, the 1942 Ontario juvenile champions. That was when juvenile hockey, with its age limit to eighteen, and not midget, was the stepping stone to major junior hockey. "It's a wonder Bill could play at all because he had very bad eyes," Mary says. "It took him three years to get out of grade eight. He couldn't see the blackboard properly. In those days they never thought it might be something like his eyesight. They just let him struggle on his own. He worked very hard, but he always liked hockey more than school."

"Bill Barilko could hardly skate when I first met him," says Frank Sicoli, who was on that juvenile team. "I never expected him to get anywhere, specially with those thick glasses. That was long before he got his contact lenses." He laughs. "Just shows what kind of a scout I'd have made." He goes on, "We were the only juveniles in the north so we had to play in a Junior B league. I think we only lost two games all year. One of the guys we played against was Bep Guidolin and he went on to a helluva NHL career. The final was at Maple Leaf Gardens. Jesus, what a thrill! Most of us had never been south before. We weren't used to artificial ice. It was so sticky and slow, but we won, we beat St. Catharines."

Following juvenile, Sicoli played junior in Stratford. "The people were really nice and we got free restaurant meals, but I was homesick sometimes," he says. Next, after two years in the army, he came home and worked underground for Dome. He played in the mines' league with the Carnegie brothers, Herb and Ozzie, who never got a shot at the NHL because they were black, and two other great local players, Eddie Brown, who had only one eye, and

"Bummer" Doran, both of whom eventually played in the old Maritime senior league. "Eddie lost his eye when he fell and a skate caught him," Sicoli says. "One night in a tavern I was sitting beside him and he had his standard order of eight drafts in front of him. He drank four of them and asked me to watch the rest while he went to the men's room. I instinctively looked over and his glass eye was bobbing around in one glass, staring up at me. Sometimes it would pop out when we were playing and we'd have to stop the game to try to find it. I don't know why he played with it in, but he did. The thing was, eye or no eye, Eddie — and Bummer, too — liked the good life too much to take hockey seriously. They were awfully good, by any standards. But there was no money then so some guys didn't think a career in hockey was worth working hard for."

A big plus for a kid in the north, Sicoli says, was the racial mix. "I was on a team with a Finn, a Croatian, a Ukrainian, as well as Scots, Irish, Italians, and French." The Sicolis moved from South Porcupine to Peterborough when they had to send their two sons, born deaf, to a special school near Belleville. "We wanted to be near them," Sicoli says. "Not so near they could run away home if they're homesick, and like I said, I know what it's like to be homesick, but near enough we could see them a lot. We couldn't do that and live in Timmins, but I went back to a school reunion and saw a lot of the guys."

As for Carlo Cattarello, Sicoli says, "He looked after us for years, in hockey and in baseball. Every Sunday morning, all winter, we'd pile in his car for seven o'clock practice at the McIntyre. Every Sunday morning without fail. If it hadn't been for Carlo we'd probably never have played. He was wonderful to us."

Allan Stanley and Pete Babando were also on that 1942 juvenile team. Babando went on to play with Boston, Detroit, and Chicago and Stanley spent twenty-one years in the NHL, ten with Toronto. He says, "We were just kids when we started, maybe twelve years old or so, and we were together with Carlo for five years, the last two playing juvenile. The first year Kirkland Lake beat us for the northern Ontario championship. Ted Lindsay was on that team. The next year we won. The team was called the Holman Pluggers because it was sponsored by Holman Machines, a company that supplied diamond drills to the mines.

"Carlo was the greatest thing that ever happened to us. We'd had coaches before but Carlo was exceptional with kids. He treated us with real respect. He's a very good man. And he did it for nothing, for years and years."

Carlo says, "Stanley played centre when he came to me but as a centre I don't think he'd have made a senior team. I put him back on defence and as a defenceman he carried the puck well and hardly ever got caught out of position."

Pete Babando scored Detroit's overtime goal to beat the New York Rangers for the 1950 Stanley Cup. As a kid he lived two houses down from Carlo, and he still does. "When we were growing up Carlo's front porch was full of baseball equipment in summer and hockey equipment in winter," he says. "If you needed something, skates, a stick, a ball glove, you went to Carlo's. It was always like that."

Mary Cattarello says, "Pete is awfully nice. But he's also very shy and very quiet, probably the shyest person I've ever known."

"I sort of took him under my wing," Carlo says. "His family came from the same part of Italy as my father did. Besides, he was already a bit of a loner. When he was a youngster and I was playing senior for South Porcupine, the rink was really cold and I'd come off the ice and Pete would have a blanket to keep me warm between shifts. I was the only one he'd let have the blanket."

Ernie Keefe is sixty-eight and a pastor in a French Baptist church in Repentigny, on the outskirts of Montreal, and a part-time teacher at a Baptist seminary. He's back in Timmins to visit friends, including Carlo. "Carlo was the kind of coach you wanted to win for because you liked him so much," Keefe says.

Keefe's father was what was known as a Barnardo boy, one of the children sent from the Barnardo orphanages in England to work, largely on farms, in Canada. He found his way to Timmins around 1912 as the mines were opening up. "When my mother came to join him and tried to buy a train ticket in Toronto they couldn't even find Timmins on the map," Keefe says. His mother was very religious. "She wouldn't let me skate on Sundays, but all day Saturday I never took my skates off. We lived opposite a rink and she'd spread newspapers on the floor under the kitchen table when I came in to eat."

Keefe played for Carlo a few years after the Stanley-Babando team. "I'll always remember how he used to stress backhand passes," he says. "He'd tell us not to turn our bodies to try to make the pass on the forehand. Not only did it telegraph the pass, it left you open for a bodycheck." Sitting over a coffee near the Timmins *Press*, for which he wants to write an article on Carlo, Keefe says, "I remember when we were just kids, a team official, much older than Carlo, started to boast to us about his relationships with women. Carlo told him to shut up. He didn't want any talk like that in front of us. He really looked after us. He's a man of principle."

After a year of junior in the Northern Ontario Hockey Association, Keefe went south to the Barrie Flyers. One of his teammates was Real Chevrefils, also a Timmins native, who went on to Boston and Detroit before drinking himself out of hockey, and to death. "He could have been one of the greatest players ever," Keefe says.

In December 1948 the Flyers traded Keefe to the Galt Red Wings, and in his first game he suffered a serious skull fracture. "It was against Stratford and I faced off in our end with Danny Lewicki," he says. "I got the puck to one of our defencemen and broke for a pass but he tried to clear it; he really drove it hard, and it hit me in the head. When I came to in the dressing room I couldn't remember what had happened after the faceoff. I tried to talk but I couldn't. Part of my brain was paralysed. I heard the doctor say to the manager, 'We have to get him to hospital in a hurry.' Then I heard the ambulance siren. It was at that moment I realized that maybe this is what it's like when you're dying. And I was thinking that one second after death, the fact that I'd signed a 'C' form with the New York Rangers or that I'd played Junior A hockey, one second after I leave this life, those things don't count any more." But Keefe made a surprisingly fast recovery and even played the last two games of Galt's schedule. "I had to wear a helmet, of course, they were leather then. Not much by today's standards," he says.

That summer he began to think seriously of joining the ministry. "On the one hand was the childhood dream of playing professional hockey, on the other the call from God." Keefe says that in the fall he went to Buffalo's AHL training camp in Fort Erie, but didn't play very well, "and I'd lost ten pounds over the summer worrying about what I should do." He was assigned to Washington in the Atlantic league but he said he wanted to go home to think about it. "I was only twenty, it was a big decision, but I decided to follow the Lord."

Father Les Costello is one of those who went down that hockey pipeline to St. Mike's. He's back now and around Timmins he's 'Father Les'. After St. Mike's Costello played in the AHL and for a bit with the Maple Leafs before he entered the priesthood. His brother Murray played in the NHL and another brother, Jack, played senior hockey. Les Costello is seventy. His eyes sparkle and his voice is loud, whether he's talking or laughing, and he does a lot of both. "I love the north," he says. "I was born here and when I had a chance to pick a diocese I chose the north. I've been all over up here and now I'm back home in Timmins. I have a brother in Ottawa and one in Windsor and they ask me what the hell I'm doing up here and I tell them I'm here because I like it. The people in the north are great." His church, St. Alphonsus, is on a hill amid the small white stucco and wooden houses built years ago for miners, within sight of the old McIntyre mine shaft and the McIntyre Arena.

Thirty-four-year-old Frank Zimperi used to work at the McIntyre Arena. "Father Les would skate every day and he'd get me to skate with him. He always wanted to play hit the goalpost or crossbar for twenty-five cents a pop. I'd usually lose five or six bucks but if I ever got ahead he'd say, 'Double or nothing,' and then he'd hit the crossbar."

Costello leans across his desk, thrusting his broad face forward to make his point. "They're spoiling the game with all that stickwork, the holding, and the interference. And the hitting from behind. We never hit from behind. I was at a game with Carlo and he said, 'They're bigger and faster and shoot harder today.' I said, 'So what?' and Carlo said, 'I didn't say they were smarter.'" He sits back, laughing.

After a moment he goes on. "My father was a dynamic man who worked at Dome for forty years. When I was growing up he'd stress how important education was. I could have played junior in Galt, but my father said no, school was important, and I ended up at St. Mike's. I was influenced there by two men, Father David Bauer and Father Ted McLean. They told me that there was a lot more to life than hockey. So I owe my education to hockey and to my father. My education made me realize that I had an obligation to other people, not just to myself. When I turned professional I was sent to Pittsburgh, a Leaf farm team then. We were treated well, had free passes to all the nightclubs, anything we wanted. It was fun. I was young and I loved hockey. But I had this nagging feeling that I wasn't fulfilling my potential. I wanted more education, for one thing. I guess the church was in the back of my mind all the time. But, in the Catholic tradition, it's not you who chooses, but God who chooses you, and I got the call. There's no better, fulfilling life than the priesthood. A lot of people said I was crazy, but what the hell, how long do you last in hockey? Here I am, forty years in the priesthood and still going strong."

Sitting in the McIntyre Arena's coffee shop, Lou Battochio, a retired phys. ed. teacher and municipal politician, says, "The people here love Father Les. His services are always jammed. You know why? He never lectures. He tells the odd joke, and you're out in twenty minutes."

Battochio is with Fred Salvador, a former recreation director who played football in the '50s for Toronto Balmy Beach in the old Ontario Rugby Football Union and briefly for the Montreal Alouettes and the Ottawa Rough Riders in the days of Peahead Walker and Kaye Vaughn and Tom "The Bomb" Tracy. Salvador and Battochio are trying to put together a hall of fame at the arena. They've started with pictures of hockey players. And there's one of Barbara Ann Scott, the world and Olympic figure-skating champ-ion of the '40s. She came from Ottawa but she trained at the McIntyre. "She was up here six or seven years in a row when the Mac was the only rink in Ontario with ice in the summer," Battochio says. "They ran the Schumacher Figure Skating School here. And the guys would come over from Kirkland Lake and even Noranda to skate before training camp: Ted Lindsay, Wayne and Larry Hillman, Willie Marshall, Tod Sloan."

The Toronto Maple Leafs inaugurated the arena in 1938. McIntyre's president, J. P. Bickell, had built it for his employees and their families. Bickell was also the Leafs' president and he brought them in for an inter-squad game, the Blues against the Whites. "I was a rink rat and I was there that night," Battochio says. "The next day they came to the our school and there was a special assembly and we met them all — Syl Apps, Turk Broda, Red Horner, Gordie Drillon. For a kid, you can't beat that."

Pete Babando is seventy-two. He wasn't at that first game at the McIntyre, but ten years afterwards he was playing against Apps, Broda, Nick Metz, and other Maple Leafs. Babando is about five foot nine and still has his broad-shouldered, powerful hockey build. He has a thatch of white hair and heavy, black horn-rimmed glasses. After six years with Boston, Detroit, and Chicago he came home to repair ore cars. "I like it here, even the cold winters," he says. He speaks very softly and he seems as shy as Mary Cattarello said he was. He admits that he likes to keep to himself. "Our hockey contracts had clauses that we'd be available for community gatherings or public speaking," he says. "I hated that. I don't like crowds. My tongue always felt thick if I had to talk in public. That's why I'm not much for team reunions or anything like that."

Babando was born in western Pennsylvania where his father was a miner. His father, as Carlo's father did, took his family back to Italy for a while. When he returned to North America it was to Timmins. Pete Babando was scouted by Baldy Cotton, of the Boston Bruins, during that 1942 juvenile championship game against St. Catharines at Maple Leaf Gardens. "He came up to me between periods, asked me my name and whether I wanted to play pro," Babando says. The Bruins sent him to Galt for junior. After that it was the Boston Olympics in the old eastern league, and then the Hershey Bears in the AHL. He was called up to Boston and was on a line with Billy Taylor and Don Gallinger in 1948 when Taylor and Gallinger were caught dealing with gamblers.

"One day I was called into the office of Art Ross, the general manager," Babando says. "Dit Clapper, the coach, was there, too. It turned out they had Taylor and Gallinger on tape talking to gamblers before a game. They wanted to know where I was at the time. I didn't know anything about it but I was really scared. I didn't know what they were thinking. Anyway, I was okay."

Babando's most memorable moment came in his one season with Detroit, where his teammates included Gordie Howe, Ted Lindsay, Red Kelly, and Sid Abel. Babando scored at 8:31 of the second over-time period to give Detroit a 4–3 victory over the New York Rangers in the seventh game of the 1950 Stanley Cup final. It was his second goal of the game. "The faceoff was in their end and George Gee was our centre. I remember it clearly. He waved me into position so he could draw the puck to my forehand, but it came to my backhand. I shot right away, a low shot. I don't think Chuck Rayner ever saw it."

Babando drops his voice even more. "It's funny," he says, "but I hadn't had a very good season. I don't want it to sound as if I'm making excuses, because I don't like people making excuses. But first I broke my thumb. I played in a cast but I couldn't shoot properly. Next I got chest pains. It turned out my tonsils were infected and the poison was dripping into my chest. Jack Adams wouldn't let me have them taken out until after the season. I took painkillers, but I was weak."

Babando, like Ernie Keefe and others, thinks that Real Chevrefils, who died so tragically, might very well have been the best player he played with. "It was sad," Babando says. "He had everything." Another good one was Joe Graboski, whose brother Tony played for the Canadiens. Like Eddie Brown, Joe had lost an eye. "Otherwise, he'd have made it. He ended up playing in the mines league here. When he skated it was as if he were on wings. Ask Carlo about him."

As for himself, there's really only one thing Babando would change. "I wish they'd left me alone to play defence, but Boston moved me up. I was a really good skater; maybe that's why. The thing is, I loved hockey and I never expected to make the NHL. I would have been happy to play for South

Porcupine. So I've always felt very fortunate to have made it because I never thought I had the ability. Yes, very fortunate."

Allan Stanley played hockey at six feet two inches and nearly two hundred pounds, which was very big for his day, and at seventy-one looks as if he could still play. He's not grey, and he hasn't put on any weight. He divides his time now between Florida and south-central Ontario, near Lindsay, where he developed a housing estate and golf course. In his living room is a picture of that championship juvenile team coached by Carlo Cattarello. He says that nine of the team went to NHL training camps the next fall.

"We were lucky as kids," he says. "Timmins built rinks all over town. All outdoor, but they were regulation size. And if the lakes and ponds froze before the snow fell, we'd skate on them. And the town would scatter those big steel drums around and light fires in them and we'd skate at night and if we were cold we'd skate over to one and get warm. You couldn't beat it for fun. I guess it's hard to get kids to skate outdoors now. If you suggest it they'll probably think you're crazy."

Stanley went to Boston's camp, which was in Quebec City, and then, at sixteen, signed with the Boston Olympics, Babando's old team. He was playing for Providence in the AHL when he was sold to the Rangers.

"The Rangers were a tough team to play for," Stanley says. "The gallery gods would single out one person and really get on him. Before me it was Ab Demarco. Ab had a cousin who was a boxer, built like a tank. If he was in New York for a fight he'd come to the dressing room. One night he asks Ab if he wants him to straighten those guys out and Ab says sure. So he goes up and sits right in the middle of them and says that the first guy who yells at Ab goes over the side. Later, he asked me whether I wanted the same and I said no. I thought afterwards maybe I should have let him throw them all in the East River. The funny thing is that after the game I'd run into these guys on 48th Street and they'd say, 'Al, it's nothing personal.' It was hard to figure sometimes why they'd get on you, but when they did it was no fun."

Among Stanley's favourite players was Henri Richard. "Henri had a huge heart," Stanley says. "He didn't need anyone to look after him. His brother, the Rocket, was ready to, but he didn't need him."

Unlike many of his peers, Stanley likes today's hockey. "They shoot harder and they pass better," he says. "And everybody's a skater. The equipment is so much better, too. I carried twenty-six pounds around, dry. I bet they don't carry half that and they have better protection. And the sticks are so much better. We had lumber, they have sticks."

He also likes the Russians because of their skating and play-making. "There's hardly a bad pass with them," he says. "No matter where it hits them they direct it to their stick. I like Don Cherry but he should knock off his criticism of the Europeans. They're making a helluva contribution."

Mike Mulryan is an assistant coach with the midget team that was practising the night before at the McIntyre Arena. He gave up full-time coaching to become the team's general manager. He owns Quinn Sports on Third Avenue. Many downtown stores have suffered at the hands of the huge Timmins Mall on the city's outskirts, but not Quinn Sports. "We do well because of hockey," Mulryan says.

Mulryan is thirty-nine. He's in a T-shirt, baseball cap, and jeans. He played hockey until Junior B and then began to coach. He's nursing a Pepsi and a cigarette — "Yeah, I still smoke" — in "Dimples." In spite of its fern-bar name, it's a big, old-fashioned restaurant with red vinyl booths. "We have eighteen corporate sponsors, including this place," Mulryan says. The team is in the nine-team Great North Midget League that includes Sault Ste. Marie to the west and North Bay and Sudbury to the south, a big area. Mulryan is strict with his team. "We really work them. We figure if we make the practices hard, then the games will be easier." Off the ice, for travel, there's a jacket-and-tie dress code.

Mulryan is animated and enthusiastic, rocking back and forth in his seat. The night before he addressed more than forty coaches in the Timmins minor hockey association. "I told them that they had to be well prepared to coach, to know what they were talking about, both in theory and in application," he says. "Kids, even the little ones, recognize bullshit in a hurry." He says that he also told them it was important to get into coaching for the right reasons. "Make sure you love the game, that you have something to teach. Don't go in just because you think the guy who coached your son last year was a jerk who didn't know anything. And I told them that they must take coaching seriously. They are the most influential people in those kids' lives apart from their families."

As his playing career wound down, Mulryan says that he found he was getting a greater understanding of the game. "I played for some really good coaches," he says, "and I know what coaches can do."

One of the things that bothers him today is the slashing and spearing. "Some guys think that's sort of funny coming from me because my nickname was 'Hack' and 'Stick' but that was before the full visor so when you gave the guy the stick it was on the legs and the lower body. You never went for the head because it wasn't protected. Now, with all this equipment, they don't seem to care. That's why head and neck injuries are going up like hell. And you go to a peewee game and the sticks are flying around and the kids are banging each other on the masks and there's nothing to it. When we were kids, without masks, you had to be in control of your stick the whole time."

Trevor Morden, a blond kid of nineteen, is a power forward with the Timmins Golden Bears of the junior NOHA. He played two years of midget for Mulryan and works part-time for him at Quinn Sports. Morden has gone to three Sudbury Wolves camps but didn't make the team. Tonight he's at the Timmins Sportsplex waiting for the Zamboni to get off the ice so the Bears can begin their practice. The Bears are affiliated with the Sault Ste. Marie Greyhounds and wear Soo practice jerseys. A ghetto blaster in their dressing room is cranked up about as far as it will go and can be heard all over the near-empty arena. "I'd like an NCAA scholarship," Morden says. Between the music and the noise from the Zamboni, he has to shout. "But it's hard to study when you're playing hockey." He is two credits short of grade thirteen. The music dies and the practice begins.

Frank Zimperi is in charge of maintenance at the arena. He's the man who used to work at the McIntyre Arena and played hit-the-crossbar with Father Les Costello. He's sitting in his glass-fronted office at the end of the rink watching the practice. His door is open and the office is full of the popping sound of pucks bouncing off the boards and the swish of skates against ice. The coaches have the Bears skating hard down one side. When they hit the blue line they drive the puck into the near corner, cut across, and pick up their own shot coming off the opposite boards. As the players move through the drill, one of the coaches, standing on the red line, keeps slapping his stick on the ice and yelling, "C'mon, c'mon, rip it in there, go, go. Heads up for Christ's sake. Keep your goddamn heads up or you'll be killed!"

"Timmins can be funny," Zimperi says. "The crowds here go up and down. Right now we're lucky if we get three or four hundred. The Bears tried real physical hockey and the fans liked that for a while. But then that died down and they switched to a finesse game. That worked for a bit, but it's hard to know what the hell the fans want."

A few days later, in Quinn Sports, Trevor Morden is feeling upbeat. He says he's playing well following a slow start. "I wasn't scoring. I was running around hitting everything in sight and often taking myself out of the play. So I was benched for a couple of games. I'm still playing tough, but I'm playing smarter and the points are coming." He says that he was upset about being benched, "but there's not much you can do about it."

As well as being back playing, he says that Ohio State has written to him asking for the Golden Bears' schedule. He assumes they want to scout him. If he fails to get an NCAA scholarship at Ohio or another American school, he'll try to go to college or university in Canada. He is also ready to ride the buses in minor pro hockey. "Sure I am, anytime," he says. "I'll play for anybody who'll take me, anytime, anywhere."

11

Victoriaville, Quebec

October 1997

THE MAYOR OF VICTORIAVILLE, Pierre Roux, bypassed his town's hockey team in the late '50s to play for the Toronto St. Mike's, joining those youngsters who came down the pipeline from northern Ontario. Bob Davidson, the veteran Maple Leaf scout, recruited him. "Davidson came to Victoriaville with a junior team," Roux says, "and a friend of my father's, who'd been at St. Mike's, told him about me." His teammates included Gerry Cheevers, the goalie whom the Maple Leafs later let go to Boston, and Dave Keon, who went on to play fifteen seasons with the Leafs and become their captain. Roux played one season with St. Mike's. Early in his second season he injured his back and that finished his career. About then his father died. Young Roux was only nineteen but he came home to run the family's construction business and he's been here ever since.

Victoriaville is two hours east of Montreal, on the south shore of the St. Lawrence. It makes up a hockey triangle with Drummondville and Sherbrooke; all three are in the Quebec Major Junior Hockey League.

In the past they've had senior and intermediate teams and at one time Sherbrooke was the Canadiens' farm team in the AHL. All three have won Allan Cups, which, in the old days, was hockey's biggest prize after the Stanley Cup and the Memorial Cup.

Farther to the east is Thetford Mines, where Gilbert Perreault, a Victoriaville native, and Réjean Houle, the Canadiens GM, played junior in the mid-'60s, beginning their climb to the NHL. Thetford now has a senior team in a league which includes St-Gabriel, Princeville, and Acton Vale. All these towns are within an hour or two of Quebec City, but the smaller ones, particularly those in the Beauce region south of Quebec, almost seem to be a couple of generations away. They're farming and forestry communities with a bond between the inhabitants that's rare these days.

In Victoriaville, on a bright autumn day, municipal elections are coming up and Mayor Roux is well prepared. At fifty-nine he's trim, and conservatively dapper in his blue blazer, white shirt, and grey flannels. It's around eleven o'clock in the morning and he's back in his office at City Hall for an hour or so following a civic function. He has another one at lunch. It looks like nobody will be running against him, but he's not taking any chances. Cockiness can hurt as much in politics as it can in hockey. However, he's not so rushed that he can't take the afternoon off to play golf with an old pal, Gilles Marotte, the former NHL defenceman. Marotte was born in Montreal but lives in Victoriaville. "Pierre Roux was the first person I met when I came here to play junior," Marotte says. "I was sixteen, and we've been friends ever since."

Victoriaville is a town of forty thousand, built with railway, farming, and lumber money, as were so many Canadian towns. Most of its old buildings are red brick or stone. The Nicolet River runs through it and in the countryside around it are more rivers, and ponds and farms and, now, golf courses. Victoriaville gave its name to a company that made hockey sticks, but the company has changed hands, changed names, and moved down the road to Daveluyville. There is some furniture and textile manufacturing and the Lactania dairy is a big employer, but the main street, Notre Dame, has its share of vacant shops and offices and papered-over windows. "Drummondville is way ahead of us in the electronics industry," says Christian Paquin, of the newspaper, *La Nouvelle*. "They've adapted better to the times. It's tough around here. People are hurting."

General Maurice Baril, the Chief of Defence Staff, comes from St-Albert-de-Warwick, a couple of miles away. *La Nouvelle* quotes the general as saying that he still sees himself as a local boy and he's proud of it. The same edition carries eleven sports stories, including one each on women's volleyball, girls' soccer, and speed skating. The other eight are on hockey. The gist of the hockey stories is that this could be the year of the Victoriaville Tigres, particularly since their best players, forward Daniel Corso, and goalie Mathieu Garon, have returned for their last year of junior from their NHL clubs, the St. Louis Blues and the Canadiens.

"Hockey is important here and it has been for years. This is a solid hockey area," says Roux. "Let's face it, it's very good for a city our size to get coverage in newspapers, on radio, and TV because of hockey — win or lose. But hockey is very expensive. Our team is well managed and we can have pride in it, but it also needs a good piece of the population to back it up and that's always a worry in a small market.

"There is a solid fan support of maybe two or three thousand. But they don't all go to the game at once. And we don't have a very big rink anyway. There's just over two thousand seats. It'll hold another thousand standing, but I think we'd have to be playing for the Memorial Cup to get a full house. The trouble with hockey here is the same as anywhere: there's too much of it. Every night there's a game on television. It's hard on teams in small towns. People stay home in winter. There's only so much hockey anyone can take."

The general manager of the Tigres has the same name as the mayor, Pierre Roux, which causes some confusion because the mayor was not only a hockey player, he is also a shareholder in the team. The Tigres' Roux has his office on the upper level of l'Amphitheatre Gilbert-Perreault, in a corner overlooking the ice. It's very tidy. There's a rug on the floor, pictures of hockey teams and players on the walls, and cups and trophies and framed pictures on the bookshelves. Roux's desk is stacked with papers; and there's the ubiquitous computer.

Roux is thirty-nine, stern and business-like. He's sitting at his desk, wearing a denim shirt open at the neck with the sleeves rolled up. He looks like a man used to working. He's been with the team for ten years, beginning as an assistant coach under Guy Chouinard, the former Calgary Flame and St. Louis Blue. Roux is happy that Daniel Corso and Mathieu Garon are back but, like the mayor, worries about operating in a small market. "We're not like Granby or Hull," he says. "We can't afford to buy a Memorial Cup, and even though Granby did, the team still folded. We don't have the big market or the silent, rich partners. Hell, we have fourteen-hour bus trips."

Roux points out, however, that a place the size of Victoriaville does have some advantages. "We have twenty-five players on the roster, and twenty-three of them are attending CEGEP (community college) and it's only five minutes from the rink," he says. "It's an ideal set-up. They're all here for practice at three o'clock. More of our kids are at school, I think, than almost any other team in the league."

Roux, like all junior-club GMs in the '90s, emphasizes the importance of education, and unlike some, he sounds as if he really means it. "When you're between sixteen and twenty you have to have more than hockey in your life," he says. "Most of the players aren't going to make a career in hockey, so they must have an education. As well, a kid who's disciplined enough to get ahead in school will probably make a better hockey player than one who isn't. We've had kids go through here who have gone on to study business, accounting, medicine, you name it.

"But there are far more leagues now than there were twenty-five or thirty years ago, the International Hockey League and the East Coast Hockey League and the United (Colonial) League. There are leagues out west and there's Europe — all kinds of choices — so some players will put their education on hold for a while and take a chance."

Not so long ago, Roux says, NHL teams preferred English-speaking players over francophones because a single language in the dressing room was easier to deal with. The invasion of the Europeans changed that. "Now you can have four or five different languages on a team," he says. "It's no longer just the Québécois who have the communication problem." Nevertheless, it can still be intimidating for a francophone player from a small town to have to go suddenly to Los Angeles, for example. "They'll get homesick anyway; if you don't speak the language, it can be even harder. That's why a lot of players in this league take English conversation courses. They want to be better prepared than the players were ten years ago."

However, according to Roux, language isn't the only difference between a player from Baie Comeau and one from Brandon. "The players in our league, the French Canadians generally, are smaller than the players in Ontario and in the west, and we play a more wide open game. There's less holding, less obstruction. We have a lot of shooters. Our stars are usually guys who can really fly, like, for example, Alexandre Daigle, who played here. That's why, maybe, we turn out so many good goalies. They get lots of shots. We don't seem to produce the grinders because we aren't big enough."

Roux sits back and clasps his hands behind his head. "I believe that hockey is 50–50 mental and physical," he says. "To succeed you have to be up to it mentally. And after the players leave hockey, it doesn't matter what they do, if they had the character to do well in the rink, that'll serve them off it, too."

Down under the stands, in a corridor outside their dressing room, a handful of Tigres are standing around talking. One of them is taping a stick. Their practice begins in about half an hour. Mathieu Garon, the goalie, is there. He's big, as most goalies are these days, and serious-looking. He breaks away from his pals for a moment. He says his selection by the Canadiens "was a dream I've had since childhood. It's the dream of every Quebecer, to play for the Canadiens. It's unbelievable when I think of it. Most people, including my parents, won't make as much money in their whole life as I'll make on a three-year contract. But I have to remember that if a team is prepared to pay that much, it's because I'm an investment for them. They hope to make money because of me. And I have to prove that I'm worth it."

One month later, on a blustery November night, a block from l'Amphitheatre Gilbert-Perreault, the Tim Hortons is busy. But it's not a hockey crowd. Les Tigres are up north. They have three games in three nights: Val d'Or, Rouyn, and Val d'Or again. Most of this evening's customers, who include girls with figure skates over their shoulders, are youngsters. Hot chocolate and hot soup are selling well because of the cold. The skaters belong to the Victoriaville Figure-Skating Club, and they've just left the ice. A man named Yves looks at his watch. "They'll be starting soon," he notes. "They're always on time." He's referring to a bunch of men, ranging in age from twenty-eight to fifty-four and including two ex-NHLers, who play hockey every Wednesday night after the figure skaters have finished. "It's a real treat to watch them play," he says. But Yves can't stay tonight; he has to get his daughter home.

A few minutes later, the game begins — whites against blues. Four people are watching, including one of the Tigres, not on the road trip because of an injury, who is exercising by running up and down the arena's steep stairs. Overhead hang three banners, celebrating Jean Béliveau, Gilbert Perreault, and Gilles Marotte. All three played here. On the ice, the players are having a good time, laughing and kidding each other, but they're skating hard, playing their positions. This isn't pond hockey. Just then, one of them, flying across the red line, takes a pass that's behind him and, without breaking stride, steers the puck from his stick to his skate and back to his stick.

It happens click-click-click, in a split second. "You won't see the Russians do it any better," says a rink worker.

"Who is he?"

"I didn't notice. Most of these guys are really good. They're fun to watch. It's all skill with them."

The players belong to a team called Les Essouffles — literally, 'the Out-of-Breaths'. It was formed nearly thirty years ago. As well as every Wednesday night in Victoriaville, they play in tournaments where they've raised more than $100,000 for local charities. The hockey *really* is for fun; the teams are shaken up each week so there's not much chance of it becoming too competitive. "We don't need that at our age," says the team's president, Yves Lemieux.

According to Lemieux, the players seldom miss a game. "They've built hockey right into their work schedule." Apart from ex-juniors and ex-pros, two Essouffles are from top-ranked universities, the University of Moncton and the University of Quebec at Trois-Rivières. "We let young guys in with us because we want to keep up a fairly fast pace on the ice," Lemieux says. "This year, we have five new additions. It's very rare we get that many at once. The guys hate to give up their spots. Believe me, there's a long waiting list to join us."

Yvon Poudrier, who played junior for Victoriaville in the '60s, joined Les Essouffles in 1970. He's one of the older ones. "I dropped out of hockey for business reasons for four years," he says. "God, I missed it so much. It's like a religion to me. Here, with these guys, we're a big family."

Gilles Marotte, an old-time defenceman, built low to the ice, was a teammate of Poudrier's in Victoriaville before Marotte moved on to the Niagara Falls Flyers in the OHA. At fifty-three, he's the second-oldest player on the team. He is in a blue sweater, number ten, and although he's at play, when he gets the puck in his own end and takes charge with his hard, pinpoint passing, it's easy to see how he spent twelve years in the NHL.

The Essouffles' games are split in two. After half an hour, the players leave the ice while the Zamboni gives it a fresh flood. Marotte, sweating slightly, goes to the bench. He takes off his helmet and wipes his creased face. He's the only one playing without a face mask. "I tried one but I couldn't adjust to it; I couldn't even breathe properly," he says. "Hell, I never even wore a helmet until I started coming out with these guys. But we play half-decent hockey. We keep our sticks down. We let the young guys out with us as long as they behave. This is meant to be fun. Good hockey, but fun. Afterwards we go for a few beers."

Marotte was born in Montreal and came to Victoriaville for his first year of junior. "Hockey has always been good around here. Victoriaville, Drummondville, Thetford, Sherbrooke, over the years they've all had good teams," he says. "I met my wife here and I've always liked it here so this is where I've settled down. It's a good, friendly town, there's lots of golf, and it's only an hour or so from Montreal." Marotte is a broker for several sporting goods manufacturers.

He says that his biggest single thrill in hockey, bigger even than being called up to play for Boston, was winning the Memorial Cup. Marotte was an assistant captain when the Niagara Falls Flyers beat the Edmonton Oil Kings four games to one in 1965. "And we did it in the west, on their turf, their ice," he says.

In Marotte's opinion, that Niagara Falls team was one of the best junior teams ever assembled.

Not surprisingly, the single-minded Hap Emms, one of junior hockey's most successful executives, was the owner and manager. Emms had already won Memorial Cups with Barrie. Besides Marotte, he had goalie Bernie Parent and forwards Derek Sanderson, Don Marcotte, Bill Goldsworthy, and Jean Pronovost. Parent, now in the Hall of Fame, played for Boston, Philadelphia, and Toronto. Sanderson, Marcotte, Goldsworthy all went up to Boston, too. Pronovost spent fourteen years with Pittsburgh, Washington, and Atlanta and now coaches Rouyn in the QMJHL.

"Bill Long was a good coach and Emms was great to play for. He was really tough, really strict, but he was fair," Marotte says. "He'd turned out so many NHLers over the years that you knew he had to be doing something right, and it was with him that I began seriously to think I had a shot at making the NHL."

He continues, "Overall, Victoriaville is a great hockey town for kids. But I don't always agree with the minor hockey system now, here or anywhere else. This Double-A or Triple-A, whatever, puts far too much pressure on them. As well, they have to travel too much. It takes them out of the community. I'm all for competitive hockey, but for God's sake let them have some fun before they get into really stiff competition." He laughs. "I have two daughters. They figure-skate. Come to think of it, I don't really have to worry about boys' hockey."

A few moments later, as the game resumes, the biggest man on the ice, who until now hasn't been doing much, suddenly takes the puck from behind his own net and, skating smoothly, and fast, moves the length of the ice. He feints to his backhand, pulls the goalie out, comes back to his forehand, and then, grinning broadly, doesn't shoot. Instead, he goes behind the net and flips the puck to one of his wingers. By this time the goalie is back in position and makes the stop.

The rink maintenance man says, "He can still do it, eh?"

"Who?"

"Perreault."

"That's Gilbert Perreault? Someone told me he lives in Buffalo."

"No, no. He does some work for the Sabres, but he lives here."

"Jesus, he's put on weight."

"Yeah."

Then, as if to leave no doubt who he is, Perreault again goes end-to-end. This time he scores.

Later, sitting in the stands while another group of recreational players have the ice, Perreault says, "Yeah, I weigh about 250 now." He chuckles. "But I'm much stronger." He has showered and is wearing a blue cotton windbreaker and smartly pressed khaki chinos. His thick hair is neatly combed. In spite of his size, he looks like an Ivy Leaguer, much younger than his forty-six years, still the fresh-faced kid Buffalo drafted first overall from the Montreal Junior Canadiens in 1970. Perreault is Victoriaville's favourite son. Jean Béliveau was born here, too, but Perreault has stayed around longer.

"I don't miss the big cities; that's why I'm back here. My wife's from here," he says. "If I ever did go to live in the States I'd go to Buffalo. I mean, I was there for sixteen years, I have friends there. I was very happy in Buffalo and I still work for the Sabres, but this has always been my home."

He turns to watch the players on the ice below. "Victoriaville is like a lot of hockey towns. You have to have a good team if you want people to show up. Hockey at the junior level is very, very expensive. You have to get the crowds or you'll die. And this is a small rink. When I was fifteen and playing in Thetford, before I went to the Junior Canadiens, the rink had about 2,500 seats but we'd get three or four thousand in there. Then, with the juniors in Montreal, when we were winning two Memorial Cups, we'd get sixteen, seventeen thousand at the old Forum. You can't do that here."

Like Gilles Marotte's Niagara Falls Flyers five years before, the Junior Canadiens of '69 and '70 had a number of players who went on to solid NHL careers. Among them, besides Perreault, were Réjean Houle, Richard Martin, Guy Charron, Ian Turnbull, Moose Dupont, Jocelyn Guèvremont, and Bobby Lalonde.

"The player I admired most when I was growing up was Jean Béliveau," Perreault says. "As a French-Canadian kid you had to like Béliveau. But there was also Howe, and Bobby Hull, and later I played against Bobby Orr and Marcel Dionne. Lafleur, Gretzky. It was a great thrill to be with Guy and Wayne for that Canada Cup in 1981."

For years, to try to ensure a French presence in Montreal, the Canadiens were allowed first crack at French-Canadian hopefuls. That ended with expansion. "I was lucky," Perreault says. "If I'd been picked by Montreal I might have ended up on the bench for two or three years. That's what the Canadiens could do because of all their depth. In Buffalo, I got to play right away. We were an expansion team, but we did well from the start.

"I didn't speak much English when I went to Buffalo and that made it a bit hard at the beginning, but I was never homesick. I'd left home when I was fifteen for Thetford and then I'd had three years in Montreal, so I was used to being away from home."

Perreault says he was also lucky with his first coach, Punch Imlach. "He was good to play for. He gave me confidence, let me play my own game, that is, to score goals. He'd say, 'That's why you're here, to score goals.'" However, the days of the Imlachs are over, he feels. "Coaching is different now. In the old days the coach was like a general commanding his troops. 'Do it my way or go to the minors.' Now you have to keep your players on your side or you won't last very long. Punch and Toe Blake and I guess Dick Irvin demanded respect. Now, with players like Wayne or Mario Lemieux or Eric Lindros, you better be able to communicate with them. That's what it's all about: communicating. Roger Neilson was like that. He cared about his players, he was a good communicator. I liked playing for Roger. He was a gentleman. But I respected all my coaches. I never had any trouble with them."

As the game goes on below, Perreault becomes reflective. "I have no complaints at all," he says. "I had a great career and I still enjoy the game. I have two sons. One is playing Junior B, the other is twelve and is playing here. But I think Mario Lemieux put it right the other day. There's too much hooking and grabbing. It made me mad when I'd be hooked and grabbed and there'd be no call from the ref. It's hurting the game. I don't think they have to make the rinks bigger, just get rid of the red line. That would open things up for the skill players. But with twenty-six teams, and soon thirty, that's more than six hundred players. The product is going to be even more diluted. There just isn't enough talent. And that's sad."

12

Cape Breton, Nova Scotia

October 1997

GLACE BAY, SYDNEY, NORTH Sydney, Sydney Mines, New Waterford, New Victoria, Dominion . . . coal and steel towns on the rocky lower arm of Cape Breton Island, hard by the Atlantic Ocean — a compelling region of Canada, magnificent in summer, bleak and unforgiving in winter. In the '40s and '50s, when coal was king and the mines were being worked and the steel mills roared, life was better in Cape Breton than it had ever been before, and likely ever will be again. Young men from across Canada flooded onto the island looking for work, just as the generations that followed went west during the oil boom.

Some of these men came to play hockey, for the pay was good, for the Sydney Millionaires or the Glace Bay Miners or the North Sydney Victorias. And when the season ended, most of the hockey players would hurry home to Winnipeg, Saskatoon, Timmins, or Sault Ste. Marie, or wherever. But there were also those who were offered jobs and who stayed behind and settled down.

One of these was Lou Medynski, who comes from a small town in Manitoba called Stonewall, about twenty miles north of Winnipeg. Medynski got to Cape Breton after stops playing hockey in New York and on the coast of British Columbia and in Truro, on Nova Scotia's mainland. Today, he and his wife, Margie, live in Sydney, on King's Road, which becomes Highway 4 and runs down to Bras d'Or, a saltwater lake in Cape Breton's unspoiled and splendid interior. In front of the Medynski house is the Sydney River, which enters the ocean a few miles away, and in the back, on the lawn, on this autumn morning, is a family of ducks. "They're here again, are they?" Medynski says, looking out from his back door. Then he says, "I love it here. I love being near the ocean. Prairie people love the ocean."

Lou Medynski is seventy-six. He has heart trouble and he moves slowly because of a nerve disorder, but he still looks like a hockey player — the easy smile, a crooked nose, and the loose-limbed build that marks so many athletes. He's friendly and self-effacing, as are a lot of hockey players of his era. "My dad worked at the quarry in Stonewall," he says. "A streetcar used to run into Winnipeg and he'd give me money for it so I could go in to play hockey, but I don't think he ever saw me play. It was different then. My parents were from the old country; they were Polish. They worked very hard all the time. For them it was a new life and they expected to work hard. It was difficult for people like them to understand games.

"My older brother 'Bink' was a good hockey player. He came down here in 1935 or '36 to play for the Moncton Hawks and then Saint John. He also played for the Springfield Indians. He was back in Winnipeg at Canada Packers and playing hockey for them when he was electrocuted at work. He was twenty-eight. My mother blamed hockey because he'd got the job at Canada Packers through hockey, so she was never crazy about me playing. She never understood it."

Medynski played junior for the Winnipeg Rangers. "There were ten or eleven teams in the Manitoba junior league, including Kenora. It was tough as hell to get out of our own province let alone win the whole thing. Chuck Rayner was with Kenora and 'Sugar Jim' Henry with Portage. They both wound up with New York. That was the first team, I think, to carry two goalies."

The Winnipeg Rangers won the Memorial Cup in 1941, beating the Montreal Royals, who were led by Kenny Mosdell, later a Montreal Canadien. To reduce travel, because of the Second World War, the Rangers played their "home" games in Toronto's Maple Leaf Gardens. It was a best-of-five series and Medynski wasn't expected to play much. He'd suffered a gash on his forehead in practice and it took eighteen stitches to close it. "It happened in Saskatoon during the western final," he says. "We got off the train and went for a skate right away and I collided with our spare goalie, Sonny Peters, and wound up in hospital." This was before antibiotics, and the cut hadn't healed properly by the time the series began. But Medynski came off the bench to score the winning goal in game three with less than two minutes left. "I was on a line with Bernie Bathgate, Andy's older brother. The puck gets to your stick and you shut your eyes and let it go and something happens."

Besides Mosdell, the Royals had Jimmy Peters, who played nine years for the Canadiens and the Red Wings. Glen Harmon, who also went on to play for the Canadiens, was with Winnipeg. Medynski says, "One summer Harmon and I worked at a pickle factory in Winnipeg. We smelled so much of vinegar and brine that on the streetcar going home the other passengers would move the hell out of our way. We always got a seat."

Hughie Millar, who played a few games for Detroit, was on that Winnipeg team. Like Medynski, Millar came from Stonewall. "The town gave a banquet for Hughie and me and we each got a set of golf clubs," Medynski says. "It was a helluva thrill for a kid back then. It's hard to explain these days with everything changed so much just what it meant, but it was really something. I still have my golf clubs."

In Winnipeg, another ex-Ranger, Sam Fabro, remembers that Memorial Cup series well. "Lou got that goal to put us ahead 5–4 and I scored an empty-netter," he says. He also remembers Medynski's accident. "I was right there when they banged into each other. They had their heads down. It was awful. Blood was everywhere."

Fabro turned down an offer to play in the New York Rangers' farm system — "Jesus, considering what they paid in those days, I was better off working" — and joined McMahon, a large, successful carpet-distributing company in Winnipeg. He retired as CEO. On the wall over his desk in his den is the Order of Canada. Fabro says he got it for community service, but he'd rather talk about hockey. A recently published book says that the stars of that Memorial Cup series were Bill Robinson and Les Hickey, who both went on to distinguished minor league careers, and Sam Fabro. Fabro isn't so certain.

"In the first game I got two goals and we won 4–2. I picked up a couple more in the next two games. We were ahead 2–1 in the series and it was the fourth game. I scored the third goal and we're winning 3–2 with about a minute left. Ten seconds later I get a penalty — this was when a player served the *whole* penalty regardless if the other team scored — and they ganged our net and scored twice and we lose 4–3. I went from hero to goat. No matter what I do, I can't forget that. It's a good thing we won the fifth game."

In the fall of 1941 Medynski went to the New York Rangers' training camp in Winnipeg. "Lester Patrick was running the Rangers, and I showed them enough that they asked me to go to the New York Rovers in the old eastern league," he says. "Neil and Mac Colville and Babe Pratt were on the Rangers and after camp broke the Rangers went off to New York by train. They were going to play exhibition games along the way. They couldn't take their cars but they wanted them in New York so some guys drove Pratt's down and I and a couple of others drove the Colvilles'." He smiles. "I remember it was a Nash. Anyway, we got to New York at three one morning. The Rover trainer was with us and he took us to an all-night automat. You put in a nickel or a dime and got a piece of pie, sandwich, whatever you wanted. Probably sounds silly today, but we'd never seen anything like it. New York was really something for kids from Stonewall — hell, or even Winnipeg."

Medynski played one season with the Rovers. Then, from 1942 until the end of the war, he was in the navy. His last posting was on the west coast, where there was some wartime hockey. After he got out the Rovers wanted him back. At this time they occasionally played two games on a Sunday. There would be one in the afternoon and then they'd take the train to Baltimore or Philadelphia for an evening game. "We were on the road nearly all the time and I didn't like the travelling," Medynski says. "About then I'm having a few beers with a guy and he said he'd fix me up to play for the Truro Bearcats. So down to Nova Scotia I came."

It was in Truro that he met Margie and was married. When the team folded after three seasons — "the rink was too small; you couldn't make a dollar after expenses" — Medynski moved to Sydney. "It was an ideal set-up," he says, "a three-team league: Sydney, Glace Bay, and North Sydney. We slept in our own beds every night. And the rinks were usually packed. They loved hockey here. And I was at the steel plant for twenty-five years."

He leans forward in his chair. "My good friend Joe Watts was a helluva defenceman. He didn't work at the mill. He got paid to play, but he still had to get up at five o'clock in the morning to deliver milk to make ends meet. The Sydney Millionaires were millionaires in name only. Guys making millions today and here's Joe Watts, a really good hockey player, up at five o'clock in the morning, delivering milk."

Joe Watts lives in Kingston. "I was in Sydney two years," he says. "We were Maritime champions both years and Allan Cup quarter-finalists both years. It was a tough league. We played four times a week. We'd played ninety-six games before we got into Ontario. When we went into Glace Bay on a Saturday night it was always wild. The place would be packed to the roof. It was a heck of a rivalry. We even had to be careful where we parked. The Glace Bay fans would put sugar in our gas tanks and, believe me, it was very rough hockey.

"I didn't want to work in the steel mill so I got the job delivering milk, seven days a week, up at five. I got thirty-five dollars a week from the dairy and around $125 a week from the hockey club. It went up a bit my second year. I needed the money: I was married and we had a baby on the way.

"As a kid in Kingston I wanted to play junior. I thought for sure I was on my way to the NHL. I was ticketed to play for Oshawa in 1943 but instead I ended up in the navy. I was really disappointed. And then I injured my knee playing for the navy and that was the end of it."

Lou Medynski says, "When I look back I wish I'd stayed in school and gone on to university the way boys do now. Hockey was all I ever had growing up. But I don't have any real regrets. I had three good years in Truro, met my wife, and then came up here to Cape Breton. Yeah, it's all been good."

For most of the settlers arriving en masse in Cape Breton in the 1800s, largely from Scotland, life was only marginally better than the poverty they were fleeing. In his book, *The Company Store*, John Mellor writes that Cape Breton miners suffered "under abominable working conditions and [the mine owners'] intimidation. . . ." And up through the 1920s bloody labour battles divided the island, breeding, in some communities, a dislike of their neighbours which lasted for years.

The island's economy boomed through the Second World War and into the '50s, but now mines have closed, and Sydney Steel, loser of millions of dollars, employs only a fraction of the number of people that it used to. The population is falling, and there's an uneasy stillness in what used to be one of the most industrialized parts of the country.

Roger Hill works for the Glace Bay Development Association. He says that unemployment has been as high as 27 percent amid continuing regional feuding. However, in 1995, eight municipal governments were rolled into one. "If it had been only a hockey rivalry it would have been okay," he says, "but the local governments fought all the time. Politicians were interested only in their own turf. There was no plan. Money was wasted, things weren't getting done. Maybe things will start to change now."

Angus MacDougall, a seventy-three-year-old retired machinist, lives in Glace Bay. Sitting in the Glace Bay arena watching a midget practice, he tells one of his favourite Cape Breton hockey tales, one that shows the bad blood that existed for years between Glace Bay, the rough mining centre, and its bigger and more polished neighbour, the steel city of Sydney. The fact that coal fed the steel mills, making the two places dependent upon each other, never entered the equation.

The pivotal figure in the story is Earl "Leaky" Boates, the inept backup goalie for the 1941 Glace Bay Miners. When the league declared Glace Bay's regular goalie ineligible on the eve of the championship series against Sydney, it looked like the Miners would be stuck with Leaky. But lo and behold, just before the first game, Leaky disappeared. Heavily favoured Sydney needed the money that the series was bound to make. "The Millionaires had a big payroll so they weren't going to demand that Glace Bay forfeit," MacDougall says. "And they figured they'd win no matter who was in goal." So Sydney agreed that the Miners could use Bill "Legs" Fraser, the magnificently colourful and crazed Winnipegger, and perhaps the best goalie never to play in the NHL. Fraser had been playing for North Sydney, who hadn't made the playoffs.

For Sydney, it was a poor call. In front of Fraser's

acrobatics — he earned his nickname "Legs" because of his kick saves — Glace Bay won the first three games of the best-of-seven, 4–1, 1–0, and 5–4. "I saw one of those games," MacDougall says. "A neighbour took a bunch of us youngsters in. What a thrill! It was all Fraser. He was outstanding. Without him Sydney would have beaten Glace Bay easily."

Meanwhile, Leaky remained among the missing. Some said he was enjoying the bright lights of Halifax. Others maintained that he'd been hidden away in a cottage in the back country with a case of Scotch. At any rate, Sydney was now scared stiff. The best team it had had in years was on the way out under very suspicious circumstances, so it protested, demanding that Fraser go and the three games be washed out. "It was an explosive situation," MacDougall says. "You could feel the tension. There was a real fear it might become violent around here. It's hard to believe it was all because of hockey, but it was." After much squabbling the Nova Scotia Hockey Association washed out the three games, and they washed out Fraser, too. Instead of another best-of-seven series, a new best-of-three series was declared, and the Miners would have to find another goalie. The people of Glace Bay were furious. They set up roadblocks of wagons, trucks, what have you. Nothing moved over the twenty miles between Glace Bay and Sydney, the two most important industrial centres on the east coast, which were vital to the war effort.

Dan Willie Morrison, Glace Bay's mayor, pleaded with the Canadian Amateur Hockey Association to intervene. His telegram warned that unless something was done, ". . . this may result in a stoppage of coal shipments to Sydney." The telegram found its way to the federal labour minister. Ottawa was petrified of any threat to coal mining or steel production. It ordered the blockade lifted and threatened to send soldiers in if it weren't. Miraculously, about then, Leaky Boates reappeared. He never revealed where he'd been, and if others knew, they didn't let on. The new series was begun and five thousand people packed into the Miners' Forum in Glace Bay on a foggy March night for the first game. Sydney beat the Miners, and Leaky, 9–1. No second game was played. Glace Bay gave in.

Sydney went on to the Allan Cup final, where they lost to the Regina Rangers. "People don't realize how important the Allan Cup was in those days," MacDougall says. "Sugar Jim Henry and Garth Boesch both played for Regina. That's how good Regina was. But Sydney was a hell of a team, too. All Glace Bay wanted was to beat them. We would have been happy." About then, Legs Fraser joined the army. After the war he played for the old Ottawa Senators of the Quebec senior league.

(Sammy Koffman, the late great Ottawa barkeep and raconteur, was walking by the Montreal Forum early one evening and Fraser was leaning against the box office and calling out, "Buy your tickets here, buy your tickets to see Legs Fraser shut out the Montreal Royals." Sammy went to the game. "You know, the son of a bitch won 4–0.")

Bruce Gallagher, like Lou Medynski, came to Cape Breton to play for the Millionaires and like Medynski he stayed. He's seventy-one and loves to talk about hockey. "I liked it down here right away," he says. "This was a small town, everybody knew you. It was a great place to play."

Gallagher comes from Toronto. His two brothers went to St. Mike's. He went to De La Salle, another

Catholic school, and then to the Oshawa Generals, where he played with Sid Smith, who was the captain of the Maple Leafs in 1955–56. Charlie Conacher was the coach. "Now there was a guy who loved hockey," Gallagher says, "and everything that went with it." He begins to laugh.

"We're playing St. Mike's or the Marlies at Maple Leaf Gardens and there's a fight," Gallagher says. "Everybody's fighting except this big guy on our team, Barry Sullivan. In the dressing room between periods Conacher, who'd scare the shit out of anyone, pins Sullivan to the wall and says, 'If there's another fight and you don't get in it, you'll get this,' and he drives his fist just past Sullivan's head, misses it by an inch, right through the wall. Sure enough, the next period there's a fight and Sullivan's out there swinging like there's no tomorrow, whether there's anyone near him or not. I can still see him. Like a windmill. God, it was funny."

Gallagher went to a Boston Bruins camp in Quebec City. "We stayed at the Château Frontenac and I remember seeing this big crowd of reporters and fans in the lobby and they're all around Bill Cowley. God, what a hockey player he was. I was eighteen or nineteen. It was a thrill just to be part of it." During a scrimmage Gallagher was on a line with Cowley and Herbie Cain. He says, "Cain tells me to fake a pass, but hold the puck. I did. I beat Pat Egan and I scored, and he was a great defenceman. A couple of minutes later I tried it again and the next thing I know Egan's standing over me in the corner asking, 'You okay, kid?' You might fool him once, but not twice. The Bruins gave me a real good shot and I thought I might make it, but I was awfully small."

Gallagher says he could have gone to the Boston Olympics, in the eastern league, the league the New

York Rovers were in, but he decided on another year of junior. "Then the war ended and there was a surfeit of good players and I guess I got lost in the shuffle," he says. "A New York Ranger scout, I forget his name, talked to me once but I never heard from them.

"I think Sydney got my name from Father Mallon, who was the athletic director at St. Mike's. They wanted me and one of my brothers, but he wasn't interested. He stayed to play senior in Kitchener. I was in a commercial league in Toronto. I quit my job and came down, which didn't make my mother too happy. But I was young and I thought it was a good chance to see another part of Canada. I worked for twenty-five years as an electrician at the steel plant."

Among his Sydney teammates were George Robertson, Don McCrae, and Jack Gibson, a goalie. All three had been with the Winnipeg Monarchs, who'd beaten St. Mike's in 1946 for the Memorial Cup. "Robertson was so good that when he went up to the Montreal Canadiens he was on a line for a while with the Rocket," Gallagher says. "But he liked a good time too much so Frank Selke sold him to Eddie Shore. Robertson sure as hell wasn't a Shore-type player. I guess that's why he ended up down here."

Don McCrae died recently in California. As a player his nickname was "Red." He was an electrical engineer, a graduate of the University of Manitoba, and the most fabled junior of his day. He came down to work at the steel plant. "He loved hockey, but he loved engineering more," Gallagher says.

In those days a player could play three games in the NHL without compromising his "amateur" status. The Maple Leafs, run then by Conn Smythe, wanted McCrae badly. "He'd show me letters from Smythe begging him to come to Toronto," Gallagher says, "but Don would insist that if he got hurt the Leafs agree to pay him for the rest of his life. He wanted a lot of money, so finally Smythe stopped asking. I know why they wanted him: to kill penalties. He wasn't a great scorer, but he could handle the puck and he could skate all night. He was outstanding."

Gallagher remembers when Murph Chamberlain, the former Montreal Canadien and a truly free spirit whose nickname was "Hardrock," was coaching the Millionaires. A Cape Bretoner, Johnny Myketyn, was on the team. "Myketyn later became a high school principal in Halifax," Gallagher says. "God he was tough. He'd throw these short punches, bam-bam-bam. He always seemed to cut the other guy. I never saw him lose a fight. I was in a lot of fights but I never got hurt because for most of us it was too hard to set your skates to punch hard, but that never bothered Johnny. He could have been in the ring."

Gallagher relates how the Millionaires were playing Sherbrooke in Sherbrooke in the Allan Cup playoffs when Myketyn got in a fight. "In those days there was only one penalty box so Johnny and the other guy are in there with a cop between them. I was on the bench and I look over and for God's sake, the cop is holding Johnny and the other guy's hitting him. I said, 'Hey, Murph, look,' and Chamberlain said, 'Jesus Christ!' and he took off. There was a two-by-four running down behind our bench to the penalty box. I don't know if he could have done it again, but he jumps up on it, like a goddamn tightrope walker, except he's running. When he gets to the penalty box he dives in and wallops the cop, really belts him. The cop's cap goes flying onto the ice. Johnny's loose by now and he's beating the hell out of the other guy. Finally, order's restored and

Chamberlain walks back to the bench, straightening his tie. I said, 'Jesus, Murph, you're lucky you're not in jail.' He looks at me as if I'm crazy and says, 'Put a Montreal Canadien in jail in Quebec? Are you goddamn nuts?'"

Russ Doyle is the sports editor of the *Cape Breton Post*. He's fifty-six years old, slim, with grey hair. He's a quiet man, given to thinking about Cape Breton, where he's spent all his life. "All we ever had were the coal mines and the steel mills," he says. "But there's a mindset here. I guess other parts of Canada can say the same thing, but when you're a Cape Bretoner, this is where your life is, this is where you want to be. My advice to my children, to any young person, is to leave. But this is still the place you'll come back to, and some come to stay."

In his jacket and tie and behind his glasses he looks more like a professor of sociology than a sports writer. He's having a sandwich at the new, flashy Sydney casino. He glances at the gamblers and says resignedly, "This is about the only viable thing left here." Doyle loves harness racing and owns five horses. He doesn't gamble at the casino. "It doesn't interest me," he says. "But lunch is okay." He nods to a couple going by. "The sad thing is that there's so little going on here now that people build their social life around the casino." Doyle vividly remembers "Black Friday," November 13, 1967, when Dosco announced it was closing down its steel plant in Sydney, which would create the government-run Sydney Steel that has been losing money ever since. "That was the beginning of the slide of our industrial base," he says.

According to Doyle, it was that industrial base, before the slide, that made hockey so important to

Cape Breton. "For years there was nothing for the miner or the steelworker after work besides hockey and baseball and that's why the mill and the mines brought in the players," he says. Of the 1941 Millionaires, the team that beat Leaky Boates but lost the Allan Cup final to the Regina Rangers, Doyle says, "I wasn't around then but I've checked and nearly all of them were from Ontario or the west, including Johnny McCreedy, from Winnipeg, who played for the Leafs the next year."

Doyle is old enough, however, to remember some of the glory days, particularly the 1949–50 season when the Millionaires met the old Toronto Marlboros in the Allan Cup playoffs. To cut down on travel, all the games were played at Maple Leaf Gardens. "I was eight but I was allowed to stay up and I was glued to the radio," he says. The Marlboros had brought up two juniors, the heady, hard-working George Armstrong and Danny Lewicki, one of the best skaters of his day. "They also had Flash Hollett," Doyle says, "on his way down from the NHL but still the Bobby Orr of his time. And Hollett came from here, North Sydney." Toronto won that series and eventually the Allan Cup. "They were a fine team," Doyle says, "but the Millionaires, from a place the size of Cape Breton, weren't far behind."

Doyle says it was a real blow to Cape Breton hockey fans when the Edmonton Oilers pulled out their AHL team. "People didn't realize just how good the hockey was until they'd left." He says right up until the end the team was averaging crowds of 3,900 even though it wasn't playing well and there was little promotion. However, by then the city had sold its 50 percent share of the team to the parent Oilers. "And that gave Glen Sather carte blanche to do what he wanted, to look for a better deal," Doyle says.

The Cape Breton Screaming Eagles of the Quebec Major Junior Hockey League arrived in the fall of 1997. "They haven't filled the gap the Oilers left yet," Doyle says, "but they're paying their bills and they'll make a go of it if they start to win over the next few seasons."

The Screaming Eagles are the brainchild of a Halifax businessman and expatriate Cape Bretoner, Harold MacKay. He's also the man who put the Halifax Mooseheads — named for Moosehead Breweries, for whom he used to work — into the Quebec junior league. With Halifax in, MacKay felt it would be natural to have another team from Nova Scotia, and Cape Breton seemed to be the right place. Bill Sidney is the Screaming Eagles' president and CEO. "MacKay did the work, it took him two years," Sidney says, "and we got the investors." He and other local businessmen came up with $1.25 million to buy the troubled Granby franchise. They had to come up with another $90,000 to put into the league kitty for travel. "It's a long way for the Quebec teams to come so they want something up front," Sidney says. "I didn't like it, but if I were them, I'd have done the same damn thing."

Sidney comes from Oakville, outside Toronto. In 1950 he followed a Cape Breton girl back down here from Ontario, married her, and stayed. His company, Modern Aluminum Products, did very well and now, at sixty-seven, he can devote himself to hockey. He got into it first, years ago, making public announcements at the old Miners' Forum in Glace Bay in the Maritime major league. When the league folded Sidney operated the Junior B Miners out of Glace

Bay for a couple of years. He switched to minor hockey as his kids were growing up and then, in 1968, he put a Sydney team in the Nova Scotia Junior A league. "We had our own plane and flew to all the games," he says. But the league didn't last. "The Voyageurs moved into Halifax and that killed it," Sidney says, referring to Halifax's AHL entry, then a farm team of the Canadiens.

Before the game, in his arena office, shifting back and forth in his chair behind his desk, Bill Sidney looks as anxious as his players. "I usually get here an hour and a half beforehand and do a check of the building," he says. "Then I go and stand in the lobby and say hello. I know most of the people and I listen to their bullshit, what they like and what they don't. . . . It's important in a place like Cape Breton."

Dave Huntington, the team's vice-president, can be heard in the next office. He's on the phone to a maintenance worker. Something is wrong. The PA system has broken down. "They don't know what happened," he tells Sidney, and goes off to see about it.

"Jesus," Sidney says, "we can't make any announcements or anything." Then he says, "You'll see a lot of grey heads out there. That's the only complaint we have; it's an older crowd. Our young people are moving away because there's no jobs. In Halifax, they figure about 50 percent of the fans are young. Here, we worked it out to 13 percent. But the older people know their hockey. They're a good base."

The Centre 200, which was opened in 1987 to mark the City of Sydney's bicentennial, can hold just under five thousand, and there must be nearly four thousand for tonight's game.

Bill Sidney promotes the team as a Cape Breton team, not a Sydney team. "In the old days, Sydney,

North Sydney, and Glace Bay were all separate enti-
ties," he says. "They didn't want anything to do with
one another. They fought at every sport. They hated
each other. We used to dress for a fight when we
went to a hockey game, we really did. Now, that's
over, the animosity has disappeared."

So have the days, Sidney says, when young hockey players split their time between the pool hall and
the rink. Like junior teams everywhere now, the
Screaming Eagles are all at school or community
college. "We have an education coordinator who
sees that the kids from the various provinces,
Quebec, P.E.I., Newfoundland, here, meet the
requirements for college or university back home,"
he says. "In the early '50s another guy and I were
scouting here for Detroit and we'd take kids up to
the junior camp in Hamilton. The odd one would
make it. The others would drop back into B hockey,
and most of them never went to school again. I still
feel guilty about it."

But it's not always smooth skating. Bill Sidney
says two boys quit the team this fall. One of them,
from outside Montreal, "got on the team bus to go
to Quebec to play and told the coach that he wasn't
coming back, and he didn't. He said it was personal,
whatever the hell that means."

The other was a native from Mistassini Lake, a
reserve 250 miles north of Quebec City. The season
was well underway when he joined the team and he
lasted only about two weeks. Sidney says it's hard on
the native kids. "They really miss home," he says.
"I'd seen it before, with this boy's older brother, when
he was here. This one got an apartment in town and
his girlfriend moved in with him. We couldn't allow
that because the other players are in billets. But
before we could do anything, he'd gone home."

The PA system is repaired; the trouble was a faulty transformer. That makes Barry McKinnon happy. He handles the music: "Some nights country, some nights Beatles — you know, nostalgia," he says. Tonight it's Celtic, a safe choice in a place where the phone book lists more than three thousand names with the prefix "Mac." And that's not counting the "Mc"s, never mind the Fergusons and the Stewarts and the Mathesons.

Benoit Vézina is a big, good-looking eighteen-year-old with intense coal-black eyes, a touch of acne, and an injured shoulder. If it weren't for the shoulder, he'd be down on the ice playing for the Screaming Eagles. And tonight would be a special treat. The Rimouski Oceanic are in town and that means Vincent Lécavalier. Most hockey people feel Lécavalier, who wears Number 4, Jean Béliveau's number, will be hockey's next big star.

"I like playing against him because he's so good," Vézina says. He's standing in the press box. "It's always good to play against the best. That's the way you'll get better yourself." Vézina comes from St-Jerome, about forty miles north of Montreal. He was with the team last year in Granby, before it moved to Sydney. "This is a real good hockey town," he says. He swings his hand around at the crowd. "In Granby we'd get a thousand, maybe less."

Down on the ice, the Screaming Eagles could have used Vézina. They led the Oceanic 2–0 but then allowed four unanswered goals — Lécavalier picked up only one assist, but seemed to dominate each time he was on — and lost 4–2. The Cape Breton coach is Dan Dubé. He's from Trois-Rivières and was coaching the French national team when he applied for an assistant's job with the Montreal Canadiens. He didn't get it, so Cape Breton signed him for two years. He blames injuries for tonight's loss. "It's frustrating for us, although you have to respect the fact that they beat us," he says, sounding almost philosophical.

Brad Rowe, the hockey writer for the *Cape Breton Post*, is also philosophical. He doesn't expect Dubé to be in Sydney for long. "He's ambitious," Rowe says. "He wants the NHL. You can't blame him."

Rowe, like his boss, Russ Doyle, is from Sydney. And like Roger Hill of the Development Association, he hopes that the Cape Breton infighting is over for good. "The Screaming Eagles aren't just Sydney," he says, "it's Cape Breton. They're for the whole island. People know that." Warming up, he goes on, "They come in from all around, not only Glace Bay, but Port Hood, Ingonish, Baddeck, Inverness. Randy Copley comes from Inverness. People are always coming down from Inverness to watch Randy play. Watch for him. He's going to be great."

Antigonish is in farming country about halfway between Sydney and Truro. It's a college town, home to St. Francis Xavier University, Brian Mulroney's alma mater, and it looks like one. There are lots of trees and the big houses on the quiet streets off the main street have wrap-around verandahs and expansive lawns. The university, with its statue of St. Francis, was founded by the Jesuits but now is nondenominational. It's made up of older grey stone buildings and newer red-brick ones. There are three thousand students.

A couple of blocks away, opposite a pub filled with students, are the fairgrounds, "Home of the Eastern Nova Scotia Exhibition," where the hockey arena is. Being autumn, the arena is getting busy. Last night, St. FX beat St. Mary's University from

Halifax. Tomorrow, a Sunday, there are two junior games. Tonight it's the Rural Hockey League, reputedly one of the oldest country leagues in Canada, St. Andrews against Heatherton. The other teams in the league are St. Croix and Pleasantdale. The standard is what used to be called "intermediate."

A young, overweight man in thick glasses is at the door taking tickets and stamping the backs of hands so people can get back in after going out for a smoke. He promises a good game with lots of fights. Fewer than fifty people have taken him up on it. One of them, forty-seven-year-old Kevin Bonvie, is sitting high in one corner from where he can see the whole ice surface — the place where people who know about hockey sit. "I played in this league for fifteen years," he says. "The kid at the door is wrong about the fighting. There used to be lots of it but not now. These guys all know each other. There's not the village rivalry like the old days." Then he adds, "Nobody gets paid. You play in this league because you want to play hockey." He says the crowds will grow as the season gets going, when all the crops are in and the farmers have less to do, and winter has a lock on the place.

Bonvie works in a paper mill. He lives in Frankville, about thirty miles away. That's near the causeway to Cape Breton, not far from Port Hawkesbury, which has a Junior B team. "Whenever I get a night off I go to a game, Junior B or A or St. FX," he says. "There's always a game somewhere."

Bonvie's son Herbie, twenty-one, is on the ice, playing for St. Andrews. He was with the North Bay Centennials in the Ontario Hockey League for two years, until a badly separated shoulder finished any serious hopes he had of a pro career. Kevin Bonvie smiles as Herbie finishes off a two-way passing play.

"That's it, that's it," the senior Bonvie says. He pauses, then continues, "He should have done that years ago instead of fighting. Herbie can be too much of a fighter. It's okay but sometimes it puts him off his game." St. Andrews wins 8–1. Given that these guys are meant to be friends, they play a hard game with a handful of penalties, but it's mostly clean. Herbie ends up with two goals.

His older brother, Dennis, preceded Herbie in North Bay. Dennis came back to Nova Scotia after junior and in 1994–95 racked up more than four hundred minutes in penalties with the Cape Breton Oilers. The next year the Edmonton Oilers called him up.

Bonvie says his sons are very close and that Herbie may have tried to play as roughly as his older brother does. "I told him to be himself, but Herbie is a scrapper. He looks up to Dennis so I guess he thought he could do the same thing. I told him, 'You can't do that. You got to be Herbie.'"

(About three weeks later, halfway through November, Dennis Bonvie phones his parents to tell them that the Oilers have demoted him to their AHL team in Hamilton. "They told him that he's going down for a week or two, maybe longer, maybe a trade," Kevin Bonvie says. "Whenever the dust settles he says he'll fly us up to see what's going on." He says that Dennis was very upset at first. "But he's over it now. He said, 'Dad, I got to go. That's the nature of the beast, that's hockey.'")

13

―

Lantz, Nova Scotia

October 1997

LANTZ IS JUST OFF HIGHWAY 102, one of Nova Scotia's major roads, about thirty minutes north of Halifax. It's referred to as a "rural area." That is, it's neither a town nor a village. It's in the municipality of East Hants. And in the East Hants Sports Complex, which is on the edge of Lantz, about three hundred people are waiting for a Maritime Junior A hockey game to begin. It's a Wednesday night and the East Hants Molson Penguins are playing the Truro Bearcats. The league has ten teams, six from Nova Scotia in one division and two each from P.E.I. and New Brunswick in the other. At the snack bar, which smells strongly of mustard, ketchup, and disinfectant, a woman with grey hair tied back in a bun is making hot chocolate. Another woman is complaining that there's only one phone. "The RCMP took out the other one because of all the false 9-1-1 calls," says the woman behind the counter. "They said they'll take the other one out, too, if there are any more. It's the kids."

In a small, bare room under the stands a young man in a dark suit, white shirt, and tie is pacing while his team is taking its pre-game skate. Paul Currie is in his second year as East Hants coach. "Our team is so-so," he says. "There's lots of room for improvement. We've only won one game out of seven, but we've tied two and our goal ratio is not bad. They're young players. They have a lot to learn."

Currie comes from Kingston. He played Junior B there and what he says was "a little bit" of major junior with Guelph and Brantford. Then, after stops in Pembroke, Aurora, and Newmarket, he came down to play for Dalhousie University in Halifax and to study sociology and criminology. Now he's in the waste removal business.

"I like the competitive part of hockey. And because I don't play any more, it's the best way to get that feeling," he says of coaching. "And I like working with young guys. I think I have something to teach them or I wouldn't be doing this. It's not for the glamour, I can tell you." He stops pacing and goes over the lineup with his assistant, Stu Hennigar, a veteran of Newfoundland senior hockey and the AHL.

It's a good, fast game. Truro take a 1–0 lead when one of their forwards steps around the Penguins' defenceman and puts the puck between the goalie's legs. The East Hants president, Melvin Nelson, curses under his breath. He's a big man who used to work for CN. He's sitting, hunched over, about halfway up the rink near centre ice. "I was never much of a hockey player but I spent a great deal of time around the rink because I've always liked it," he says. "I have two boys and one of them got as far as a Montreal Canadiens' training camp. I refereed hockey for years." When he came home after working for CN in New Brunswick he agreed to take over a senior team in East Hants. Two years ago, when the juniors came in, he became their president. "This is a community team," he says. "The gate took in $76,000 last year and bingo netted us a little over thirty thousand and we raffle off items. One last year was worth ten thousand dollars. This year we're building a house and we'll put it on the market and that'll give us some more money. Hockey is expensive. We need every nickel."

Up in the lounge, Steve Bates is leaning against the glass, looking down on the game. He's a baggage handler for Air Canada at the airport in Halifax. "I love hockey," he says. "When I put the ball glove away, I bring out the skates. I love the competition in hockey and no matter what anybody says, it's Canadian." He plays intermediate and used to coach, too, but gave it up. "It was too goddamn hard to keep everyone's parents happy. You want to win, but you also want all the kids to play." Bates is wearing a Toronto Maple Leaf cap. "Hey, you know something?" he says. "I got a cousin named 'Teeder', after Ted Kennedy who played for the Leafs. I'm not kidding. He's named 'Teeder'. It's his real name."

Back on the ice, East Hants ties up the game but Truro scores in the third period and wins 2–1. The Truro coach, Steve Crowell, is pleased. "That was good, defensive hockey," he says. "That was Bearcat hockey. We'll take a win like that any day."

(Three months later, Paul Currie was replaced as coach of the East Hants Molson Penguins. Currie says that he quit because of interference from the team's president, Melvin Nelson. Nelson says he fired Currie because Currie wouldn't tell him what was going on. And in December, the Glace Bay Islanders folded. They were in the Maritime junior league with the East Hants team and the junior Truro Bearcats. The Islanders found it too tough competing for fans with the Cape Breton Screaming Eagles, the major junior team based in nearby Sydney.)

Lyle Carter, at fifty-three, is a lanky, easy-going, fair-haired man with glasses. The word "shambling" fits him the way "graceful" fitted Fred Astaire or "sweet" fits Georgia Brown. His trousers are baggy and he's wearing a rumpled, red nylon windbreaker with "Mr. Kool" printed across the front. Carter used to describe himself as a "journeyman" goal-tender. That term, too, was a good fit. Now, he's a businessman, the owner of two car-parts shops; one of them, "Mr. Kool," which specializes in radiators, is in Truro. A second shop is in Bible Hill. And when Carter is not at one of his shops, and the races are on, there's a good chance he'll be at the track.

"I live such a rushed life with the shops and a weekly sports column and getting my son into hock-ey that I get over here and just relax," he says. It's a bright and crisp fall day and Carter is sitting in his big car in the sun a few yards from the finish line at the Truro raceway to watch the standardbreds. In the front seat beside him is Stan Rath, the father of a friend. Rath is in a wheelchair and needs to be lifted in and out of the car. Carter takes him to the track regularly. Today, a horse Rath has a piece of, Warm Weather, is in the sixth race. He finishes third. Stan Rath's son, Stu, who is Carter's friend, made a lot of money in cable TV and owns Truro's junior and senior Bearcats hockey teams.

But right now, Carter wants to talk about racing. "I'm not a trainer or driver but I know how to har-ness a horse and that's interesting and I can care for horses," he says. "I guess over the years I've owned thirty or more of them. In 1989 I sold one, P. H. Terminator, for $51,000. That's a lot of money in the

Maritimes. The only time I've ever driven in a race was an exhibition in Barrie. Eddie Shack also drove." Carter looks around. It's a thin crowd. "The casinos are really hurting racing," he says. "A lot of people are doing their betting there. It's too goddamn bad. Where'd you rather be on a day like this? In a bloody casino or here?"

After the race card's finished, Carter takes Stan Rath home and then goes to Mr. Kool. It's a Sunday, so there's no one around. On an office wall is a print of a portrait of Dan Patch, the famous American pacer, painted in 1904. And there are dozens of hockey and baseball photos. One is of Babe Ruth surrounded by children in the nearby village of Westville. It was taken during the Second World War, when Ruth was on a goodwill tour.

"They say he gave a hitting demonstration but the only one he hit out of the park was a foul ball," Carter says. "He blamed the bats and the balls and the light, every damn thing. An old guy who was there told me." A scarred goalie stick, thick with tape, is standing in the corner. "Lift that," Carter says. "It's like a goddamn tree. The sticks now are so much better and lighter."

Carter was scouted while playing intermediate for his hometown Brookfield Elks, a few miles from Truro. "The Elks gave me my start," he says. "I guess it was then that I began to dream of a hockey career." He was sent to Toronto and the junior Marlboros. Turk Broda was the coach. "I was awed by him," Carter says. "I've heard people say since that he wasn't a good coach, but he was very good to me. He certainly knew how to handle goalies, and he was a helluva nice man." The Marlies dealt Carter to Brampton. After junior he kicked around in the minors for a while until he reached the NHL with the

California Seals. It was 1971 and California was owned by Charlie Finley, who also owned the Oakland Athletics, then one of baseball's premier teams with Reggie Jackson, Rollie Fingers, and Catfish Hunter.

Carter says, "I guess my biggest thrill was when Charlie said, 'Welcome aboard, son.' I know he said that to hundreds of hockey and ball players, but it was still a big thrill." He laughs. "It took me almost as long to make it as it did Johnny Bower. I just wish I could have done even half as much when I did make it." Carter played fifteen games for California in the 1971–72 season and allowed fifty goals. His team-mates included Carol Vadnais and Bert Marshall, both fine defencemen. Then it was back to the minors, for good. Over his career he played for about as many teams as it seems possible to play for. All in all, unless he's forgotten any of them, and not necessarily in order, they were the Brookfield Elks, Toronto Marlboros, Brampton 7UP, Cleveland Barons, Houston Apollos, Oklahoma City Blazers, Baltimore Clippers, New Haven Nighthawks, Montreal Voyageurs, Nova Scotia Voyageurs, California Seals, Salt Lake Golden Eagles, Clinton Comets, Muskegon Mohawks, and Syracuse Eagles. Then there were the senior teams, the Orillia Pepsis, Windsor Maple Leafs, New Glasgow Rangers, and Moncton Hawks, and from the old Newfoundland senior league, the Gander Flyers and Buchan's Miners. That's all Carter can think of for the moment. "They were always looking for goalies," he says. "I sure as hell was never out of work for long. One season I played for three teams."

He puts away the goalie stick, locks up the shop, and heads for Truro's Colchester Legion Stadium to watch the Truro senior Bearcats practise. He wants to do his weekly *Daily News* column on them. It's his second arena of the day. This morning, after church and before the track, he scouted a goalie at a midget game in Brookfield. "Jesus, I never seem to stop," Carter says. He grins. "You see now why I like to take it easy at the track."

Inside the arena, Stu Rath, the team's owner, Jim Foley, the general manager, and a couple of others are watching the Bearcats work out. "This is one of their first practices," Carter says, "but they'll be good this year, you'll see. They got some talent. Anyway, I hope like hell they are because they're hosting the Allan Cup in April, then that's it. They're the only senior team in Nova Scotia and they're closing down. It's a damn shame."

14

Stonewall, Manitoba

December 1997

AT BUCKINGHAM PALACE, ON September 4, 1918, King George V awarded the Victoria Cross to 2nd Lieutenant Alan McLeod, a pilot in the Royal Flying Corps, for "very gallant" action in an air battle over France. A photograph shows a fair-haired young man, more of a boy really, in uniform and holding a swagger stick, staring unsmilingly, and uncomfortably, into the camera. When McLeod came home to Stonewall on a glorious fall day several weeks later, a holiday was declared. Shops, businesses, and schools were closed; the children were given balloons, and little Union Jacks to wave; there were speeches from the town fathers; and there was a parade with McLeod in an open car. Six weeks later he was dead, felled by the 'flu that ravaged Europe and North America as the First World War wound down. Alan McLeod was nineteen years old.

Stonewall remains the tidy prairie town and farming centre that it was when McLeod was driven through it in triumph that afternoon long ago. There are a couple of shopping plazas and a brand new hospital, and a bar with slot machines. But it's still small: only about three thousand people live there, and few of the buildings on the main street, Main Street, are more than two storeys high. The limestone quarry, once Stonewall's major employer, where Lou Medynski's father worked, has long been quarried out. And the Winnipeg Electric Company's streetcar line, which Lou would ride over the twenty frozen miles to Winnipeg for hockey, is no more. It's been replaced by a four-lane highway. Down by the railway tracks, across from the RCMP station and not far from Alan McLeod VC Avenue, is the rink. It's nearly fifty years old, built after Lou Medynsky headed for Nova Scotia. "I remember Lou well. We grew up on the same street," says Chuck Hubbard. "He and his brother were both good hockey players. I was just a kid but I'd see them play. I remember that Lou left town after the war."

Hubbard is sitting in the Rockwood, Stonewall's only motel. Outside, in the failing, late afternoon light, a cold wind slaps snow against the window. Hubbard is a soft-spoken, small man of sixty-seven with glasses, who still plays hockey. He's wearing a Detroit Red Wings cap. "Yeah, they're my team." This weekend he'll be in a tournament in Winnipeg against players in their thirties. "I played forty-four games last year, sixty the year before. I have the kid in me. I just can't get away from it," he says, without the hint of a smile."

At only fifteen, he says, he made the intermediate team in Stonewall. It was hard-hitting, no-holds-barred hockey, an example of the rural rivalry that pitted town against town. "I never minded the rough stuff," Hubbard says, "but I can't stand the hooking and holding today. We never had that bullshit." It was 1948, Hubbard says, when Bryan Hextall retired from the New York Rangers and came home to play. Hextall, the father of Bryan Jr. and Dennis and grandfather of Ron, was from Poplar Point, fifty miles west of Winnipeg. "My old coach put me on him," Hubbard says. He gives a proud chuckle. "I was a pretty good skater and Hextall'd get so goddamn mad he could have killed me. I was always under his feet."

Hubbard was far too small for professional hockey, even the hockey of fifty years ago, but he says that he was asked to play in England, for Nottingham. "But I didn't want to. I guess I was a homebody." When he heard that a pulp mill in Pine Falls, northeast of Winnipeg, was putting together a team, he tried out. "Eighty-five, ninety guys at the old rink in Winnipeg and Jesus, I made the bloody team and I was given a job," he says. "We were in with Portage, Brandon, Minnedosa, Neepawa, Dauphin. That was the top hockey in Manitoba. We won five provincial championships."

Among Hubbard's teammates one year was the rambunctious Bill Juzda, who'd played with the New York Rangers and the Toronto Maple Leafs. "We called him 'the Beast'. He could hit like nobody I've ever seen. Dauphin had Chuck Lumsden. He played for the Blue Bombers but he was a helluva hockey player, too. He was big, and a wonderful skater, and one night he winds up behind his own goal and you could see the Beast almost pawing the ice, getting ready to meet him, both of them breathing fire, and away they went. They hit each other at centre ice. Hardest goddamn hit I've ever seen. You could hear it, 'Thwack!', all over the rink. It's a wonder the building's still standing. But nobody was hurt. They were two tough boys. Juzda and I played defence together. He'd get the man, and I'd get the puck."

(Juzda is seventy-seven and lives in Winnipeg. "Sure I remember Hubbard," he says. "He was a little bugger. He could skate like hell.")

In 1967 the Pine Falls rink burned down, so Hubbard and a friend joined Stonewall, because it was Hubbard's hometown, for the season. "We drove eighty-five miles from Pine Falls to Stonewall for home games, sometimes further for away games," he says. "No matter what the weather was like, we did it. We didn't miss a game. And that year we won a championship here, in Stonewall."

It's Friday night, hockey night in Stonewall. The wind is up and the temperature is down. In the tin-sided arena a handful of old and young, including girls who've just finished figure skating, are milling about drinking coffee and hot chocolate. In about twenty minutes the Stonewall Flyers play the Peguis Mohawks, an Indian team from a reserve a couple of hours north of Stonewall. The teams are in the South Interlake Senior League — "Interlake" because it's a region between Lake Winnipeg and Lake Manitoba. The Stonewall coach, Wayne Isbister, says the league is really intermediate or Senior B, below the only legitimate Triple-A senior team in Manitoba, the Ile des Chênes North Stars, that challenges for the Allan Cup.

Tim Williams, who handles the cash for the Flyers, is selling tickets at the door. It costs three dollars to get in. Most of the ticket money will go to the three on-ice officials and for ice rental. What's left goes towards team expenses, including gas for the Flyers' bus when they're on the road.

"Maybe 150 here tonight," Williams says. He's fairly happy. "But they don't bring many with them." He's referring to the Peguis team.

Williams is thirty years old. In his rugby jersey and with his short hair, he seems more L.L. Bean than small town, prairie hockey. By day, he's a general accountant in Winnipeg and by night, when there's no hockey, he's at Just the Faxx, a restaurant a few blocks from the rink. He's part-owner. Williams has been with the Flyers for eight years, but he hasn't been on skates since he fell on the ice and suffered a severe concussion when he was ten. "I like working with the team because it's as close to the ice as I can be without going on it," he says. "My father coached and I spent a lot of time skating before my accident. I grew up in rinks."

Williams says it costs $10,000 to put the team on the ice and that fundraising and selling advertising is difficult. Stonewall is close to Winnipeg, which siphons off a lot of interest. "This isn't like Fisher Branch," he says, "where they can pack the rink for every game and take in a thousand dollars. Some nights we barely cover ice rental."

The Flyers have finished their pre-game skate and have clumped down the wooden stairs into their pokey dressing room, which smells like any old hockey dressing room, of ammonia, sweat, and mildew. They've taken off their sweaters, loosened their skates, and are sitting on the benches that run around the room, legs outstretched. Most of them are in their twenties. A couple of them are re-taping sticks.

Wayne Isbister is sitting on a bench in the narrow hallway outside the dressing room. He's forty-four years old, thickset, with horn-rimmed glasses. He has on a black leather windbreaker with the Flyers' logo. Isbister has been around the Flyers for years. He played for them and his older brother, Ike, also coached and played for them. So he's done all this before; he doesn't get too excited. Tonight, for example, he's neither up nor down, sort of in neutral. "We haven't had enough practices," he says in a low key. "It's tough to get all the guys out because of their jobs. This is a good skating team they're playing tonight."

Dana Kapusta, a big man with an earring, comes out of the dressing room. He's swearing to himself and rubbing a bare elbow, but he's smiling. "It's always goddamn sore," he says. "Since I hurt it when I was a kid. It's been operated on." He didn't have his elbow pads on during the warm-up, he says, and he fell on it. Isbister looks up. He shakes his head in bemusement, but he doesn't say anything. Kapusta sits down on the bench beside Isbister and lights a cigarette. "I smoke out here," he says. He nods towards the dressing room. "I don't want to bother anyone in there."

A woman's voice calls from upstairs: "Aren't they going to have their warm-up?" She's talking about the other team.

Isbister looks down the hallway. The Peguis Mohawks are only now filing into their dressing room at the other end of the hall, with their big, black hockey bags, like body bags, over their shoulders. "They're just getting here," he calls back.

"Well, they won't get it then," the woman calls again.

"That's not my problem," Isbister mutters, to nobody in particular.

Isbister works as a machinist in Winnipeg and doesn't get a dime for coaching. The Flyers even pay to play — $150 each. On top of that, they supply their own sticks. That's why there's resentment towards the Mohawks. The word is that they pay some of their players as much as two hundred dollars a game. "It can screw up the league," Isbister says.

Carl McCorrister, who runs the Mohawks and once played for them, says that none of his players is paid. However, unlike Stonewall, the players don't have to pay to play. McCorrister expects to spend between $20,000 and $25,000. "Once a guy signs his card, we supply pretty well everything," he says. That is, except skates. "But sometimes we'll give a guy $150 or so towards skates if he's short."

Gladwyn Scott, who lives within a couple of hundred yards of the Stonewall rink, is president of the South Interlake League. He says that players *are* being paid and that in some cases they're moving from one team to another for money. "It's hard on the rest of the teams that play for fun and have trouble even paying for sticks," he says. "When you go into a game thinking you have a chance to win, that's one thing. When you go in knowing you're going to get plastered by a bunch of hired guns, that's not good for the league."

Scott is sixty-six, a retired school teacher, principal, and school superintendent. He's also an ex-hockey player and he used to be president of the Manitoba Hockey Association. He figures that since beginning to play hockey as a child he's been involved in it for more than fifty years. He says that paying players is only one of the problems facing senior hockey. "It's not like the '50s and '60s, when hockey was at a really high ebb," he says. "Like nearly everywhere else, there's so many things to do today it's often hard to get a commitment from players and fans. Without the commitment you have nothing." He covers league games for the Stonewall *Argus*. "If I don't do it maybe nobody will, and if they do, it's not done very well," he says. "I think it's important to discuss the people involved in sport here. Besides, I meet a lot of nice people."

• • •

Back outside the Stonewall dressing room, Isbister says it's tough at times getting players. Two defected this year to the East Coast Hockey League, two others are hurt, and others have job commitments. He says that he coaches so the team can keep going. "They might not find anyone else," he says. "I played for the Flyers, and my brothers did, and I want kids who leave Junior B here to have somewhere to play."

Brent Kapusta joins his brother outside the dressing room. He's taller and slimmer than Dana and, at twenty-four, two years older. He grins. "Faster, too." He takes a drag from Dana's cigarette. He isn't surprised the Mohawks are late. He says it's a bitch of a drive they have to make. "Some of those goddamn winding roads." The Kapustas are grandsons of Pete Kapusta, who had a great minor league career that included nine years with Providence in the AHL. They're very proud of their grandfather.

After a moment, Isbister follows the Kapustas back into the dressing room. The Flyers are tying up their skates and pulling on their sweaters. He stands in the middle of the room, surrounded by hockey bags. He says, raising his voice, but still with an air of resignation, as if he's said the same thing a hundred times, "You're taking too many dumb fucking penalties. Too much goddamn stickwork." He turns, looking for the captain, Dan Becker. He reminds him of the game misconduct that he took in the last game. "That was goddamn stupid," he says. "If you're going to get thrown out, make it worthwhile, give him a shot in the head or something, don't get tossed just yapping off at the ref. That's a goddamn waste." From upstairs comes the sound of a whistle. The players begin to get up. "Let's go," Isbister says, "and wingers, for Christ's sake, cover the points in our end."

If there are 150 people there when the puck drops, Tim Williams the man selling the tickets, will be lucky. The Stonewall Flyers are in white, with a red-and-black winged wheel, similar to Detroit's. The Mohawks are in red with the Chicago Blackhawk logo.

There's lots of hitting on the small ice surface. Dana Kapusta scores Stonewall's first goal. When the period ends, Stonewall is leading 4–1. Isbister stays in the hallway outside the dressing room. "I'm happy we're ahead," he says, "but we're sloppy as hell in our own end." He's right. Before the second period ends, the Mohawks, scoring in a flurry, have gone ahead by a goal. By early in the third — after Isbister tells his team that they better goddamn well know what to do to win — it's tied 7–7. A minute later, Stonewall goes up again. The game becomes chippy and a Peguis player runs a Stonewall player from behind. He's ejected. Then Derek Arbez of Stonewall gets in a fight. He's thrown out, too.

"It makes me sick to see this," says Holly Klimpke, a slim blonde. She goes to most of the games because her husband and her brother play for Stonewall. "This is supposed to be fun. I can't stand the fighting. But I blame the officials, too. They should have been in control of the game from the start." She's very angry. "That type of stuff stinks."

Down below, in the Stonewall dressing room, Arbez has taken off his skates. He's a tall, rangy twenty-year-old who plays all the forward positions, and defence. He looks relaxed, but from behind his easy smile the words spill out. "All I did was flick his visor and he jumped me," he says. He sighs. "Hell, fighting is nothing to me. It's routine, like eating supper. Doesn't wind me up or nothing. I don't like it, but it's a job. People might not like it. That's their right. But for me, if fighting happens, it happens."

Western kids sometimes call the WHL, which is the major junior league, the "Dub", for its letter "W". Arbez says, "Last year in the Dub with Swift Current I had 295 penalty minutes and thirty-some points. That's not bad." He's been to Detroit and Hartford free-agent camps. At Hartford, he says that in his first shift in a scrimmage he fought the hard-nosed veteran Kevin Dineen. "Hey, I got newspaper stories about it," he says, smiling. For a moment the years drop away, and he sounds like a child bragging over some schoolyard feat.

Last fall, Swift Current traded Arbez to Seattle, but he didn't want to play there. He calls it a "stupid organization." He says, "You know, they wouldn't even let us wear our baseball caps backwards? You got to figure that if they thought baseball caps were important, it'll tell you something about them. Anyways, I only stayed a week. I lost the drive to play hockey. It happens. Maybe I pushed myself too hard. I wasn't the kind who worked out every day in the gym, or spent all summer getting in shape. But once the season started I'd be the first on at practice and the last off. And if we were losing five–zip I'd play hard to the last minute, try to get things started with a fight or something. I never quit. You want to be a hockey player, you better be ready to be one. I'm not saying it's a bad thing, but all you're going to know is hockey. I still get phone calls all the time wanting me."

The last call, Arbez says, was from the Tacoma Sabretooths of the Western Pro Hockey League, offering him a furnished apartment and four hundred dollars a week. "I thought maybe I could go for this year," he says, "but when you play in a league like that and you're supposed to be a fighter, you're like the deadbeats of the deadbeats. That league is the farm teams of the farm teams of the farm teams."

Arbez says it's almost impossible to combine the WHL and an education. "They get mad at you in the Dub if you don't go to school," he says, "and you get fined. But if you look at the scholastic player of the year for each team, they're about the only guys passing, maybe with a 60 percent average. A few guys can do it, but not many. And it's probably tougher in the WHL than in the OHL or the Quebec league because we travel more. Jesus, we stretch from Brandon to Prince George.

"My advice to kids is, if they're going to play pro, I mean real pro, okay, that's one thing. But if you're not sure you're going to, then go to university. Like, I'm paying the price for not taking a couple of courses. I'm twenty. I have no money, I work as a grunt, $8.50 an hour." He stops talking for a moment. Then he says, "But I'm living like a normal kid, a normal life, for a change. I mean, it sucks going to work, but I'm getting a taste of the real world and that's good. If you ask most junior players what they think of junior hockey they'll say it's the greatest, that they'd do anything for the team. Bullshit. When you look at the guys who break curfew, or fuck each other over, or screw each other's girlfriends, backstab. The jealousy when a guy gets a good pro contract. But I don't regret it all. It was a good life. I was never a superstar. I was just a guy who worked hard."

In the fall, Arbez hopes to go to firefighters' school. He'd do so on a WHL scholarship. He's entitled to it because he played for Swift Current. In the meantime, for the first time in years, he's playing hockey on his own terms. "It's for fun again, only fun. And it's nice playing for a small town, too. The people appreciate it."

The rest of the team pushes into the room, sweating and laughing. Stonewall has prevailed, 11–10. "Sounds like football," a player says. Wayne Isbister says, "I told you. We stunk in our own end. Jesus." But he's pretty happy. After the players shower and dress they head for the bar at the Rockwood Motor Inn on Main Street, which is jammed, this being a Friday night. As many people are there as were at the rink.

The next afternoon, Saturday, Murray Couch, a sixty-three-year-old cattle buyer, drives into Winnipeg to watch Stonewall in an oldtimers tournament. He settles down in a warm, glassed-in room over the rink. He's just in time to see Chuck Hubbard move from behind his own net and put a long pass right on the stick of a man crossing the red line. "See, he's still good," Couch says. "He's older than I am, nearly twice the age of some of those guys, but he seldom makes a mistake. He's probably one of the smartest players out there."

When he was sixteen, Couch went to Colorado College in Colorado Springs on a hockey scholarship. But he got homesick and came back and played three years with the junior Winnipeg Monarchs. He was with the Winnipeg Maroons, a team loaded with ex-pros, that won the Allan Cup in 1964. And he also had a stint with the national team under Father David Bauer, when it was based in Winnipeg. "But by that time I had a job and a family and there were some real good players," he says. "I suppose if I'd been a better player I'd have been on it, the national team, and gone overseas with them, but I didn't."

Couch says that minor hockey is thriving in

Stonewall. "In every age group there are three teams
. . . twelve to fifteen kids on each team," he says. But
ice time is getting scarce. "So they also use a little rink
in a town about ten miles away, Balmoral, and they're
probably the biggest factor in keeping that rink open,
because Balmoral doesn't have many kids."

Couch used to coach but he got fed up with the
parents. "I still go to the rink but it's to watch my
grandsons," he says. "Last weekend they were both
playing, one in Stonewall, the other in Selkirk. That's
about twenty miles away. I spent my time running
back and forth from rink to rink."

Twenty minutes due west of Stonewall, on the CN
railway that runs all the way from Winnipeg to the
northern tip of Lake Manitoba, is Warren. It's a one-
church (United), one-grain-elevator town of one-
storey buildings and about nine hundred people.
Like Stonewall, it has a team, the Warren Warriors,
in the South Interlake Hockey League. They play out
of an old, tin-sided arena, like Stonewall's, that's
managed by Chuck Lefley. Lefley spent nine years in
the NHL, two of them with Montreal's Stanley Cup-
winning teams of the early '70s. He also played in St.
Louis, Finland, and Germany. Off the ice, he farms
sixteen hundred acres.

"There isn't all that much to do in the winter on
the farm except haul some grain for the cows, so
working at the rink helps keep my sanity," he says.
"A couple of guys work for me so we split things up.
I guess I'm there about three nights a week."

Lefley is forty-seven but looks younger because
farming has kept him in shape. He lives with his wife
and daughter in Grosse Isle, a few miles from
Warren, where he grew up. He had five brothers —
he was the second oldest — and a sister. The oldest

brother, Bryan, who spent five years in the NHL before going to Europe, was killed recently in a car accident in Italy, where he was coaching. "We had a memorial service for him last week," Lefley says. "A lot of people turned out, hockey people and others. He was cremated. There was also a service in Italy."

All the brothers were good hockey players and for a couple of years five of the six were on the same intermediate team. Lefley says that one year when Bryan was back from Europe it looked as if all six might be playing, but then another brother's job took him away.

Of his NHL days, Lefley says he retired young, before he was thirty, because he was burned out. "I'd just had enough," he says. He was with the St. Louis Blues at the time. "Emile Francis was the GM and he got me my release. Francis was one of the best men I ever dealt with in hockey: totally honest. I was very lucky to have had him, and Sam Pollock when I was in Montreal.

"Francis also coached us in St. Louis and until then I never realized how much work it was to be general manager and coach. I don't see how the hell the man did it. But he was just so into the game. I've never seen anyone with so much energy."

Lefley also liked playing for Leo Boivin in St. Louis, "one of the nicest people I ever met in hockey. I think that's why I played so hard for him." He calls Derek Sanderson the most unselfish centre he ever played with, and Jacques Lemaire probably the most underrated Montreal Canadien. "He was a great hockey player."

In spite of Bryan's recent death, Lefley seems fulfilled. He has a strong marriage, he likes what he does, and he's very proud of his farm. After showing off a new shed which houses his heavy farm equipment, he walks across the yard to see whether his cows need to be fed or watered. The day is clear and there isn't a whisper of wind, so the trees are still and straight. It's very quiet. "Lots of deer around here," Lefley says. "It's like a nature preserve some days." The cows lift their big heads as Lefley approaches and two of them begin to amble towards him, their brown coats thick and heavy, protection against the winter cold. "They want to see what's happening," he says. "Cows are curious. They don't just stand around." He points out that some of the cows will soon have calves. "I like cows. I don't like pigs. Cows are much easier to handle." Lefley looks down. "This is okay in winter," he says, kicking at the frozen, snow-covered ground. "If it's mild you're not up to your ankles in mud and manure."

He continues, "I've lived here all my life and I like it. I have friends from childhood here. And Winnipeg is a nice place." He looks around, beyond his new shed, into the trees, where deer forage for food. "My brother Glen and I bought the farm from Dad, before I retired, so I knew when the time came, this was what I was going to come home to. It was a nice feeling knowing there was no doubt that I was coming here."

Leaning against the fence of his cattle pen, Lefley says that if he were to have his NHL career over again he'd take hockey more seriously. "In the summer, hockey was the last thing on my mind," he says. "I think it's the first thing on players' minds today. They do it ten, twelve months a year. I did it from training camp to the last game we played. Nothing in between. I could be stubborn, too. I didn't always do what perhaps I should have. Another thing is the confidence the kids have today — eighteen, nineteen — much more than I ever had at that age.

"But although I made the NHL, won Stanley Cups,

my very favourite hockey memories are from here, when I was fifteen or sixteen, and they'd ask us to play for our intermediates at Warren. Being a kid I was so nervous because I'm playing with men, but they made us feel so great and important. The coach was Alex Stewart. His son, Johnny, played with me. Johnny went to the NHL. Alex would call us 'the kids'. He'd always bring up more than one of us so we wouldn't feel alone. And the rink, on a cold Saturday night, would be jammed: three hundred people, maybe more. And if we did well — and we didn't have to score — but if we did well playing against men, there was no feeling like it. It was the best feeling in the world. You had accomplished something really important. It was incredible, being there, playing, incredible."

Jimmy McFadden, the old Detroit Red Wing and Chicago Blackhawk, lives in Carman, on the other side of Winnipeg from Stonewall and Warren. The senior hockey team in Carman is called the Beavers. At the Carman Post Office they didn't know that Jimmy McFadden had moved. "He picks up his mail. It comes to a post box so it's addressed to general delivery," a postal clerk says. "There's no street address." He's checking the telephone book. "He was in here this morning and we were kidding each other. I know he was a pretty good hockey player even though it was before my time." He closes the phone book. "It still has his old address." Then he says, "Hey, did you know Ed Belfour comes from Carman?" Just then a man comes in who knows where McFadden lives, in a condominium on the Boyne River, which seems suitable for a boy from Belfast.

Jimmy McFadden got a late start in the NHL. He

didn't play his first game until the 1947–48 season when he was twenty-eight, but he won the Calder Trophy as rookie of the year. Over seven years he scored a hundred goals and another ten in the play-offs. He played at about five foot eight, but was sturdy and his opponents always said he was hard to knock off his skates. People who saw him play say he was a magnificent skater.

He's seventy-seven and he appears in good health, although he suffered a stroke two years ago. McFadden's wife died a little while ago and that's why he moved. He lives alone. He says that he misses his wife very much. He has lived in southern Manitoba, when not away playing hockey, since 1930. That was when his father brought the family from Northern Ireland on something called the Veteran's Land Act. "Moving my mother and six kids over here and starting up wasn't easy," McFadden says. "He got a quarter-section a bit south of here. We started with a few horses, that's what you farmed with in those days, and some cows, some pigs. They had some hard years. During the Depression we just had what was on the farm. Some people had nothing. I remember driving a stook (hay) wagon, two horses, when I was only eleven. That was man's work." McFadden's three sons live in Manitoba and he's very proud of them. One of them farms with him. They have twelve hundred acres. "I've always liked farming," McFadden says. "I still get out there on the tractor."

This winter McFadden says he's been going to three or four hockey games a week. He sees all his grandson's games and he also goes to watch the Beavers. "Let's face it," he says, "there's not much else to do here in the winter. The senior hockey isn't as good as the old senior hockey, you know, in the

'50s and '60s, before the leagues started folding, but it's okay, and the Beavers are doing well. Crowds are down but if they keep winning, the people will start coming again."

McFadden was already ten when the family settled in Manitoba, and he had to make up quickly for his late skating start, certainly late for a prairie youngster. "It wasn't like today, with rinks open all the time. It was just natural ice and it lasted only four months, so I skated as much as I could," he says. He went to school in Opawaka, near Carman. "I still remember the teacher's name, Andy Bailey. He would let me keep my skates on in class. I used to sit in the back row of the schoolroom, keep the old blades on, all ready to go. Whenever noon hour came or when school ended I'd be zipping to the rink. I'd be skating before school, at recess, after school. And it made me a good skater and that's what it takes to be a hockey player, skating, and that's what I did best. If you can skate, the rest will kind of fall into place."

McFadden's parents disapproved of hockey. "They were very religious, Pentecostal," he says. "They didn't want anything to do with dancing or sports. But we lived only a couple of hundred yards from the school and in the winter my dad was the part-time school caretaker and he had to look after the rink. That's the only reason he let me skate, I guess. But they were real good Christian people. Some around here still tell me how much they loved my mother and dad because they were kind to them, especially during the Depression. I didn't bring up my boys the way I was brought up, but they all turned out well."

McFadden's first venture into serious hockey foundered, but not because of his late start at skating. "I tried out for Portage in the Manitoba junior league," he says. "I made the team, but coming from Ireland I didn't have a birth certificate so I couldn't prove my age." He returned to Carman and played for the intermediate Beavers, and they won a provincial championship. By then McFadden had been spotted by the Montreal Canadiens so, following four years in the army, he was invited to the Canadiens' training camp in Montreal. "We were billeted in the old Queen's Hotel and when I got there I found a letter from Tommy Gorman," he says. "He was running the Ottawa Senators in the Quebec league. In it was a cheque for two thousand bucks. Jesus, that was a lot of money. I didn't even bother with Montreal. I don't think I even unpacked. I just got out of there and went to Ottawa. I remember Legs Fraser, from Winnipeg, was our goalie. He'd throw his stick into the crowd after a game. Goalie sticks were expensive and that really pissed Gorman off, but he kept doing it. It was hard to tell Fraser anything. He was something else. I played in Ottawa for a year and a bit and then I went to Buffalo in the American league and afterwards to Detroit.

"Let me show you something." McFadden gets up, goes to the dining room, and returns with a silver tea tray. "My granddaughter found this and shined it up. I'd forgotten about it." The inscription says it was a present from the Detroit Red Wings in 1948 for winning the Calder as rookie of the year. "Okay for twenty-eight, eh?" he says. He points out that Ed Belfour, who won the Calder in 1991 with the Blackhawks, comes from Carman. "I know him to see him," McFadden says. "But I've never talked to him. Someone told me that he knows that I won the Calder Trophy, too. Good, eh? Two Calder winners from Carman."

• • •

Gladwyn Scott played for the Miami (Manitoba) Rockets when McFadden, back from the NHL, was the Rockets' playing-coach. "Jimmy was an outstanding player for years after he left the NHL," Scott says. "He made a big impact in the southeastern league around Morden, Altona, Winkler, Pilot Mound, and Portage. He was one of the dominant hockey players in Manitoba in the late '50s and '60s. Nobody could catch him once he had a stride on them. And he had a very good shot, very quick getting it away.

"As a coach he'd have us on the ice for an hour and a half every night. We were in mid-season shape before the season began. He was strict: no smoking, no drinking. It was all business. We would pack the rinks. Miami was a small town but we'd take on Brandon and Selkirk and we'd come within a goal of representing the province. Most of this was due to Jimmy."

Back in Carman, Jimmy McFadden puts away his tray and comes back to the sofa. "Because of my years in the army I never even thought I'd make the NHL," he says. "I was twenty-eight when I went up, getting old. So in that way I was lucky." He pauses. Then he says, smiling, but meaning it, "But it wasn't all luck. I guess I had to be pretty good, too."

15

Bienfait, Saskatchewan

December 1997

FRANK PASTACHAK IS SIX FOOT three and weighs 275
pounds. He has hands the size of hams and the face
of a defensive tackle from the days before face
masks. But his game isn't football, it's hockey. "I can
hardly wait until fall comes and the ice goes in and it
starts again for another year," he says. His voice is a
cross between a bark and a growl. "It's the travelling,
it's the crowds, it's the people in hockey, it's everything. It's even better when you have your boys playing. I love hockey's intensity. And you've got to be
tough to play, but you've got to have finesse. It
demands everything. You got to be able to take your
bumps and bruises. There's not a game can touch it.
Not even goddamn close."

Frank Pastachak's team is the Bienfait Coalers.
Bienfait — pronounced *been-fate* — is in coal-mining
country a few miles east of Estevan, tucked into that
tidy corner of the map where Saskatchewan,
Manitoba, and North Dakota meet at right angles.
There's not much to it, although its story has its
colourful, and tragic, chapters. In 1920 there was a

gangland slaying, never solved, which apparently was connected to the booze that was trucked through Bienfait and into the United States during Prohibition. And in the cemetery, are the bodies of three coal miners. The miners died during a strike in 1931. A headstone says simply, "Murdered by the RCMP."

Pastachak is retired. For years he was the town of Bienfait's chief maintenance man. As a young man he played some senior hockey and then he got into officiating. "The referees were always neutral but the teams would supply a linesman each and pay him ten dollars a game," he says. "That's what I did. I'd leave work at five o'clock, get on the old school bus we'd fixed up for the team — sometimes I'd drive it — and we'd be off eighty, ninety miles to play. I'd officiate, drive back, maybe two or three in the morning, some nights snowing so bad you could see better with the headlights off, and go to work at seven o'clock. I'm not an on-ice official any more, but I do some goal-judging and I try to line up prizes from local merchants like gift coupons and stuff for the draws between periods. Anything to make money for the team. And I'll still travel when the team does. I get excited as hell at games. I got in a fight last year with a ref, because he wasn't calling anything. Some of our guys could have been damn near killed, but no penalties. But the cops couldn't do anything to me. They didn't see nothing. It was my word against the ref's."

Tonight, a Sunday night, Pastachak is getting excited. It's the Coalers' first game of the season. They are playing the Carnduff Red Devils in Bienfait. The rink is just across the street from the Pastachak house. "Not bad, eh?" he says. "Some nights I don't even bother with a coat." The Coalers are in a senior league like Stonewall's. It's called the Big Six, which is something like the Group of Seven. That's to say, the number doesn't mean much. This year the Big Six has eight teams; one year it had five, and it's had as many as twelve. It's been around a long time. "It's a tough league, believe me," Pastachak says. He leaves his house for the thirty-second walk to the rink. It's mild for early December so he's wearing only a light jacket. "Jesus, I hope we get some people tonight," he says.

Pastachak estimates the Coalers' budget at $10,000, most of it going on travel and sticks. Echoing Stonewall's complaint, he says that some teams pay their players as much as three or four hundred dollars each a game. "That's horseshit for a league like this," he says. "We can't afford it. We give them sticks and tape, that's it. We don't draw that good, maybe a hundred or so."

Both of Frank Pastachak's sons, Kevin, who is thirty-two, and twenty-five-year-old Kelly, play for the Coalers. Kevin was asked to join another team for pay, but stayed at home. He has two children and he works for the Prairie Coal Corp. as an oiler-operator on a dragline, the huge mechanical bucket used in surface mining. He's tall, like his father, but slim, and much more relaxed.

"I was always at the rink when I was a kid, tagging along after my dad when he was officiating," Kevin says. "I'd have my skates and some of the players would come out on the ice and show me a few things. And when I was around fourteen four of us would go to the rink at one in the morning on weekends and play two-on-two. And we'd clean the ice between periods at Coaler games before they got a Zamboni. We'd wear skates and push scrapers. Growing up, a bunch of us always competed with each other, and that's bound to make you a better player. In the summer, when the ice was out, we set up nets and we played with a ball."

Frank Pastachak says, "One year, when Kevin was playing juvenile in Lampman, right after the game he and three others jumped in the car, didn't even take off their skates, drove twenty miles to Bienfait, changed sweaters, and went out to play for the Coalers. They got there for the second period and we're losing 4–1. We won in the end and it was because of Kevin and the three others."

Kevin also played for the Estevan Bruins in the Saskatchewan junior league. One of his coaches was Gerry James, the great running back with the Winnipeg Blue Bombers in the '50s who'd played a bit for the Toronto Maple Leafs.

"He knew how to get the best out of us," Kevin says. "He knew that everyone is different and had to be treated differently." He says that James was one of the first coaches he'd heard of who used aerobics. "I think we were doing them long before other teams.

"But I could get mad at him. One night we're in North Battleford and I'm on the number-one line. We scored on a power play but that wasn't good enough because we hadn't done the power play his way. So he sat us out for a whole period. I was on ninety-nine points for the season. I really wanted a hundred, but I didn't get it. I didn't say anything, though, and neither did he."

As Frank Pastachak enters the rink a number of people greet him. A woman asks for his wife. "She's coming in a few minutes," he tells her. At the snack bar, the coffee comes in china mugs. "How many rinks have you been where they serve it like this?" asks a young woman. "People donate them. Better than Styrofoam or paper cups, eh?"

Frank says the Coaler players' jobs make it difficult for them all to get out to practise at the same time. "They're working shifts in the oil fields, for the mines," he says. "They don't get any breaks from their employers." He says the teams are allowed rosters of twenty or twenty-one but that only sixteen have signed with the Coalers and they can only count on ten or twelve on any given night.

James Wrigley, a squat man in a wool coat, likes hockey as much as Frank Pastachak does. For a living, he drives a truck for the Estevan Coal Corporation. When he lived in Calgary he says that he'd occasionally drive the bus for the New Westminster Bruins — who used to be the Estevan Bruins — when they were on their prairie swings. "Just being around hockey players is good," he says. James' son, Jamie, a defenceman built like Tie Domi, is the Coalers' captain. Right after the game he has to report for his night shift as a drag-line operator with Prairie Coal. James Wrigley worries that there aren't enough players coming up with his son's kind of dedication to what he calls "good old hockey." He says, "That's sad because small town hockey used to be the best thing going on. It's what kept towns together, gave them their identity."

The Bienfait rink is an old rink with the dressing rooms upstairs. The players must walk down to the ice through knots of spectators. But the ice is good and there's more of it than in many rinks. Kevin Pastachak played seven years in Germany. He likes the European-sized surfaces. He says the Bienfait rink is eighty-seven feet wide. That's two feet wider than the standard NHL rink. Kevin dropped back from forward to defence a couple of years ago. Like Jamie Wrigley, he's able to control the pace of the game.

"When we went to see Kevin in Germany they

treated us like royalty," Frank Pastachak says. "There'd be six or seven thousand at a game and Kevin would be picked as most valuable player and they'd all stand and cheer him. You're so goddamn proud. There's nothing like it."

Craig Kickley, who says he's lucky to be walking, is a slight, fair man of thirty-three. He's been playing in the Big Six since he was sixteen. This would be his seventh season with the Coalers, but he's out with a serious neck injury. He was checked into the boards from behind in an exhibition game. He says, "The doctor told me a fraction closer to the spinal cord and I'd be in a wheelchair now and —"

Frank Pastachak interrupts. "They didn't even call a goddamn penalty," he barks. "The guy should have been kicked out of the league. The officiating is goddamn awful sometimes. They don't know what the hell they're doing."

Kickley says that people have advised him to quit. "But I hate just watching. I want to play. Hell, people have come back from neck injuries." Until he can play again, he's putting together a book on the league's history. "When you're a kid you'd look up to senior players with stars in your eyes," he says. "It may sound crazy, but they were like gods. People from the cities don't understand how important hockey is to places like Bienfait."

Kickley, Frank Pastachak, and James Wrigley are standing with a handful of other men on the balcony at the end of the rink, outside the dressing rooms. Nothing is between them and the Carnduff goal about fifteen feet below. "You got to be goddamn quick to duck if the puck gets deflected up here," Frank says.

Duane Kocoy, who's doing play-by-play for CJSL Radio in Estevan, is up there, too, mike in hand, with no protection. His equipment is on a chair in front of him. Downstairs, behind the glass, there's maybe seventy people. A few more are scattered in the two rows of unheated seats along the boards. Frank Pastachak gives the house the once over, like a veteran vaudevillian. "Crowds'll pick up after Christmas," he says, almost with certainty.

In the first period Bienfait has three power plays. During a two-man advantage, Kevin moves in from the point and lets go a hard, rising shot. The puck is deflected. It hits the goalie's arm and bounces well over his head. He loses sight of it. He still hasn't found it when it drops down behind him, trickles off the crossbar, and falls harmlessly into the mesh at the back of the net. "Jesus Christ, can you believe that," Frank Pastachak says.

A moment later a Coaler breaks in alone across the Carnduff blue line. A linesman stops the play: a two-line pass. The crowd boos. At rinkside, a skinny young man with a beard and wearing a grubby Philadelphia Flyers windbreaker leans towards the linesman, who's against the boards, about three feet from him. "I hate to say it," the skinny man shouts over the booing, almost into the linesman's ear, "but that was a good call." The linesman looks up, winks, then skates away, following the play. "I don't give a shit if it was against Bienfait," the skinny man says to his companion. "It was a good call. He took the pass over the line."

Gradually, the Red Devils take control. In the second period they score three goals, two within a couple of minutes. "I think this is their fourth game," Pastachak says. "Not like us." He's not a good loser. With the score 5–0 in the third, Pastachak and some others begin to taunt the Red Devil goalie, just below them. Play is stopped. The goalie says something to the referee. "What the hell you crying about?" Pastachak yells at him. The goalie has told the ref that they're spitting on him. "Christ, we're not god-damn well spitting on him," Pastachak tells the RCMP constable who has come up to check things out. He's a youngster, in glasses, about half Frank's size. "Yeah, no one's been spitting on him," James Wrigley agrees. Frank Pastachak says loudly, as much to the goalie as the RCMP constable, "For Christ's sake, can't the little baby take some yelling?" Another man says, "Yeah, poor baby can't take it." The goalie never turns around. The young cop sighs audibly and raises his eyebrows in mock resignation. "Just take it easy then," he says. "Let's have no spit-ting." He moves off down the stairs. Duane Kocoy, the broadcaster, has been doubled over his equip-ment, trying to protect it from the people pushing around him. The game ends and in spite of the chip-piness, the players shake hands. Kelly Pastachak, Frank's second son, goes over to the boards and picks up his infant daughter, Jessica Blair, and takes her for a little skate, holding her up to be seen, and the crowd cheers. Frank watches his son and grand-daughter. "That's nice," he says.

The crush of bodies begins to thin and Duane Kocoy sets about packing up his equipment. He says that he learned broadcasting at school in Regina and moved down to Estevan's CJSL about ten years ago. He says that Bienfait is the hardest rink to work from. "The other rinks, some have areas designed for me," he says. "But to be fair, even here, the guys standing close are just listening to me call the game. They seldom give me any trouble." Then, trying to choose his words carefully, he says that Frank Pastachak and James Wrigley can be difficult in the heat of a game. "That shouldn't surprise you, though," he says. "You've seen them. But they're sure as hell the most dedicated fans. You can't fault them there. There's no one like them. I guess that's what hockey needs in places like this."

Kocoy used to broadcast the Estevan Bruins games. He gave them up because he didn't like the travel. He's thirty years old, married, and has two young sons. "With the senior hockey it's an hour and a half on a bus at most," he says. "That's a far cry from five hours to Yorkton with the Bruins or a weekend northern trip. And I realized that if I can't hack the Junior A travel, I sure as hell couldn't handle anything higher than that. So for now at least, I'm very happy here. I love calling games.

"We're a little down on the dial so we don't have the greatest reach, so we might get maybe two hours north. And it's not a huge money-maker, but it's important. They can listen to their kids and grandkids play senior hockey. That means a lot to the parent in Oxbow or Redvers. I hear about shut-ins in Carlyle who like nothing better than to listen to the Carlyle Cougars on the radio. For me it's a bit like being a big fish in a little pond, but it's still nice.

"And remember, for some of these guys this is their NHL. For some of them, to have their games broadcast on the radio is a big deal. Sometimes they'll tape the games, play them back, and if they don't like something I've said, they'll let me know.

"I think the hardest thing I ever did was a quadruple overtime game by myself. It was a playoff between Bienfait and Carlyle two years ago. It was here and the rink was packed. God, they were stacked in, breaking every fire law in the land. I couldn't move for five hours. I was on the air from eight o'clock to after one. All by myself, even the between-period intermissions."

Frank Pastachak has said his goodnights and is on his way across the street to his home. "Ah hell," he says. "That's just first-game jitters. A few more practices and a few more games and we'll be fine." He's calmed down. It's hard to believe he was so worked up only a few minutes ago. "I can't explain it," he says. "Hockey does that to me. It always has." It's getting colder. Most of the fans have gone. For a moment, it's very still and quiet. There's no moon, but beyond the arena, under the pale light from the stars, the prairie stretches to the horizon. And out on it, perhaps miles away, a train really does whistle, and a dog really does howl.

16

Nanton, Alberta

December 1997

HIGHWAY 2 RUNS DUE SOUTH from Edmonton, skirting oil and gas fields, brushing past Red Deer, and going right through Calgary, where it becomes the Macleod Trail. On the other side of Calgary it swings by Okotoks and Joe Clark's old hometown, High River. To the west is prairie and beyond that are the Rockies, with the snow on their distant peaks glowing pink in the approaching twilight. At one point, Highway 2's southbound lane become the main street of Nanton, while its northbound lane is Nanton's second street.

Sixteen hundred people live there. The new library is lit up, busy with children this early evening. At one time Nanton boasted "Canada's finest drinking water," a claim based on spring water so pure it didn't have to be treated. Ten years ago a drought put an end to that. There's a weekly newspaper, the Nanton *News*, a Chinese restaurant, two bars, a big Esso truck stop and a small motel. There's a sixty-strong choir, a theatre group and a senior hockey team, the Palominos.

A hundred years ago, though, winter couldn't have been much fun. "The people who settled here must have been exceptional, they must have been survivors, very courageous and dedicated," says Brigit Jones, one of the founders of the choir. "The frontier populism that built Nanton, and other western communities, sets great store by acts of individual bravery and, like Trail and Stonewall, Nanton has a Victoria Cross connection.

The Nanton Lancaster Society Air Museum honours Bomber Command, the offensive that turned the tide in the Second World War, and the thousands of Commonwealth aircrew who trained at bases under southern Alberta's high skies. Among the museum's vintage aircraft is a Lancaster bomber, dedicated to the memory of Squadron Leader Ian Bazalgette, from Calgary, the only Albertan to be awarded a VC during the war.

The hockey arena is across the highway and down a block from the air museum. Hockey has been played in Nanton for nearly a hundred years. Local history says that the Nanton Skating Rink Association was created in 1903 "for the purpose of building an open air rink east of the railway tracks, above the C&E Dam on Mosquito Creek." The first hockey game, in 1904, "if such it could be called," cautions a newspaper report, "was between married men and bachelors. They used a football for a puck, drop kicks were forbidden, and wedge formations were barred." By the late '20s Nanton had a new arena that was considered among the best in Alberta. Over the years it was added to and kept up to date, but in 1967 it burned to the ground. The one in use now opened in 1969. Like most small town arenas, one end is glassed-in and warm. Beyond the glass, there are seats down only one side. Electric bars hang over them for heat, but it's still cold. The rink's capacity is around six hundred.

The Nanton Palominos have been around for fifty years in one league or another. They are now in the eight-team Ranchland Hockey League, which used to be the Foothills Hockey League. "The league name changes depending who will be in it," says Blair Martin, thirty-three, who runs a drywall and stucco business. Martin played for the Palominos and is now their coach. He's been involved in hockey since he was a kid, except for the year he left high school and took off for New Zealand. His wife, Joan, does public relations for the team and fundraising and keeps the books. "And everything else, too, right down to washing the jerseys and making sure there are bandages in the first-aid kit," she says.

The Martins have finished dinner. They're still at the table in their big kitchen/dining room/living room. Blair Martin seems tense and preoccupied. Twice he's called to the phone. "We have a team meeting later," he says by way of explanation. Then he adds, "Between work, hockey, and three kids we're both going hard all the time."

In spite of the troubles facing small town, senior hockey, Blair Martin is confident about its health in Nanton. The Palominos, he says, are a tradition. "All any kid around here wants to do is play in the NHL." He pauses for a moment. "If they don't make the NHL, they play for the Palominos," he adds, laughing.

He stops laughing and goes on, "But we know there are problems. When I started playing fifteen years ago we had enough fan support that our sticks and tape were paid for. In three or four years the costs of the ice and the officials were going up and fan support was dropping, so we had to pay for half our sticks. Now we're at a point where the players have to sell so many season's tickets, buy their own sticks, and pay ten dollars each towards bus trips."

"We supply the sweaters and socks," Joan says.

"Yeah," Blair says. "We still do that."

The team carries fifteen players. About half of them are from Nanton and most of the others from nearby communities. The league allows each team two imports, that is players from Calgary or north of Calgary. "We had to put a limit on them," Martin says. "City players were coming down here and our kids were getting cut and then the city players would get tired of travel and not show up and before you'd know it the team would fold." He says each autumn he crosses his fingers that there will be enough players, "but then training camp comes and we're all right for another year."

Later that night at the arena, as the Palominos are dressing for practice, Martin is leaning against the rink's glass watching the Zamboni. He apologizes for his preoccupation an hour earlier. He says it was because he'd decided to kick a player off the team. "He got into some trouble and I didn't want him with us any longer," Martin explains. "It was my decision, but the team backed me up. Anyway, it's over." He nods towards a dressing room. "I've just told them." Martin won't reveal what the player did, but he's more relaxed, now that it's over.

He will say that he's proud of the team. "Nobody comes into our dressing room with an ego," he says. "That is, they may come in with one, but they sure as hell won't leave with one. The players don't pay attention to game sheets and stats, who's beating who in scoring. Everyone's the same. That may sound corny, but that's the way the dressing room has been for years. And when we go to the bar after a game, everybody goes. We have fun."

As the players make their way onto the ice, Martin says, "Here's what I mean. Last week we were in Crowsnest. We're losing 5–3 in the third period and our goalie races out to clear the puck. The other guy beats him to it, skates around him, and flips it into the empty net. Our goalie is so god-damn mad he throws his stick. It ends up in the crowd and he's kicked out of the game. Hell, we only brought one goalie with us. So this kid on our team, Grant Wideman, volunteers to play goal. He says he's never done it before. You know what? We won, 8–6." Martin laughs. He's definitely feeling better. "But nothing beats us beating the NHL." That was ten years ago, he says, when an NHL Oldtimers team came through. "Their tour ended something like 40–1 and we were the one," Martin says. "Tom McMasters scored the winning goal. And they had Lafleur and this was the year *before* he made his comeback with the New York Rangers."

Outside in the arena's lobby, Tim Boyko and Mike Sears, retired Palominos, are waiting for their lift to Fort Macleod for a recreational (non-contact) game, the only hockey they play now. On the wall beside them are pictures from Nanton's hockey past. One is of the 1954–55 Palominos that included Johnny McKenzie, later the feisty Boston Bruin. He's grinning, and with his round face that gave him the nickname "Pie," he's easily recognizable.

Boyko and Sears are talking about hockey and youngsters. Boyko doesn't like the elite classifications, Double-A and Triple-A. "It ruining kids' hockey in towns our size," he says, bringing up the same argument Gilles Marotte did in Victoriaville. He's angry. "Jesus Christ, we don't have enough elite players to make a team, and when we do get one or two, they're encouraged to play somewhere else.

Besides, it puts too goddamn much pressure on them. Hockey at that age should be fun, too."

Standing with them is Brett Grant. He's a tall, thin youngster who was eighteen when he joined the Palominos two years ago. This season, at twenty, he's back playing Junior B in Stavely. "The Palominos have guys who played major junior and in Europe and minor pro," he says, "but they'll always be here. I can play for the Palominos for ten years. Right now it's nice to play with guys my own age again.

"I was like every kid who in the back of his mind has the dream of making the NHL. But unless you get a break, get spotted — plus, of course, have the talent — you aren't going to make it. I play now just for fun, because I love it, because it's the best game in the world."

Inside, on the ice, the Palominos are throwing the puck around with the confidence of young men who not only do it well but are having a good time doing it. They're laughing and shouting, like children on a schoolyard rink. There's a mishmash of sweaters, including one from the Notre Dame Hounds, Father Murray's great hockey school in Wilcox, Saskatchewan. Some of the Palominos haven't bothered with helmets and are wearing baseball caps.

Thirty-nine-year-old Tom McMasters is a good-looking, powerfully built former player who is in charge of the arena. He grew up in a hockey family. He and his three brothers played junior and two went on to play professionally. One, Jim, got as far as the Cleveland Barons in the WHA. Tom McMasters is a thoughtful man and when he talks about hockey he seems to embody what it means to small towns such as Nanton. Sitting in his office off the rink's lobby, wearing an old, beat-up Seattle Mariner cap with the simple "M" on it, he says quietly, "I'm from Nanton and I grew up a rink rat. I was always at the rink. When I was a kid the man who ran it would let us on the ice whenever he could. He was really decent to us, encouraged us. That's why if the ice isn't rented for a game or practice I let the kids know and turn it over to them. I know what it means to them. I try not to rent to outsiders. I want our kids to have it."

He continues, "A man I know here wanted to put his boys into the Calgary minor hockey program. He said the competition was better. I said maybe but that they wouldn't get nearly the ice time that they'd get here. I knew that they wouldn't. And I told him that it's the practices that make players, not the games. Anyway, they're still here." He stops talking, pushes his cap back, and scratches his head. After a moment he says, "It's hard to find the words, to explain it, but I just love being around hockey, being around kids, helping them."

After junior hockey McMasters played for the Palominos until he had to retire at thirty because of a bad knee. "Doctors kept telling me to quit, and then I got to the point where I'd had enough of tape and bandages to last me forever," he says. "I also had a family to feed." He coached the Palominos until Blair Martin took over two years ago.

(Martin says, "I don't know half what Tom knows. I'll go to him for advice and then have the guys practise it and they'll think that it's me, that it was my idea, that I'm such a smart son of a bitch of a coach.")

McMasters says that when he coached he had no particular method. "But I always tried to be positive," he says. "You tell a guy what he's done wrong, but for God's sake, tell him when he's doing something right, too. It's a wonderful game. Fast, intense, everything you want. Something is always happening."

Mark Greig, a veteran of the NHL and the IHL, is a close friend of McMasters'. "Mark comes home in the summer and brings the kids down here for ball hockey. He's a real hero to them," McMasters says. "And he helps with a hockey school in Okotoks and he drives them back and forth from here. He's really, really fantastic with the local kids. It means a lot to them and it's great to see."

Mark's older brother, Bruce, played a few games for the old California Seals. "He's quite a story," McMasters says. "He had a lot of talent, but I guess they only wanted to use him as a fighter and he resented it. He's had his problems. Phil Crowe, from here, is another fighter. He's up and down with the Ottawa Senators. His brother's a fighter, too. He's with Dayton. I know a lot of people don't like fighting, but that's what they get paid to do, fight. Fighters usually didn't get that much ice time, but I think they're getting more now and because of that their skills have to improve."

McMasters thinks many people don't realize the dedication needed for hockey players who are trying to reach the top. "Hell, they ride buses forever out here, maybe fifteen hours, and then they're supposed to play a game," he says. "This is their big shot, and maybe they screw up, give up the puck, miss a check, whatever. And that means there's a good chance they won't get on the ice again. That could be it for their dream. It's a very, very tough life."

Another Tom, Tom Hornecker, worked at the rink for twenty-six years and managed it until Tom McMasters took over. Hornecker is sixty-nine, tall, thin, and has leukemia. It's in remission, but he had to stop his oldtimers hockey. He comes to the rink nearly every day for coffee with McMasters.

"My father was an American on his way to Alaska when he got sidetracked. He hit Nanton, married my mother, and stayed," Tom Hornecker says. "When I was a kid we'd ride out on horseback to find a good slough and play against the Indians. They'd wear chaps and they'd stuff their coats in for padding. We'd use a scoop coal shovel for a goal stick. You had to make sure it was turned the right way: if it wasn't, the puck would fly up it and nearly take your goddamn head off."

Hornecker says that his American father knew very little about hockey, but that they'd listen together to the Toronto Maple Leafs radio broadcasts in the late '30s. "Syl Apps was my favourite, and I'd hide behind the sofa and cry if the Leafs lost," he says. He guffaws and slaps his knee. "Jesus, I'd be crying a lot today."

He goes on, "I remember when Nanton was in the league with Lethbridge and Drumheller and Calgary and there'd be doubleheaders at the old Calgary Corral on Sundays and dozens of cars would go up from here. There'd be crowds up to four thousand. That was all the hockey there was in Alberta then after junior. It was pretty goddamn good. And you felt close to it. It was part of you. We're losing that today."

Bill Greig, who spent years in hockey as a coach, scout, and manager, is the father of Mark Greig, Tom McMasters' friend, and his older brother, Bruce. Bruce has been battling drug addiction and alcoholism. "He's done well," Bill says. Another son, Garth, played for Victoria in the WHL. Bill Greig is sixty-nine and lives in a beautiful old stone house that he converted from a barn on a farm a few minutes northeast of Nanton. As on Chuck Lefley's farm near Stonewall, there are deer about, standing by the road, nibbling grass where it pokes through the snow. Unlike Lefley, Bill Greig doesn't farm any more. He did for nearly thirty years but when costs kept mounting he rented it out and worked for Calgary's recreation department until he retired.

On this sunny morning he settles back on his living-room sofa with a mug of coffee. Shredder, his big white malamute with blue eyes as clear as glass, is lying on the floor beside him. On the living room's west wall is a huge picture window looking across the prairie to the Rockies. Bill Greig is going to talk about hockey, something he says he doesn't do much these days. "I'm not as interested in it as I was. I often don't like what's going on." He's big, with a lined face and only one eye. "I was a goalie. I was on an All-Star team from here playing against the branch of the Veterans of Foreign Wars in Great Falls, Montana. It was before goalies wore masks and I got hit by a skate. I was twenty-one." On a chain around his neck is a gold cross. He touches it. "I'm not really religious. I was in a bad car accident and somebody gave it to me when I was in hospital." He shrugs. "I haven't had any trouble since, so I figure I might as well keep wearing it."

Greig says he got into coaching largely because of a man named Elmer Piper, a major influence on hockey in the foothills of southern Alberta. Piper arrived in Okotoks in the fall of 1938 after coaching the Trail Smoke Eaters to an Allan Cup victory the previous spring. Until then, Greig says, hockey had been a local affair. "But he brought three or four very good players with him. One of them was Bill Flett, the father of 'Cowboy' Flett. You remember that

Cowboy played in the NHL for years. Anyway, what this meant was that an average hockey player was just an average hockey player. If you were going to compete you had to raid to get the better players.

"That season Okotoks went into the Alberta Senior Hockey League because they were too good for anything around here." He pauses. "The Drumheller Miners were in the league and in 1938 they had five Bentleys playing for them, including Max and Doug, before they went to Chicago."

Greig says that Piper was one of the first coaches to use the point man on offence. "It may seem strange now, but they didn't do it much before then," he says. "Piper did it in Trail and I think that's what got them the Allan Cup. It was called the checkerboard play. He always had very strong teams. He was a real competitor. But he was also a very decent man. He knew a lot and he shared it with anyone who was interested. But when you played for him, you made a commitment."

After Greig lost his eye, he says that Piper encouraged him to go into coaching, and he eventually reached Hockey Canada's level five, about as high as you can go. Among the then very young men who were studying coaching with him were Dave King and Pierre Pagé. Glen Sonmor, who had played professionally and went on to coach in Minnesota, was also there. "I really like Glen," Greig says. He laughs. "He has only one eye, too, so we had a lot in common."

Still smiling, thinking back, he says, "I was coaching junior one year in Brooks and at camp there was this one big kid, a very nice kid. He was close to making the team, but in the end I had to cut him. He was bitter as hell about it. Well, a couple of months later we're coming home from a game in Hanna and our bus runs out of gas. We're in the middle of nowhere in the middle of the night and it's twenty-five below. We sat for an hour waiting for someone to come by, and it's getting colder and colder. Finally, a half-ton comes along. The driver gets out, opens up the bus door, sticks his head in, and who the hell is it but the big kid I cut. 'Greig,' he says, 'how're you doing on a nice night like this? I thought it was you guys.' Then he says, 'What do you think I should do, go off and get you some gas or leave you here?' I said that getting gas sounded like a hell of a good idea. So he says goodbye. 'I might be back or I might not,' he said. 'Anyway, it was nice talking to you.' Well, we waited, and it was *cold*. And we waited. Then, about three-quarters of an hour later, he's back with gas."

And there was the time Greig says he was at a WHL camp in Calgary, looking for players. "I remember Father Bauer was there checking guys out for the national team. There's a scrimmage and these two brothers are really working over this guy, slashing him, tripping him, really doing a job on him. Finally he gets mad, there's a fight, and he knocks one brother out. The second brother comes off the bench like a shot and the guy knocks him out, too. The brothers' father is sitting a couple of rows in front of me. Jesus, before you know it he's over the boards to help his boys. The guy turns and levels the old man. Ends up all three of them are lying there in a pile. One of the funniest goddamn things I ever saw."

However, Greig says, the higher up he climbed in the coaching ranks, the less fun and the more difficult he found the job. "There's no tougher business," he says. "You want to grow up in a hurry? Get into hockey. It starts to get really hard in junior. One time a Calgary team was playing in Regina and this young guy was told to get out there and take care of someone. He'd already been in two fights that night and he said that he didn't want to get in another, so the coach left him in Regina with two dollars. How could someone do that to a kid?

"And you know, you've got to be a con man. For example, fringe players are needed to complete a team. But how do you keep fringe players interested? You got to lie to them. You got to tell them they have a chance to make it big, when you know goddamn well they haven't a chance in hell. I didn't like having to go into a kid's house, maybe he's fifteen or sixteen, paint a rosy picture, tell him and his parents that he has a real shot, that it would be worth it for him to give up two or three years of his life. And when he doesn't make it, of course, those important years are wasted. And the kid has to leave home to play and that, to begin with, is a hell of a shock. Some kids handle it well, others don't. I found it hard to do that."

Greig says that he briefly considered going to the New Westminster Bruins in the WHL when they were owned by Scotty Munro. At the time, Munro and Ernie "Punch" McLean, who had both been in Estevan, were forces in the league. "I used to talk to Scotty in Calgary and he said he'd see about it. We got on well," Greig says. "But Scotty and Ernie were tough. One guy used to say, 'You know, Bill, if Hitler had had Munro and McLean on his side he would have won the goddamn war.' Anyway, I thought it over. I would either go back to the farm or try to go on in hockey. And I decided no, the hell with it. My two youngest were still at home so why move to do something I really didn't want to do? Instead, I went to Vulcan to coach, near home, and I thought, well, that'll be satisfying, the Junior B level."

An experience he had at Vulcan, Greig says, underscores hockey's unpredictability. "We're having an inter-squad game and this kid comes on, as much talent as I'd ever seen, dominated, another Bobby Orr, scored six or seven points. The team owner gets all excited. 'Bill,' he says, 'every once in a while a guy gets lucky and we just did. We've got to sign him.' But I had a funny feeling. I said no, he's too obvious, there's got to be a book on him somewhere. If he's good here, he's got to have been good somewhere else. We'll wait, see how it goes in the regular season. You know, once the league started, he never touched the puck, three goddamn games. He was scared. The inter-squad game was different; he knew he wasn't going to get tagged too hard. Otherwise, he was scared stiff, just petrified. And you know, I found out later that he'd been cut in Saskatchewan for the same reason. And he never played any good hockey, anywhere. That whole thing was an eye-opener to me. I figured, boy, nobody has all the answers to this game."

Greig says that by now he's nearly hockeyed out and watches it only occasionally on TV. "I've coached all over the place and when my kids were growing up I practically lived at the rink. And when I worked for the recreation department in Calgary I saw hockey from six o'clock in the morning until I came home at night." He pauses. "But I did like coaching young kids, up to about sixteen. They can be very responsive and they give you an honest effort. I think I was good at that."

As for hockey today, Greig has an increasingly familiar complaint: he doesn't like what's happening to skilful players. "If you go to a game it's the smaller players that bring you to your feet because of their speed and finesse," he says. "But every rule now takes away from that. The rules favour power." He says the league is doing this to try to achieve parity

among teams. "They don't want any team to dominate the way, say, the Canadiens used to. They don't
care that the Canadiens and a few other teams are
fast and exciting. They stack the rules against them.
That's why there's so goddamn much hooking and
holding in the neutral zone. And Jesus, they're some
big guys out there and I often wonder how the hell
they tie up their skates they're so uncoordinated."

Greig would like to see pension money distributed
throughout hockey. "They should cut back those goddamn multi-million-dollar salaries," he says. "I don't
care if a guy gives five years to junior, the AHL, or the
IHL, he's entitled to realistic compensation for his years
in hockey, even if he didn't make the NHL. The NHL
players shouldn't have it all. These players that didn't
make it made their contribution to hockey, too."

That night, a Friday, in Nanton, the Palominos, in
their yellow-and-black Boston Bruin-like uniforms,
are playing the Lomond Lakers. The Lakers are in
blue and white. There's not much of a crowd, maybe
150. That's about the same as the whole population
of Lomond, a dot on the map forty miles to the east.
But, as in Stonewall and Bienfait, Nanton's hockey
people seem sure that the crowds will pick up after
Christmas. "They always do," Joan Martin says. She
knows her husband is still a bit stressed, although the
matter of kicking the player off the team is well
behind him. "Blair had to sit some of the guys out
tonight because of numbers," she says. "And he
hates doing that. It's hard to tell them. It's not as if
they're being paid. They come out because they want
to." According to her, the players include ranchers,
hired hands, an engineer, electricians, a printer . . .
"You name it, we have it."

Standing with Joan is Ralph Frost, a twenty-nine-
year-old who's had to quit the Palominos because of

an injured shoulder. "I've had three reconstructions and eight 'scopes," he says. "This is the first game I've been to this year because I can't stand not being able to play."

The rink is ringed with advertising signs. Over the Palomino bench one reads, "Wild Rose Taxidermy, Preserve Your Memories". The game is fast, with a lot of hitting. At the end of the second period, with Nanton having scored two power-play goals, one of the Lomond coaches, red-faced, almost spitting with anger, approaches the officials as they leave the ice. He is screaming and swearing over the penalties called on the Lakers and he can be heard over most of the rink. The officials ignore him, going directly to their dressing room, but an RCMP officer calls out, "You, shut up! It's a criminal offence to swear in public. Do it again and you're coming in." The coach shuts up.

The crowd has grown to about two hundred and now includes a dozen or so God-fearing Hutterites. Similar to Mennonites, with their roots in nineteenth-century eastern Europe and Russia, the Hutterites are from a colony in nearby Cayley. They're leaning on the rail behind the seats at centre ice. Their clothes are homemade, wool and cotton, and the men's distinctive dark caps with high fronts stand out among the baseball caps, toques, and cowboy hats. The women, largely teenagers, are in babushkas — scarves worn tied under the chin — and long dresses under their coats. The rougher the game, the more fun the Hutterites are having.

"I'm here every Friday night. I never miss," says one of the Hutterites, Ed Walter, a small, excitable man in his forties with a nut-brown face. Walter is cheering for Lomond, making more noise than anyone else in the rink, except for the brief burst of profanity from the Lomond coach. "I want to see a game of it," he says. "I don't want one team running away with it. I like a contest." Just then Lomond scores. "That's it, Jesus, that's it," Walter shouts in joy, punching the air in celebration.

The men are shouting; the women seem shy and they giggle together, cheering when a goal is scored but, unlike Walter, they don't look around; they keep their eyes on the ice. Stories abound about the Hutterites' love of hockey, such as Hutterites coming into town, even though it might be forbidden, to play pickup games. "They were enthusiastic as hell, but they had only bare-bones equipment," Bill Greig says. "They'd go home with pretty sore shins." Some of the colonies are stricter than others. Hutterites have had to sneak out to cars they've hidden in the hills to drive into games, or ride tractors to them, no matter how cold it was. Ed Walter says that when a Hutterite boy was hurt playing hockey on a pond at the Hussar colony, its leaders ordered that the hockey equipment, including the skates, be burned. "But I don't think they got it all," he says. "Some was squirrelled away."

One time ("I guess they'd been in the wine," Bill Greig says) three or four of them lassoed the referee during a game. They were banned from the rink but Greig says he'd see them in town and they'd plead with him to try to get the ban lifted. "They'd say, 'Goddamn it, Bill, we've been out three weeks now. Can't you get us back in? We miss our hockey.'"

Ed Walter says, grinning, "Yeah, I knew those boys." Another time, several gophers were released onto the ice and the game had to be stopped while they were chased down. "Yeah," Walter allows again, "I knew those boys, too."

Sitting with a blanket over his knees, directly across the ice from the Palominos' bench, below the

Hutterites, is eighty-six-year-old Howard Kent. He says, "I started coming to hockey games in Nanton in the '20s by horse and buggy and I haven't missed many." He's here tonight to watch his grandson, Mark Kent, who plays for Nanton. "He got four hundred a week to play junior and he could have gone down east this year, to the ECHL, but he didn't want to leave his family," Kent says. "He doesn't mind playing here for nothing because he loves hockey. But he lost seven teeth last year and that'll cost him ten thousand dollars."

After the game, which the Palominos won 7–5 to run their record to ten and one, Mark Kent says, "It was actually eight teeth and it's going to cost me about eight grand by the time they're finished with me. We were on the road, winning 7–0, middle of the second period. I guess the other boys were getting frustrated, because one of them decides to play baseball, swings his stick like a bat, and hits me square in the mouth."

The player was kicked out of the league for the rest of the year. "But it didn't help my teeth much," Kent says. Then he adds, "It's an expensive sport. We'll be in debt for a while. I'm not going to quit, but I'm taking a few more precautions. I wear a mouthguard now."

Kent has just turned twenty-two. This is his second year with the Palominos. He played Junior A for Fernie and Nelson in the Rocky Mountain Junior Hockey League. "My granddad used to drive three hundred miles to watch me," he says. As his grandfather said, Kent could have gone to the ECHL for seven thousand U.S. dollars, plus expenses. But he's a carpenter and he has a girlfriend and a very young daughter and he's happy playing in Nanton for nothing. "Yeah, I guess I like hockey that much," he says.

When the game ended and the Palominos left the ice, the usual case of beer was waiting in their dressing room, and in Lomond's. They came from the Auditorium, a bar down the street from the rink. "That's our support for the team, for hockey," says Larry Wynnyk, the Auditorium's owner. He reckons it's hard to say how much hockey means to his business, "but it's always good to see ten or fifteen guys from the team come through this door after a game." Wynnyk says the Auditorium has gone through a few names, including El Coyote and Wylie's. "But when I bought it I changed it back to what it was when it first opened as a hotel in 1902," he says. "Yeah, 1902; there's quite a history around Nanton."

17

Okotoks, Alberta

December 1997

TWENTY-FIVE MILES NORTH OF Nanton, back towards
Calgary, is the town of Okotoks. The name means
"rock" in the Blackfoot language. It comes from the
huge ice-age boulder on the prairie about four miles
to the west. Ten thousand people live in Okotoks
and even though the Sheep River winds through it,
the town is so close to Calgary that it has the look
and feel of a prosperous and sleek suburb. A few
years ago *Chatelaine* called Okotoks "One of
Canada's top ten towns". According to City Hall,
that's because Okotoks has "a small town atmosphere and urban amenities." For example, the
Western Wheel, its weekly newspaper, has a circula-
tion approaching nine thousand and is fat with
advertising; a chic French restaurant, *La P'tite
Table*, attracts people from Calgary, fifteen miles
away, and it's a good idea to make a reservation.
There's a flashy new mall and the old CPR station
has been turned into a "cultural centre" and art
gallery. But not everybody is thrilled. "I worry that
we're getting too big," says Marg Cox, who is with

the administration of the Okotoks recreation centre. Cox comes from Watford, near Sarnia, in south-western Ontario, and has been in Okotoks for nineteen years. "This is a very friendly and caring place," she says. "I don't want to lose that and become just an extension of Calgary."

Okotoks' main hockey team, the Junior B Foothills Bisons, apparently hasn't lost it. They still have that friendly, small town, part-of-the-community appeal. The Calgary *Sun* has called them "One of the finest amateur franchises in the province". The *Sun* based this on the team's "sound management, solid coaching and dedicated players".

John Barlow, who covers hockey for the *Western Wheel*, says that local Junior B was in danger of becoming simply goon hockey. "I'd like to think that teams like the Bisons that are built on speed and finesse are forcing the other teams to get rid of the goon stuff," he says. "Junior B around here used to be called 'jungle B'. The Bisons and Aidrie and some others are trying to change that."

The Bisons play in the twelve-team Heritage Junior Hockey League. Their owner, Bill McFarlane, runs his own insurance business in Okotoks. He's a large, ruddy-faced man who looks as if he might have been a hockey enforcer. He says no, he wasn't much of a player at all. "But I grew up in Drumheller and it was an honour there to be a rink rat, to clean off the ice for the Miners," he says. "I've always been interested in hockey." His two sons, who work in the insurance business with him, played for the Bisons. The older one, Jay, is a Bison assistant coach.

Bill McFarlane notes that most of the Bisons are at college or university. He believes it's very important to have hockey for youngsters who don't want to make it a career, who know that they'll never make the NHL. "Some B players move up towards it," he says, "but it's a real stretch. What our players get is good, hard, competitive hockey. They don't want to play in a beer league."

Although Okotoks is much wealthier than most small hockey towns, its hockey people still have to hustle for the bucks. "Fundraising is tough all over, I suppose, but those video lottery terminals here have been a killer," McFarlane says. "We used to have bingos for the team that would take in two thousand dollars a month. VLTs finished them off." To make up for this, the Bisons sponsor a rodeo with bucking broncos, bull-riding, and calf-roping. "It doesn't make a whole lot of money," McFarlane says, "I think we netted seven thousand dollars last year. But it raises the team's image and helps the community."

McFarlane says the team's budget is around $35,000. The Bisons aren't paid, except for meal money — seven dollars — when they're on the road, and hotels if it's an overnighter, which it rarely is. They are given their exterior equipment — except skates and gloves — that is, sweaters, socks, pants, helmets. The team pays for skate-sharpening, and the sticks are half-price.

"If we moved up to Junior A we'd have to pay a $50,000 initiation fee and expenses of $200,000 a year," McFarlane says. "And farther up, in major junior, you're looking at $1.5 million. That's right out of the question."

The Bisons have twenty-three players on their roster. They're allowed to dress twenty for a game. "I sit down with each player we want to sign," McFarlane says. "I get to know them, and a lot of them already know my boys, which makes it easier." As well, he says, most of them are local — "High River, the Turner Valley. That's important for the community."

Darren Corbin, at twenty-one, is the oldest Bison. This is his fourth and last year with the team. He hopes to go to a community college next year. He's from Strathmore, east of Calgary, and works on a farm. His big hands are rough, the nails broken and blackened. He's six feet two inches tall and weighs two hundred pounds. He's breathing hard after a practice at the Okotoks arena. "I love the heavy going, I love the hitting," he says. "When I was younger I dreamed of playing in the NHL, but by the time I turned fifteen I knew that I never would be good enough. But these last three years are the best hockey I've played. And you make friends, guys you'll never forget. The guys who stick up for you in fights."

Landon Hurlbut, at five foot nine and 160 pounds, is a lot smaller than Corbin. "I don't see my size as a big deal," he says. "It's not as if I'm a fighter or enforcer." Hurlbut is nineteen. His hometown is High River, between Okotoks and Nanton. He's studying business at Mount Royal College in Calgary. He says that hockey demands intelligence. "You've got to use your mind on the ice all the time," he says. "Players' skills are often pretty much the same, so games are won and lost through mental errors . . . finishing your check, defencemen knowing when to pinch, anticipating plays, knowing your assignment. . . ."

Hurlbut says one of his regrets is that he didn't take figure skating. "My mom wanted me to when I was thirteen," he says, "but I wouldn't. I'm a good skater, but I could have been that much better." And he wishes he'd taken boxing. "I can handle myself okay but boxing could have been a huge asset. Maybe it would have given me a shot at the pros."

The Bisons' coach is Gary Soroka, a formidable-looking forty-six-year-old with a walrus moustache.

Like his players, he isn't paid. He went into coaching because things slow down in winter with his construction company in Calgary. "I coached in the city for eight years but I couldn't stand the political bullshit between parents and the teams and the league," he says. "I love it here, small town Alberta. City kids are spoiled. If they don't get a break right away, they sulk, they give up. We have kids who do chores, go to school, and then drive an hour to practice. You don't have to motivate them. I stress school and work first because, as hockey careers go, this is it for them. They're not going to the NHL, but the commitment is still there." Soroka is no pushover, though. "We lost in Drumheller one night, stank the place out," he says. "We got home around 2 a.m. and I had them out on the ice for an hour."

On Elizabeth Street, which is Okotoks' main street, Wayne Madson says that hockey accounts for most of the income at his store, Classic Sports. Madson grew up in Whitby, east of Toronto, and played some Junior B hockey and junior football for Oshawa. He moved first to Calgary and then down to Okotoks. The Bisons buy most of their sticks and equipment from him, and there's also the minor hockey program. Including skate-sharpening and equipment repairs, Wayne Madson estimates that hockey last year accounted for nearly $200,000 of his total sales, more than 60 percent. "We sharpen two hundred pairs of skates a week, maybe more," says seventeen-year-old Duane, the Madsons' younger son. And there are the other sports — soccer, baseball, tennis, lacrosse, roller hockey, field hockey — all good for business, although Madson has reservations.

"These days everything is organized. I really notice it in the store," he says. "When I was young you might buy a football or a baseball glove to fool around with. Now, it's all part of a team. And parents want the very best for their kids, even if it's overkill. It's good business for me, but it's sort of sad that the kids can't just play for the fun of it. Another thing I notice is that if a kid hits fourteen and he's not playing at the top level, he loses interest. Maybe their pride or self-esteem is hurt, whatever, but if they don't have that team jacket they often quit. There's less and less room for the kid who just wants to play."

Bruce Greig, the older son of Bill Greig, owns the Back Alley Gym, for weightlifters, a few doors along from Classic Sports. If Greig is somewhat at peace with himself, he'll say that that's in spite of hockey, not because of it. Hockey took him across the United States and Canada, from the east coast to the west, from Edmonton to San Diego. Yet, after all that, here he is in Okotoks, within a few miles of the family farm outside Nanton. "What the hell was I to do?" he says. "When I was done playing I was a complete alcoholic and drug addict. You can ask my dad. So where am I going to go but home?"

Greig played hockey at about 215 pounds. Now, at forty-five, he weighs 300. He's a world champion weightlifter in his class and has just returned from England, where he led a team from his club at the world championships. "We took thirteen lifters over," he says, "and we got six firsts, five seconds, and two thirds."

As he talks, in a high-pitched but husky voice, sitting in the front of his gym, a teenage boy comes in and asks about enrolling in a lifting class. He has a cigarette in his hand. It's not going, but Greig asks him to put it away. He answers the boy's questions and says that he'll see him later. The youngster leaves and Greig, referring to the cigarette, says, "I don't even want to see them in here, lit or not." He laughs, sourly. "Sounds funny coming from me."

As a hockey player, Greig was largely a fighter, which suited him because he says that he was a violent person. "That's why I love the weight room. Lifting was a good outlet for my aggression." He says that playing hockey up through junior to the NHL was okay, "but from then I had terrible problems. Coming out of a place the size of Nanton at nineteen and going to California wasn't easy. I was very, very immature. That's when I started into alcohol and drugs. I was an alcoholic at twenty. And when I was drinking I'd take something we called 'crank', a kind of speed. It gave you a total high. You snorted it."

One thing Greig didn't take back then was steroids, but that, he says, was because he didn't know much about them. "If someone had come up to me in the '70s and said, 'Steroids will make you stronger, make you tougher in the corners,' I'd have done them and I bet about 70 percent of the league would have done them. We wouldn't have known better back then. But to us then, steroids would just make you muscle-bound. I've taken steroids as a lifter, but I quit them in '93." He stops for a moment and frowns. Then he says, "Alcohol and steroids didn't kill John Kordic. Hockey killed him. It forced him to do anything he felt necessary to stay up there."

Greig says that after the California Seals suspended him for public brawling — off the ice — he made the rounds of the WHA and minor leagues: Cincinnati, Calgary, Indianapolis, San Diego, Dayton. His last hockey job was as playing-coach in Virginia of the ECHL. There were also stops at Edmonton's and Philadelphia's NHL camps. Greig really doesn't talk much hockey these days, but he has a story he got from Bobby Clarke about Fred Shero, the Flyers coach, and Bobby Orr, that he likes to tell. "One night the Flyers are playing Boston and Shero told them to dump the puck into Orr's corner every chance they got. Clarke said he thought Shero was nuts, but Shero said that even Orr could only skate for so long. Clarke said he was right. By the third period Orr was exhausted; Philly scored two goals and won."

Greig's father, Bill, says his son was asked to play football for the Calgary Stampeders, and that he could have boxed professionally. "He was a hell of an athlete," Bill says. "You don't make the NHL, even for a few games, unless you've got an awful lot of talent."

Bruce Greig agrees, "Yeah, I could have done a lot of things if I'd been straight but I just didn't know it then. The sad thing is that I'll never know how good I might have been. But what's more important is that today I'm sober and free of drugs and I like what I do."

The Okotoks recreation centre is on a hill looking down on the old town. It has a swimming pool, six curling sheets, and two arenas. One is named for Elmer Piper, Bill Greig's mentor, the other for the Murray family: "Bearcat" Murray, trainer of the Calgary Flames, his mother and father, both athletes, and his sister, Annabelle, the first woman elected to western Canada's sports hall of fame for track and field. Marg Cox, of the rec centre, says, "It was built with half government money and half we raised ourselves, so we're very proud of it. It was typically small town in that everyone got involved. We had raffles and barn dances, everything."

Before a crowd of about two hundred, the Bisons are playing the West Country Stars. The Stars represent

Eckville, Rimbey, and Rocky Mountain House, on the other side of Highway 2, not far from Red Deer. "It gives all three places a chance to support a home team," says Gary Soroka.

The Bisons beat the Stars 5–3, ending a three-game losing streak. Ray Travaline, fiftyish, looking smart in a white shirt and dark tie, drives the bus for the West Country Stars. "I spend sometimes four nights a week in rinks," he says. "These kids work hard at hockey. There's no quit in them." He says from what he's seen as a bus driver, young hockey players, for the most part, are responsible. "Skiers can be trouble when they're partying, but I've found hockey players to be pretty disciplined," he says. "I respect the kids, or at least I try to. I think that's where the trouble starts, with adults not respecting kids. If you don't respect them, they won't respect you." As for prairie winter weather, Travaline shrugs. "I've only missed one game in seven years, and that was because the road was closed." He says goodbye. "I got to warm up the bus," he says.

The next day, it's the Bisons who hit the highway. They're off on a four-hour drive for a game against the Stettler Lightning. Stettler, an oil town with five thousand people, is north and east of Calgary. Right after that game the Bisons will head down Highway 56, driving for another two hours to Drumheller. They'll spend what's left of the night in a hotel, and play the Big Country Raptors on Sunday. "That's Junior B hockey," Soroka laughs. "Three nights, three games."

The Bisons charter a bus. They used to have their own, outfitted with aircraft seats that tilted and faced each other so the kids could play cards. "But we were out of town and after a game we go to the bus and there were bullet holes in it," Bill McFarlane says. "The bus was all painted in our team colours and with our name on it, so they sure as hell knew what they were shooting at." The bus was empty when it was shot up, but McFarlane got rid of it anyway. "It was costing too much, insurance, finding licensed drivers," he says.

John Barlow, the *Western Wheel*'s reporter, grew up in Saskatchewan, near Yorkton. "Now there's a hockey area," he says. He spent three years with High River's newspaper and a couple of years working with the WHL, as well as with a magazine, the *Calgary Hockey News*, before coming to Okotoks. He says hockey is very strong around here. "Okotoks, Nanton, all the way to Stavely. We have good players coming out of here. Three Okotoks kids have been drafted from bantam by the Calgary Hitmen."

He says that in small towns, particularly ones such as Okotoks that are close to a major city, it's important to have local kids on the hockey team. "The Bisons have been successful with that," he says. "Most of the players are from Okotoks, Strathmore, High River, and the ones who are not from here, if they're not going to school in Calgary, they try to get them jobs here. It would be easy to bring guys in from Calgary, but in the end it would kill hockey here."

Hockey means a lot to Barlow. "I get a kick out of everything, from the first-year kids in house league, to bantam, to the NHL. And I like to watch the parents watch their kids. I know you hear the horror stories about parents, but I've never come across that in Okotoks or High River."

Roland Stewart is the Bisons' captain. He was leading the league in scoring at the end of the first week in December with sixteen goals and nineteen assists in thirteen games. He's twenty and this is his third season with the Bisons. He might have been at Harvard now if he hadn't been badly slashed on the ice. He was seventeen, playing Junior A for the Canmore–Bow Valley Eagles, when five bones in his left instep were broken. He says, "I was out for three months and that pretty well messed things up for me. Harvard had flown me down and I think I would have had a really good shot. I would have made the freshman team, anyway. Until I broke my foot, I'd always played top-level hockey." But he likes Okotoks. "It's a great club. They really look after you."

In Stettler, it's cold and wet, a good night to stay at home, but the parking lot at the recreation centre is filling up. The rec centre is an impressive building, only three years old. "Farmers put up the old one a long time ago," says a young man named Roy in a Toronto Maple Leafs cap. "It was just a huge tin Quonset hut, cold as hell. It burned down so we got this." Roy checks his program and reads aloud the names of some of the other teams in the league: the Big Country Raptors, Carstair Colts, Red Deer Vipers, Lacombe Wranglers, and Ponoka Stampeders. "With names like that you sure know you're in the west, eh? John Wayne country, eh? Hard to beat." He touches his cap and says, "Maybe this should say 'Oilers,' but the hell with it."

The Stettler Lightning are in second place in the league's north division and the Foothills Bisons are in second place in the south. It's an hour before the game's to start, but pockets of teenagers are already milling about in the lobby. Roy says that the Lightning usually attract good crowds. "We're just far enough away from Edmonton and Calgary that people can't drive in there for a night's fun." Behind him, a man is taking tickets and stamping the backs of hands. "No, you don't get your tickets here, you get them over there," he says to a middle-aged couple. "See, where it says 'box office'. No, over there." He points again. As the couple walk away, he says, "Jesus, I don't know how they'll see the game if they can't see the box office from here." He stamps the backs of a few more hands. "People will try to get in by saying they've just gone out for a coffee or a smoke or to warm up their car," he says. "So I've got to make sure."

Bill McFarlane's son Jay, one of the Bisons' assistant coaches, says that Stettler is probably number one in the league in attendance. "It's always been a mystery to me what gets people out in some places and not in others," he says. "Every place has its own distractions, but some towns just seem to need their hockey more than others."

The Bisons' dressing room is quiet; any talking is in low voices. There's no fooling around. Gary Soroka is in a big overcoat that makes him look even bigger. The assistant coaches, Jay McFarlane and Mike Hannigan, are wearing dark overcoats over blazers that have the Bisons crest, and white shirts and ties. A few minutes before the players go out on the ice, Soroka says to them, speaking quietly but firmly, "Stettler is a good skating team so let's have lots of body out there. And defencemen, watch the pinching. We almost got burned a few times last night."

Still speaking quietly, he continues, "And last night a couple of guys, every time they're hit, they're punching the guy on the back of the head. What fucking good does that do? But if you take a penalty, make goddamn sure you take someone with you. And no, I mean it, no penalties for yapping. Other than that, you know what you have to do."

Mike Hannigan adds, "Their goalie has new pads. They'll be tight so keep your shots low and watch for rebounds."

The players get up and Soroka raises his voice for the first time. "Hey," he says, "it'll be a long night in that shitty hotel in Drumheller if we don't win." The players give a big cheer and go out the door. They're already looser than they were only minutes before. "It's like anything else," one of them says as he's about to step on the ice. "I hate the waiting."

About four hundred people are in the rink, a good early-season crowd for Junior B. Many of them are teenagers, sitting together in groups. They give the Bisons a friendly boo. Bill McFarlane, the Bisons' owner, sits directly behind his players' bench, three rows up. He's wearing a windbreaker and given his size looks more like a bouncer than a businessman. The Stettler bench is on the other side of the rink.

It's a chippy first period with stickwork along the boards and in the corners. Mike Hannigan is right about the new pads: the Lightning goalie is having trouble controlling rebounds. But there's no scoring until late in the period. The Bisons, on a power play, finish off a two-on-one. Soroka isn't happy. "We're all over the goddamn place," he says. There's more stickwork through the second and third periods, with both teams scoring. Bill McFarlane, hunched over in his seat behind the bench, doesn't like the officiating, particularly when a Stettler player tries to run the Bison goalie and nothing is called. "Open your eyes!" he yells at the ref.

As the third period winds down, three big kids who have been screaming obscenities since the second period move into seats behind the Bisons' bench and begin to spit on the players. Then they reach over the glass, trying to punch them. They're still screaming and swearing, almost out of control. Two Bisons get up to push them back. The kids try to grab their sticks and there is a scuffle.

Unlike in Nanton or Bienfait, there's not a police officer in sight. Nor is there any rink security. Bill McFarlane is fit to be tied. He and two other Bison officials and some Stettler adults, try to pull them off. The original three kids have been joined by three or four more and the scuffling extends up into the stands. Finally, it's broken up. The kids involved move slowly and belligerently back up behind the last row of seats where they're joined by a handful of others. Soon there's a screaming line of twelve or fifteen of them. The game ends. Stettler has won, 5–4. As the Bisons file from their bench, something is thrown at Gary Soroka, striking him on the side of the head. It's a heavy metal staple, the kind used for fencing, about an inch by an inch and a half. Soroka is cut but it would have been worse if it hadn't struck the heavy frame of his glasses. He can't get over the glass behind the bench. A furious McFarlane charges up the aisle, but the kids have already run away.

Soroka, rubbing his head, follows his players into the dressing room. He tells them to change and shower quickly. "Let's get out of here," he says. He promises them a few beers on the bus. He doesn't seem upset. He says, "We came up here for the playoffs one year and we were showered in spit. Nobody did a goddamn thing about it." An angry Bill McFarlane is outside in the hallway. He can't find the kid who threw the staple, or the staple itself. "I saw it and someone gave it to someone and they gave it to someone and the goddamn thing's gone," he says. Soroka sticks his head out of the dressing room. Down the hallway in the lobby, thirty feet away, a crowd of young people is gathering. He goes back into the dressing room. "We're all leaving together," he says, "but don't start anything. Just keep walking." He tells the players to carry a stick each, not to leave them all in the team's stick bags. "In case we need them," he says. He laughs. He seems almost to be enjoying it. "Good old-fashioned hockey, eh? I sort of miss it." The players are quiet but they don't seem bothered either. One cracks a smile. "Jesus, can you imagine what they'd be doing if we'd won!"

The team has showered and dressed by now. Like all hockey players, they're much smaller out of their equipment. Several of them haven't bothered to dry their hair, which, for some reason, makes them look very young. "We all go out at once," Soroka tells them again. And out they go, in single file, their equipment bags slung over their shoulders, each carrying a stick. To their surprise, the crowd in the lobby applaud them. More than one of them calls out that they're sorry for what happened. "It wasn't us," a girl says. "It's only a few of them do that stuff. You played good." The Bisons go out to the bus, which is right by the door, without stopping or saying anything.

Suddenly, two RCMP officers appear in the lobby. "What happened?" one of them asks. A Stettler kid yells out, "Right on time, as usual." Bill McFarlane says, "Jesus Christ, where were you?" The officer says they weren't even meant to be there, that they were just passing by and dropped in. McFarlane still can't find the staple that hit Soroka. He'd like to be able to show it to the RCMP. Instead, he tells them, "Every goddamn time we come up here there's trouble and no one ever does a goddamn thing. I'm telling them, the next time either the RCMP will be here and do something or we'll just mail in the two points. They can have them. But we're not coming up here to take this shit." His son, Jay, takes his father by the elbow. "Come on," he says, pulling him towards the door and the bus. McFarlane takes his parting shot. "Every goddamn time," he calls to the RCMP. "We're not going to take it any more."

The bus moves off slowly from the arena, heading for the highway and the two-hour drive to Drumheller. Its tail-lights soon disappear in the big, wet snowflakes that are falling heavily.

18

Powell River, British Columbia

December 1997

IN NEW WESTMINSTER, A SLAPSHOT from Vancouver,
the Powell River Regals, last year's Allan Cup champions, are about to step on the ice at the Queen's
Park Arena. It's eleven o'clock on a Sunday morning.
The arena was built in the '30s and has a nifty art
deco front. Over the years it has been renovated
inside and out, which makes it as good as many arenas half its age. New Westminster is a lacrosse town,
so most of the signs hanging inside the arena cele-
brate Mann Cup victories by the Salmonbellies. (One
sign is of Jack Bionda's name and number, 12.
Bionda, a lacrosse great, also played parts of four
seasons with the Maple Leafs and the Boston
Bruins.) But old Queen's Park has had its hockey
moments. In the '70s, the New Westminster Bruins,
winners of two Memorial Cups, played out of there
and a generation before that, great minor leaguers
skated with the New Westminster Royals in the old
Western Hockey League.

This morning, two weeks before Christmas,
Powell River is playing an exhibition game against

the Royal City Beavers, a local senior team. It's the second game the two have played against each other in less than twenty-four hours. Last night, Powell River won 6–2, which wasn't bad as it was their first game of the season. Senior hockey on the British Columbia coast isn't what it used to be and the Regals haven't even got a league to play in. And as Powell River is five and a half hours of winding roads and two ferry rides north of Vancouver (a regular return flight on Pacific Coastal Airlines costs $170), it's not easy to get teams from the Lower Mainland to drop up for a game.

Queen's Park can hold 3,500 people. Thirty-five are there now. A dozen or so are friends of the New Westminster players. Four others are UBC students who come from Powell River. Seventeen young women, sitting off in a group by themselves, one of them writing Christmas cards, are on the hockey team that has the ice next.

This past spring, when the Regals won the Allan Cup, they did it right at home, in Powell River. In a round-robin, they beat the Warroad Lakers, who had won the cup the last three years, the Truro Bearcats, and Alberta's qualifier, the Stony Plain Eagles. Warroad, near the Manitoba border in northern Minnesota, won't be playing for the cup this time. The club has folded. But Tod English, who was born in Powell River, lives there, and plays for the Regals, is betting that his team will be, in spite of the little hockey it has played so far. "We'll have maybe twenty-five or thirty games before the playdowns start," he says. "But we can't do too much before Christmas because the guys have jobs and it makes for too long a season." In spite of his size — last year's Allan Cup program lists English, a forward, at five foot seven, 170 pounds — he has more than six hundred points in nearly three hundred games with the Regals. This experience shows even in this early-season exhibition game, although all the Regals are feeling a little wobbly after their night in the big city.

English isn't bothered by rough play, he gets an assist, and he seems always to be in position, particularly when the Regals are breaking out of their own end. And he takes short shifts. The game ends 2–2. Given that it was an exhibition game, both teams played hard. A few good punches were thrown, but the players shake hands with each other when it's over.

"Not bad, all things considered," English says. "This isn't our whole team. We'll be picking up guys, including some who were with us last year. After Christmas we'll be on the ice three times a week for practice and we'll get at least a game a week."

English is almost thirty-four. He played junior in the British Columbia Hockey League and for two years in Wilhelmshaven, in Germany. "They treated us so well over there," he says. "It fulfilled a dream for me. I never played in the NHL, but I got paid to play. That's something I've done in hockey, something I'll always have: I was a professional." This is his thirteenth year with the Regals.

The team came down from Powell River in a van and a pickup truck with a cab that can hold three people. "Most of the time we'll be flying now," English says. "We'll raise the money or pay for it ourselves." The team's captain, Shane Carlson, a big, fair-haired man, has a black eye that's almost closed from a fight last night. He's driving the van. One of the players, climbing into it, says, "I hope you can goddamn well see." Mike Andrews is driving the pickup, which is carrying the equipment. He has played nearly four hundred games for the Regals. At thirty-seven, he's their oldest player. This is his seventeenth year with them. "Andy's old enough to have fathered half the team," says Carlson. The youngest Regal, Scotty Peters, is eighteen.

As the van and the pickup pull away from the rink, the afternoon is mild, sunny, and clear, exactly the kind of weather that people in southern B.C. would like easterners to think is a typical winter day here. After a stop for a late lunch a few minutes from the arena, the Regals are off again, through New Westminster and Vancouver and then over the Second Narrows bridge to the North Shore. By the time they reach the first ferry, at Horseshoe Bay, it's becoming overcast. By late afternoon, when they disembark from the ferry at Langdale, not far from Gibson's, where TV's Beachcombers series was filmed, it's dark, and it's pouring rain.

One of the players in the van is Bobby Cripps, a tall, strong, happy-go-lucky twenty-year-old. He's a part-timer with the Regals. In January he'll go to Arizona to get a head start on baseball spring training. He spent a year on a baseball scholarship at Arizona State University and has friends there. He's a catcher who used to belong to the Los Angeles Dodgers. He explains that he was playing for Great Falls, Montana, when he was traded to the Toronto Blue Jays organization, then there's quiet for a moment. The players are tired and they're trying to nod off. The only sound is the swish of tires on the wet road. Suddenly, Cripps calls out, "Hey, everybody, I got my first penalty minutes today. I'm very, very proud of that." A couple of players laugh. Another, without opening his eyes, says, "Jesus, okay, okay," but he's laughing, too. Cripps comes from Powell River. He says, "You know, a few years ago they closed the A&W because it wasn't making enough money. Now we have a McDonald's, a KFC, a new A&W, and they've just opened a 7-Eleven. What do you think of that, eh?" Then it's quiet again.

Tod English returned to Powell River from Germany when he and his brother had a chance to buy their father's sports store. He also works for Investors Group, the financial services company. "It's a good calibre of hockey here. Most of the guys have played some pro, and a few have been to NHL camps," he says. "Now, we all have jobs." He stops and laughs. "We're looking for a drywaller who plays right wing. Then we could build a house. We already have carpenters, electricians, bricklayers, roofers . . ."

Dean McLaren is a fishing guide in the Queen Charlotte Islands in the summer and plays hockey all winter. "I have a few regrets in that I don't really have a career, but I love guiding and I love hockey," he says. "Guiding and hockey, hell, you can't beat that." He has a black eye, like Shane Carlson's. Dean's younger brother, Rick, twenty-two, is one of the Regals' best players. He played with the Powell River juniors in the British Columbia Hockey League, and for Tri-City, the former New Westminster Bruins, in the Western Hockey League. He's a logger. "I work five days a week in the bush, getting up at five in the morning," he says. "Then there are practices and games. It takes it out of you, but you got to do it."

At Sechelt, a half-hour up the coast from where the Regals got off the first ferry, they pull into the parking lot of Gilligan's, a pub. "It's better to take an hour here than sitting in the van at Earl's Cove," Shane Carlson says. That's where they catch the next ferry and where there's not much more than the terminal.

Gilligan's is packed on this cold, rainy Sunday evening, and the Regals are greeted like old friends.

"How's it going? You win?"

"Win and a tie."

"Hey, not bad."

"Not bad at all given how we felt this morning."

Gilligan's is a sports bar. On the giant TV sets are thoroughbred racing, from California, and an NFL game. There's also video gambling.

"Most people who play hockey reach a point when they play just for fun," Carlson says. "For some people it takes longer to reach that point. I like the competition. It's a physical game. That's what I like."

English says he has no plans for retiring as long as the Regals keep winning. "That's what keeps me going," he says. "I don't care if you're talking about the New York Rangers or the Detroit Red Wings, who hadn't won in a while, or Powell River or Quesnel or Trail. You might not even have been born when the Smoke Eaters won anything, but if you come from there you'll know all about them. Here it's the Regals. People know the Regals because they've won."

Over the years, the Regals have played in the Pacific Coast Amateur Hockey League, the Northwest Hockey League, the North Island Intermediate Hockey League, and the Royal City Hockey League. Teams they've played against, in and out of province, include the Nanaimo Clippers, Chemainus Blues, Prince George Mohawks, Kimberley Dynamiters, Rosetown Red Wings, Whitehorse Huskies, Chilliwack Royals, Lloydminster Border Kings, Port Alberni Labatts, Val d'Or Olympiques, Comox Totems, and Stony Plain Eagles. The Regals have played in Washington,

Idaho, and Alaska and they've been intermediate and senior champions of B.C., western Canada, and the whole country.

For Regal veterans like English, Carlson, and Andrews, the road to the Allan Cup began in the spring of 1995, when they beat the Quesnel Kangaroos in double overtime to win the B.C. senior Triple-A championship. "We hadn't beaten Quesnel in a big game for years," Carlson says. "So many times they'd stopped us. We were famous for coming second. Once, we were leading them 5–1 in a championship game and lost 7–5. So beating them was a huge load off our backs." That victory meant that the Regals qualified for the Allan Cup final. They lost to Warroad, and the next year they were eliminated in the playdowns, but the stage was set for 1997's victory. Carlson says he'll never forget the play that he feels won the cup.

"We were playing Warroad and we're leading 2–1 but Warroad was controlling the game, they had the momentum. We were really back on our heels," he says. "Our goalie skated out to clear the puck and he put it right on a Warroad stick in the slot. The Warroad guy fired high on the glove side but a defenceman blocked it. Who cares if it was luck. If he'd scored it would have been 2–2. And, as I said, they had all the momentum. That play finished them. We dominated after that. We won 5–1 and we had our bye to the final."

After a couple of drafts, the Regals say goodbye to Gilligan's until their next road game. It's raining even harder as they continue northwards. When they board their second ferry more than an hour later, the players grab a pop or a coffee and go to the lounge. Shane Carlson has to go out on the wet deck when he wants to smoke. Back ashore again, at Saltery Bay, it's slow going on the last leg of the trip. Highway 101 twists and turns and is very slippery. The windshield wipers are working overtime and Carlson is leaning forward, squinting through the rain. It's eight o'clock when they get home, nearly seven hours after leaving the ice in New Westminster.

Powell River is a pulp-and-paper town dependent on the MacMillan Bloedel mill. It looks out across the Georgia Strait towards Vancouver Island. The winter weather is mild, like Vancouver's, and the hills rising up behind the town are thick with trees. It is a beautiful part of the B.C. coast. About nineteen thousand people live in and around Powell River. (Two of its famous sporting sons are Roy and Ted Gerela, the brothers who brought soccer-style kicking to Canadian and American football.)

Powell River's Marine Avenue, which runs by the water, has some good restaurants and a couple of craft shops and art galleries. Most of them are still open although, in December, there aren't many tourists about. The West View terminal is on Marine Avenue, too. That's where the ferries leave from for Comox, on Vancouver Island, and for Texada Island. A block or so along from the terminal is Taws Cycle and Sports, owned by Tod English and his younger brother, Dean, who is one of the Regals' directors. Thirty-two dozen hockey sticks have just arrived for the Powell River Kings and Dean is helping unload them from the truck. The Kings, a Junior A team, are in the British Columbia Hockey League. They used to be the Paper Kings but the "Paper" was dropped to try to give them a slicker image. Dean English says that over the season, the Kings and the Regals will go through between fifty and sixty dozen sticks.

Besides being "Hockey Specialists", the store sells,

rents and services bicycles. It also carries a lot of hiking, fishing, and camping gear. Given the unpredictable nature of hockey in a place like Powell River, Dean says, the store had to diversify. He says that senior hockey damn nearly died in the '80s, but that it picked up again in the '90s and he's optimistic that the Allan Cup victory last spring will give it another shot in the arm. He says the Regals keep going with the help of "thirty or forty" sponsors. "And people volunteer — selling tickets, operating the hospitality room at the rink, all those things," he says. "And the players, too, like my brother, give a lot of their time. It's a hell of a community effort and I guess it always has been."

The now-defunct *Weekend Magazine* gave Powell River its first national publicity. Under the headline "This Is What Hockey's All About", Andy O'Brien wrote that as a "western hockey saga", the Regals' victory in the 1970 national intermediate championship belonged alongside Dawson City's 1905 challenge for the Stanley Cup (it lost to Ottawa) and the Penticton Vees' rowdy recovery of the world championship from the Soviet Union in 1955.

"No Stanley Cup hysteria could have been greater . . . no players could have put more into the game, than was found in the payoff to ten agonizing years of building to championship calibre," O'Brien wrote. He based his piece on the fact that ten years before that championship, Powell River not only had no hockey players, it had no ice. But it built a rink and began to recruit players from across the country. Some went to work for MacMillan Bloedel, others for the town.

One of the people responsible for hockey in Powell River is eighty-three-year-old Hap Parker. He says the only hockey he ever played was on the open-air rinks in Brandon, Manitoba, where he was born, and that he wasn't very good. "But I always liked it. I was a good friend of Turk Broda. During the Depression my dad was all right because he was a compositor at the Brandon *Sun*, but a lot of my friends, like Turk, had to go away to work up in those relief camps for about seven bucks a month. It was a tough time on the prairies. Then they brought him down to play junior."

Parker followed some of his cousins to Powell River in 1936. He got a job at the mill. He says when the first rink was built in 1955 he was put on the executive. "They assumed that because I came from the prairies I must know all about hockey," he says.

At the outset, Powell River had a three-team local league, made of players from the town. "Then a fellow wrote to friends back east telling them that this was God's country and out they started to come, and the word got around. We brought guys in from all over. We put together an all-star team and we got into a league with Alberni and Nanaimo and off we went." He shakes his head and frowns. "But the thing is, Powell River doesn't belong in hockey. Everything here is against it, starting with the climate. And look where we are, for God's sake. It costs a fortune to travel or bring in a team. In a way, there should never have been hockey here."

Parker's wife, Ina, says, "The place was hockey crazy then. When we used to play Nanaimo and other towns that depended on the ferry, sometimes the ferry couldn't make it because of the weather. And I'd stand at our phone for two solid hours saying, 'I'm sorry, but there's no hockey game tonight.' And when I got tired the kids would take over. 'Mom says there's no hockey game tonight.' For the playoffs, they'd line up for three blocks to get in. You'd have to be here to realize what a fantastic local event it was."

Andy McCallum, sixty-eight, is one of the men brought in under Parker, arriving in 1960. He'd played junior hockey first in his hometown, Brandon, where the stars were Don Raleigh and Wally Hergesheimer, both of whom played later for the New York Rangers. "I was only sixteen," McCallum recalls. He also played junior for Medicine Hat; then came senior with the Owen Sound Mercurys. After playing briefly with the Chicoutimi Sagueens and the Providence Reds, Eddie Shore bought him for Syracuse. "Shore was an experience, I can tell you," he says. "But not a good one. Discipline is one thing, but you never knew what the hell he was going to do next. I think he really was crazy, or at least partly crazy. If he didn't want you to dress for a game he'd write you a letter: 'Dear Mr. So-and-So, this is to inform you that I'm suspending you indefinitely for indifferent play.' After a couple of games you'd be brought back and someone else would get a letter and be blacklisted."

McCallum says that one Sunday afternoon Shore told the players and their wives to meet at the rink. "We figured it was some kind of a get-together, maybe a little party, which would have been something, knowing how cheap Shore was," McCallum says. "We arrived and sat down, us and our wives, to wait for Eddie. We didn't know what the hell was going on and in he comes and lectures us about it being bad to have sex the night before a game. Then he says, 'That's it,' and he leaves."

Shore told McCallum, and other players, to take tap-dancing lessons in the off-season. It would make them better skaters. "Looking back, he was probably right but tap-dancing or not, I'd had enough." McCallum sat out until Shore sold his rights back to Chicoutimi, where he played for the next two years. "That was a great league, the Quebec league. Toe Blake was coaching in Valleyfield and Punch Imlach had Béliveau in Quebec." After two years he moved on to Windsor, Ontario, and played three years for the Bulldogs. "By then I was getting tired of the east so I went and played for the Kelowna Packers for three years." In 1958 Kelowna lost to the Belleville McFarlands in the Allan Cup final. "We were up three games to nothing and they came back and beat us," McCallum says. "I had a fractured cheek, a dislocated jaw, and a broken toe, but I didn't miss a game. It was a great series."

The late Jack O'Reilly was coaching the Packers. McCallum says that O'Reilly was one of the best and most interesting people he met in hockey. Once, in a dressing room in Moscow, before the final of an important series against a Soviet club, O'Reilly didn't say a word. "He knew we wanted to win so badly that he didn't have to say anything, so he didn't, not a goddamn word, apart from the lineup, and we went out and won.

"But when he did have something to say, he had a gift for reaching his players. We were in Vernon to play on a Tuesday night. We'd been struggling with them all season. Jack comes into the dressing room and tells us that he'd overheard someone say that anytime Kelowna plays in Vernon on a Tuesday night, Kelowna loses, and that it must be a 'coincidence'. Then Jack went on, 'That's not a goddamn coincidence. I'll tell you what a coincidence is. A coincidence is when you and your wife and the alarm clock all go off at once. That's coincidence. Losing on Tuesday nights is horseshit.' We just cracked up. We were still laughing when we hit the ice. Anyway, we won the game."

It was in Kelowna that McCallum realized that his playing days were winding down. "I had to get a job," he says. "I knew I couldn't play hockey forever." When the Okanagan league died he says that Omaha, in the old United States league, asked him to coach. "But coaches are hired to be fired so I decided on Powell River. I'd never even heard of Powell River until Kelowna played an exhibition game here when we were getting ready to go to Europe, but I remembered I'd liked it, so when they phoned me I came up and they showed me around and I ended up with a job at the mill. It was a nice place to live, a good place to bring up the family, that was my main reason for coming."

McCallum became the Regals' playing-coach in mid-season when the regular coach fell ill. "I might have had trouble playing forward and coaching, but playing defence was okay," he says. "I had a good bunch of young players and a first-rate executive. The fans were wonderful. Every Saturday night that's what people did, they went to the rink." He'd retired by the time the Regals won the Hardy Cup, the national intermediate title that Andy O'Brien wrote about. His best memory as a player, he says, is of the Regals winning the Coy Cup, B.C.'s championship, three years before, in 1967. "When I came here the Regals were pretty bad," he says. "They were getting beat up physically and they weren't organized, and I turned that around. We took four cracks at it before we won the Coy Cup, but when we did, for the town of Powell River, that was my greatest accomplishment. And after that, things came a lot easier. But that first one, the one that started it, the whole town just went bananas."

To build a hockey team here took enormous patience, McCallum says, and resources. "It's a terrible location for sports teams. Everything is overnight, it's ferry rides, it's hotel rooms. It's very expensive. I mean when I played in the Okanagan league with Kelowna we had Penticton, Vernon, Kamloops, and hell, the travel was nothing. Everything was next door. Not like here."

Most of the players worked at the mill and they would get time off for games. But the mill didn't pay them. "The hockey club had to come up with the money for the missed shifts," McCallum says. "The only time the company would reimburse us is if we went out of the province or represented B.C. in a provincial final. It was a financial struggle, but the enthusiasm of the players was always there.

"As a coach I was fairly strict. Off the ice I got the guys to dress up on the road, jackets and ties, and before long some were wearing suits. I thought it really helped the club establish itself. In the past they'd been banned from some hotels. We cleaned all that up. I thought it was important that they represented the town, because the town supported them. Even bus drivers were saying that it was a pleasure to drive us."

(In 1957, before McCallum arrived, Hap Parker says there were complaints in Powell River that the Regals weren't getting much press on the Lower Mainland. People felt that the big newspapers were ignoring them. He says that when Dick Beddoes, who was writing sports for the Vancouver *Sun*, heard about the complaints, he sent the hockey executive a batch of newspaper clippings. "They were all about the Regals after a game down there getting into a helluva brawl in a restaurant in Vancouver's Chinatown, wrecking the place,"

Parker says. "Beddoes asked politely whether we were satisfied with that coverage.")

McCallum's playing career ended when he was hit from behind into the boards. "I had two spinal fusions," he says. "I paid the price." On the wall of his rec room is a photograph of him in a wheelchair. It was taken after one of his operations. "I'm very lucky that's not me today," he says.

According to Bob Crawford, who succeeded McCallum as playing-coach, "Andy brought a real sense of professionalism to the organization." Crawford's picture, taken during a game, accompanies Andy O'Brien's *Weekend* article. His face is drawn, his expression set; his sweater is spattered with blood and he has a black eye.

(Shane Carlson says, "Crawford was our hero when we were kids. Six hundred stitches . . .")

Crawford is from South Porcupine, Ontario, the hometown of Carlo Cattarello, and like so many of the hockey players from there he played a couple of years under Carlo. He stayed in northern Ontario to play junior and senior. He's fifty-six now, and looks, fittingly, like his namesake, the old Hollywood tough guy Broderick Crawford.

He says he heard about Powell River and thought he'd try it. "The biggest thing at that time was for the team to pay your way out, give you a few dollars, get you a job," he says. "Some of us knew we weren't going to make it professionally so we went this route. But I only planned to stay a year and then play somewhere else. It was 1960 and I was nineteen. But back in Timmins, if you didn't have a university education you were pretty well stuck with the mines. I'd been there at $1.35 an hour. I went to work at the mill here for $2.17 and better benefits, so I stayed."

Unlike Andy McCallum and other transplants

from Ontario or the prairies, it wasn't love at first sight between Crawford and Powell River. "I felt really isolated, really bushed," he says. "So I went to Prince George for a year and a half. I played hockey and had a job as a sportswriter, but my wife didn't like the cold, and we had two young kids, and after a while I began to miss Powell River so we came back. But I still feel isolated here sometimes, even after all these years."

The first year that he played, the Regals were in a league with New Westminster, Nanaimo, and Chilliwack. "When we played Nanaimo we had to take three ferries: two to Horseshoe Bay and then one across to the island," he says. "The big rivalry was between us and Nanaimo. Big-time bitterness. A couple of years before Andy came out, Powell River had a good, talented team but whenever they met Nanaimo, Nanaimo beat the hell out of them.

"Andy turned the team around. We still had the talent, but we became very physical. There was a lot of blood. It got ugly. They talk about violence nowadays, but I'm not sure it's any worse than it was then. It wasn't so much spearing, more old-fashioned bodychecking, boarding, elbowing." Crawford pauses for a moment. "A few sticks, though. I remember one night we were in a three-game playoff series and a guy comes up behind Andy and breaks his stick over his head. In the next game I broke the jaw of one of their players. It was a clean check, I didn't even get a penalty, but they had to carry a guy off the ice. The B.C. Hockey Association cancelled the third game. We won it by forfeit.

"But if you want spearing, that's the Cariboo league. It was an outlaw league, not sanctioned by the B.C. Hockey Association. I played there for a season and a half. Major stickwork. I mean, you dropped your gloves up there and the first thing you got was a stick in the head. I found out that in my first exhibition game. Six stitches in the eye."

Crawford had a good look at the hit that ended Andy McCallum's career and nearly left him paralysed. "I'd lost some teeth blocking a shot so I went to the hospital and got seen to, including twenty-five stitches in the mouth," he says. "I'd just got back to the arena when this guy rammed Andy into the boards from behind. He could have killed him."

Looking back, Crawford says that he wouldn't do much differently, except perhaps take better care of himself. "Maybe I should have stayed off longer when I was hurt," he says. He touches his left shoulder. "The left side of my body is pretty well shot. It's given me a lot of pain. My shoulder has been broken twice and I have a steel knee. The thing was that in those days you hated to miss a game or practice. I remember when McCallum had a broken toe and they knew if they took off the skate they'd never get it back on because of the swelling. So they put the bloody needle right through his skate to freeze the toe so he could finish the game. With me, they'd drain my knee between periods and give me shots. There were lots of us like that. You felt you'd let the team down if you didn't play. You kept going, even when you were really hurt. We all did. It sure as hell wasn't for the money, because there wasn't any. It was pride. That's what made us winners."

Powell River's old rink has been closed for several years. The new one is part of a recreation complex on the northern edge of town, in a country-club setting, at the end of a long driveway, surrounded by woods, mostly evergreens. It has a swimming pool, a theatre, a gymnasium, and two regulation-sized rinks. This morning on one of the rinks, the Kings, Powell River's Junior A team, is practising. Watching from rinkside, as he peddles hard on a stationary bike, is Wyatt Tunnicliffe. It's chilly in the rink but he is wearing only shorts and a T-shirt. He is a polite, engaging eighteen-year-old. He says that he suffered a concussion a couple of games back, which is why he's not practising. "I got to stay in shape," he says. "I'll stay on the bike as long as they stay on the ice." He peddles in silence for a minute or so. Then he says, "It's my second concussion, but they told me two in two years is nothing to worry about, so I'll be back soon."

Tunnicliffe comes from Hope, in the Fraser Valley, about a hundred miles east of Vancouver. He says the hockey there was "rinky-dink" so he went to Edmonton to play bantam when he was fourteen. "I stayed with my aunt but I was still homesick as hell," he says. "The high school seemed so big. We had four hundred in our school at Hope. In Edmonton it seemed like four thousand. And I'd never seen anything like the winter. I was used to a bit of snow, a bit of rain, and a bit of sun, not thirty below week after week."

Last month, the Calgary Hitmen of the Western Hockey League traded Tunnicliffe to Medicine Hat, but he wouldn't report. "I don't think the organization wanted to win enough," he says. "Playing against them last year, I could see it in their attitude. They'd get a couple of goals behind and they'd give up. I looked at their record this year and I just thought I'd rather go to a place where I knew I'd play and improve." So he opted for the Kings, although the British Columbia Hockey League is a step below the western league. "The hockey is good here or I wouldn't stay," he says.

After he leaves junior, Tunnicliffe says he has a couple of choices. He'll have at least two years of education paid for through the western league's scholarship fund because of his time with Calgary and before that Tri-City. "I hope I'll play pro hockey somewhere," he says, "but if not, I'll go to a Canadian university close to home and play there"; his two seasons in the WHL disqualify him from U.S. college hockey because major junior players are paid.

He's still peddling when he laughs and asks, "Ever see the movie *Slapshot*? It's awesome, my favourite movie. Hockey in Powell River is like that. In the movie they're all worried that the mill is going to shut down because the whole town depends on it. It's the same here, people rely on the mill. And our bus looks like the bus in *Slapshot*, and there are a lot of French-speaking guys on the team in *Slapshot*, the same as here, two languages in the dressing room. The whole thing is the same. It's really funny."

Three of the Kings are from Powell River. "That's not bad when you think of the calibre of hockey and the size of this place," says Joe Mastrodonato, the team's president. He says that most of the others come from other parts of B.C. and Alberta. Four are from Quebec.

One of the Quebecers is Carl Desjardins. He's from Longueuil, south of Montreal. He's eighteen, a nice-looking fair-headed kid. Next year he is off to Dartmouth, an Ivy League school, to study pre-med. Sitting in a lounge at the rink after practice, he says that he's in Powell River to improve his English. The assistant coach at Dartmouth knows the Kings' coach, Kent Lewis, and recommended Desjardins to him. Desjardins says his parents also encouraged him to come. "They told me that people can't stay at home all our lives," he says. "It's a great chance to see the country, too." Desjardins' English is accented, but fairly fluent; he doesn't have to search for words. With him is seventeen-year-old Mike Sullivan, one of the three players from Powell River. As a hometown boy Sullivan is particularly sensitive to public support for the team. "It hasn't been good lately," he says. "When we win they come out, when we don't, they don't. That hurts us. You want to play before people who care." Sullivan is smaller and slighter than Desjardins, too small for major junior let alone the pros. That's why when he finishes high school he'd like to take his hockey to the University of Alaska–Anchorage.

More than thirty Kings have gone on to U.S. schools in the team's ten years. Coach Lewis says, "Yeah, we've done a very good job there. If they aren't going to play professionally, that's where we'll steer them." Lewis is thirty-one. He's from Powell River and played with the Victoria Cougars in the WHL. When he wasn't drafted by an NHL club, he returned home to coach. He didn't want to play minor pro. "It was all or nothing for me," he says. He was assistant coach for two years; this is his eighth year as head coach. He's ambitious, but for the time being he likes small towns. "There are no hiding places here," he says. "You can't get lost in the crowd. If you're not playing well, you hear about it. If you are, it's a lot of fun."

On the road, Lewis has his rules. "There are curfews. We don't want them near bars and there's no drinking on the bus," he says. "I want their obligations to be to their families and their teammates. You know the old saying, 'Alcohol, women, and knee injuries are what'll screw you up.'"

Lewis must be doing something right. Nearly seventy Kings have been drafted by the NHL, a respectable number for a non-major junior team. He says an advantage to a small town is that the players all live within ten minutes of each other. "It makes them close, and you have to be close to win," he says. At the same time, he shares Sullivan's anxiety about crowds. And that translates into worry about money. "Sports are generally out of whack," he says. "They're all becoming too expensive."

Terry Kruger, the editor of the *Powell River News*, spends four or five hours a week covering hockey. "Because of where Powell River is," he says, "hockey costs are a concern right across the board. If you're a kid on a rep team here you're gone two or three weekends a month and you have those ferry costs. So it's not only the Kings and Regals fighting for money. On top of that, everything else is going up — ice costs, equipment, insurance. And there is only so much money in a place like Powell River. There's not much here besides the mill."

Joe Mastrodonato, a real estate broker with Royal LePage, is the man behind the Kings. Ten years ago, he and a handful of others bought the Delta Flyers, a team from outside Vancouver, and moved them to Powell River. It cost them $21,500. "That was pretty cheap," he allows, "but they weren't much of a team, either. They only had one or two players. It was just a licence to get us into the league."

Mastrodonato is in his office, in his shirt sleeves, leaning across his desk. He's big, bald, swarthy, and imposing. He's told the receptionist to hold his calls because he wants to talk about hockey.

He didn't play himself, but he's been involved in it since his son Scott, who is back home playing for the Regals after a college career in the U.S., was a child and, like Bienfait's Frank Pastachak, he takes it very seriously. Unlike Bienfait, however, Powell River, as everybody points out, is not in hockey country, and right now Joe Mastrodonato is worried about what's happening to hockey away up here.

He says the team spends between $250,000 and $300,000. As is usually the case, most of it goes towards travel. The Kings' bus is outfitted with bunks. If they're playing in Victoria, for example, after the game they'll drive to Comox, up Vancouver Island opposite Powell River. They'll spend the night aboard the bus at the ferry terminal and take the first ferry home in the morning. But they still spend more on travel than any other junior team in the British Columbia league. "Look at a map. Our league is so spread out it looks like a goddamn octopus," Mastrodonato says. "It's a continuing scramble for money. If our fundraisers die, so will we. It gets harder every day."

Mastrodonato puts the hardcore fan base at three or four hundred, "but we've got to appeal to a younger crowd and many of them don't have money. Hell, it can cost forty dollars to see a junior game. We hired a marketing person. The only problem with that is, we should have an army of people to back him up and we can't afford that so he has to do it all on his own. We're doing everything we can to get fan support except winning, which is the most important thing, because if you don't win, it doesn't matter a damn what you do."

Right now, he's angry at the NHL and he wants the world to know it. He leans further across his desk. "Look, over the years about a hundred players from our league have gone to the NHL and the goddamn NHL doesn't even recognize this," he says. "We should get some compensation. Jesus, the NHL goes to bed with major junior hockey, gives them all the seed money they want, and our league gets nothing. I know that most of the NHL players come from major junior, but a hell of a lot of kids go through our system. Our league is good for minor hockey, too, and the NHL is too goddamn stupid to realize this. Or if they do, they don't care. People across the country give away their time and their money and they get nothing in return even when our guys end up in the NHL. It's sad."

Mastrodonato feels particularly let down by Brian Burke, the NHL vice-president. "When he was with Vancouver he acted like our league's best friend," he says. "Now, when he's one of the NHL brass, in a position to do something, he won't even return our goddamn phone calls, not a goddamn call. That's not only rude, it's bullshit."

Then he says, "But when I get my teeth into something I don't let go easily. I just want to be able to say one day that we made five bucks. That hasn't happened yet and I'm hoping like hell we don't go broke before it does. . . ."

(In April, Joe Mastrodonato told the people of Powell River that the Kings lost so much money last season that unless they bought six hundred season's tickets, he'd take the team somewhere else. They bought seven hundred. In June, Brian Burke quit the NHL front office to return to the Vancouver Canucks. And Kent Lewis has left Powell River to coach in Nanaimo.)

19

Thunder Bay, Ontario

January 1998

EVERY SUNDAY, AFTER THEY'VE BEEN to Corpus Christi Church, Benny Woit, the old Detroit Red Wing, and his wife, Julie, and two other couples have breakfast at Fat Cats, a sports bar and restaurant on Arthur Street, Thunder Bay's motel and fast-food strip. Fat Cats has lots of shining black arborite and stainless steel and it's busy but, perhaps in deference to Sunday, only one of the fifteen pool tables at the back is being used.

En route to Fat Cats, Woit stopped at a McDonald's to collect one of the restaurant's commemorative Olympic hockey coins. "I've got almost all of them now," he says. "I'm missing Rob Blake."

"You've got Rob Blake," Julie says.

"Yeah, that's right. I forgot. I traded for him."

Woit passes some coins around. "They're great, eh? I still need an Al MacInnis." He looks down the table to Mike Kachur and says that he has a stack of Wayne Gretzkys and Steve Yzermans. "I'll give you a Gretzky or an Yzerman for a MacInnis," he says. Kachur was a goalie in Thunder Bay. His brother Ed played for Chicago in the mid-'50s. He shakes his head. "Benny," he says, "I'm not collecting them."

"You should," Woit says.

The third couple is Joanne and Bob Speers. Speers is a fishing buddy of Woit's. "Lake Nipigon has the best fishing in the country," Speers says. "Forty-pound trout."

"He's not kidding," Woit says.

The Woits are usually in Arizona at this time of year, but because of a death in Julie's family, they've had to rearrange their winter. "I don't mind," Benny says, "but Julie has arthritis so it's hard on her." The waitress comes by and they order their breakfasts.

Benny Woit, a defenceman, was on two teams that won the Memorial Cup — "One from the east and one from the west. Not many guys have done that," he says. He played seven seasons with Detroit and Chicago, winning three Stanley Cups with the Red Wings. He's just turned seventy. He has a broad face that smiles a lot. He was born in Fort William, when Thunder Bay was made up of Fort William and Port Arthur. "Beautiful," he says about playing hockey as a youngster, "it was beautiful." Julie Woit sighs. "With Benny, it's always beautiful, everything's always beautiful." She says it with affectionate exasperation. She's the woman Metro Prystai remembers as being kind to his father years ago in Detroit.

"Well, it was," Woit says. "You couldn't wait to get to the rink, to get on your equipment. You couldn't wait to get on the ice, couldn't wait for a practice or a game. It was unbelievable." He tells a story about the old New York Americans, coached by Ebbie Goodfellow, coming to town in the early '40s. Woit and his pal Rudy Migay, later a Maple Leaf, were beginning in junior and Goodfellow told them that they had real promise. "Holy mackerel,"

Woit says, "I'll never forget that. We felt like kings."

"I remember the day he came home after signing with Detroit," Julie says. "He told me that he'd had on a Detroit sweater. He was standing there, so happy, like a kid. Benny would have played for nothing, for zero. That was his goal, to wear the Detroit sweater. Can you imagine that now? But that was those days."

Woit says he was scouted for Detroit by Walter Adams, the brother of the longtime Detroit general manager Jack Adams. (The Adamses came from the Lakehead.) "We were playing for Port Arthur. He picked Rudy and me but for some reason Rudy ended up with the Leafs."

Woit and Migay went to Toronto together for the 1946–47 season and they won a Memorial Cup with St. Mike's. They beat the Moose Jaw Canucks four straight. All the games were played in the west — Winnipeg, Regina, and Moose Jaw. "In one game," Woit recalls, "they were throwing so many bottles at us we had to duck into the goal for protection." With them at St. Mike's were Red Kelly, later a Red Wing and a Maple Leaf, Ed Sandford, eight seasons with Boston, and Fleming Mackell, who was with the Leafs and the Bruins for thirteen seasons. Les Costello and Gord Hannigan were also on that team. "I spent a lot of time breaking up fights between Costello and Hannigan," Woit says. "For some reason they were always swinging at each other. In the shower, in the dressing room. They shared a room together, bunk beds, and they'd fight there."

Woit says his best junior memories are of the following season, 1947–48, the second year he was on a team that won the Memorial Cup. He and Migay were back home playing for the Port Arthur West End Bruins. Danny Lewicki and Dave Creighton, both future prominent NHLers, were teammates. In the semi-final they met the favoured Lethbridge Native Sons. "Nobody on that team came from Lethbridge," Woit says. "They came from all over Canada — Eddie Dorohoy, Jackie Leclair, Jack Evans. The best junior from Lethbridge was Vic Stasiuk and he didn't even play for them. He played for Calgary or somebody." The best-of-seven series was even at 3–3. Lethbridge insisted on a neutral site for the seventh game. Toronto was chosen and, in Maple Leaf Gardens, the Port Arthur West End Bruins beat Lethbridge 11–1. Then, in the cup final, they beat a very good Barrie Flyers team four straight.

"We win the Memorial Cup and we weren't even supposed to have a chance," Woit says. "We weren't even expected to be in the final. What a goddamn thrill that was."

Julie Woit says when Benny turned pro it was hard at times to adjust to big cities after Thunder Bay. "You feel like you're from a little hick town, at least at first," she says. "I was so homesick that first year when the Red Wings sent Benny to their team in Indianapolis. I was phoning home every second day. Most of us were the same, I guess. We all came from small places — Timmins, Thunder Bay, the Soo. One day, I was in the arena in Indianapolis and I saw this guy 'way in the distance coming towards me and I said to myself, that looks like Ray Ceresino. Ray came from here, and he got closer and closer and it was Ray and we ran towards each other with our hands out. He was playing for Cleveland and they were in town for a game. My God, you've no idea how glad I was to see him, to see someone from home."

She laughs. "One time when Benny was playing in Providence he dropped me downtown to shop and we agreed that he'd pick me up at such-and-such a place at such-and-such time. So I wait and wait and wait and I decide I'll wait another five minutes and then go home on my own. Just then one of the players drives by and calls out, 'Julie, what are you doing?' I tell him I'm waiting for Benny. 'Benny's at the track,' he calls back. My God, did he hear about it when he got home. But that's the way he was." She shakes her head, still in disbelief, as if it had happened yesterday. She says, "Oh, those were good days. Hockey was like a family. We had a lot of friends and a lot of fun."

Woit tells about the first time he and Terry Sawchuk ever went to the track. It was when they were playing for Indianapolis. "We asked a guy what we were supposed to do and he said you bet. So we started betting, a dollar each. We win the first six races. I'm not kidding, six in a row. I guess we got about ten bucks now, but we still don't know what the hell we're doing. We go to the window for the seventh race and suddenly there's a crowd around. The word is out that we're winning and they all want to know what we're betting. We say we don't know. Then a waiter comes over and says there's someone wants to see us upstairs in the restaurant . . . who's that singer?"

"Frankie Laine," Julie says.

"Yeah, Frankie Laine. We go up there. Frankie Laine's sitting at a table. What do you know if we don't win the seventh, too. He buys us dinner and he asks who we're betting and we said we didn't know. Anyway, we won that one, too, eight or nine in a row. There's got to be a hundred guys around us now. I think we walked out of there with about twelve dollars each. We win eight or nine races and end up with twelve dollars."

Julie Woit says, "When Benny was playing in Indianapolis, the coach, Ott Heller, said to me, 'Julie, Benny's a heck of a bodychecker. He can really hit. But would you please tell him to stop saying "Gee, I'm sorry. Did I hurt you?" when he knocks someone down?'"

"I think that's a load of baloney," Benny Woit says. Then he goes on, smiling again, "I did love to hit, but I remember when I'm with the Red Wings and we're in Montreal and I missed this guy, went flying through the air, and banged my head on the ice. I'm lying there, looking up, everything's a blur, the players, the clock, the crowd. Finally, I get to the bench. Carl Mattson was the trainer. He sticks out his hand and says, 'Benny, how many fingers am I holding up?' And I said, 'I can't even see your goddamn hand, never mind your fingers.'"

Thunder Bay is a striking part of the country, distinguished by brooding rock faces, tall trees, rushing and quiet waters. Miners and foresters have got rich from it, and painters still try to capture it. It's east and west, closer to Winnipeg than it is to Toronto, the place where in 1981 Terry Fox had to abandon his run for cancer. But, like much of the north, the economy has been taking a beating. Thunder Bay is no longer the brash inland port shipping Canadian grain to the world. The unused grain elevators are impressive eyesores standing several storeys high, some as big as a football field, rusting away while the grain now moves by rail or truck or through other ports. Forestry and mining, opened up by thousands of European immigrants, suffer too, with every fluctuation in the price of newsprint or nickel. There's no passenger rail traffic any longer, which reinforces Thunder Bay's sense of isolation. But it has more than a hundred thousand people, its unemployment is no higher than the Ontario average, and its per capita income last year ranked it seventh among the top twenty-five cities. It has Lakehead University and Confederation College. Through it all, Thunder Bay has always been a hockey town, turning out players the way Timmins has, and Sault Ste. Marie, and Sudbury, and Kirkland Lake. In the '40s and '50s it was Gus Bodnar, Bud Poile, Gaye Stewart, Benny Woit and his pal Rudy Migay, Alex Delvecchio, Danny Lewicki, Steve Wochy, Edgar Laprade, Pentti Lund, Dave Creighton, Ed Kachur, Steve Black. Later came Bruce Gamble, Trevor Johansen, Walt Podubny, Ralph Stewart, Steve Ruchin, Norm MacIver, Bill Houlder, Greg Johnson, Tony Hrkac. There have been two Lee Fogolins, father and son, two Memorial Cups, and nine Allan Cups.

On this Saturday afternoon, it's mild for the last week of January, damp and dreary. Streets are lined with blackened snow and they're nearly deserted. In the East End, on Pacific Avenue, the only bright spot is St. Mary's Ukrainian Church, with its gold, onion-shaped spires, presiding over the small, white clapboard houses. Around the corner, at the Royal Canadian Legion, Slovak Branch 129, there's only one customer, a young man. He's leaning over the bar, talking with the woman behind it, and it's not about hockey. Business at the Legion's Polish Branch 149 on Simpson Street isn't much better.

This is Danny Lewicki's turf, the few blocks where he grew up — the player whom Red Sullivan feels could have been one of the greatest players of his time. Lewicki is sixty-six. He looks ten years younger, plays golf a lot, and lives in a roomy ninth-floor condominium in Mississauga, on the western edge of Toronto. It's all a far cry from his childhood in Port Arthur, when he was the youngest of nine children to a single mother. When Danny was one she kicked out his father because he beat her. "We lived in a little shack, all of us, and she worked and worked," Lewicki says. "My father lived three blocks away. She'd send me over to see him, but to me he wasn't my father. He was a stranger. He never paid any attention to me until I began to make a name for myself in hockey."

It's mid-morning and Lewicki is having coffee in his kitchen. "Back then there were little farms about," he says. "I was four or five, too young for school, and my mother would take me with her and I'd sit in the farmyard crying because she was out in the field working and I didn't know what was happening.

"Around when I was eleven I started at a shoeshine parlour downtown on weekends. The best customers were guys coming in from the bush for a big date. A shine cost fifteen cents but they'd give you a dollar. I'd go home with at least twenty bucks and give it to my mother, and my brothers and sisters would help, too. She finally got enough money to tear down the shack and neighbours helped build a house and she took in roomers. She was a very caring and kind person."

Hockey, Lewicki maintains, made the difference for him. "We were mostly Slavs and Italians and Finns," he says. "The older guys built a rink for us, the North Star rink, and looked after it. When I was seven I'd be playing guys who were fifteen. I'd skip school and I'd skate for seven, eight hours at a time, day after day. The truant officer was a Mr. Love. I got to recognize him from a distance, how he pedalled his bike, so I'd hide under the shack where we put on our skates until he went by. I got away with it because my mother couldn't speak English. She'd come from the Ukraine when she was fourteen, but she'd never learned it. Mr. Love would come to the house to tell her that I wasn't in school and she'd smile and say, 'Okay.' And he'd say, 'Now, Mrs. Lewicki, you make sure Danny's at school tomorrow,' and she'd smile again and say, 'Okay.'" Lewicki says the first time his mother saw him play was in that 1948 Memorial Cup. "And she saw me once when I was with the Leafs. She never understood hockey. She never understood that I could make a living playing."

Lewicki takes a phone call. It's a friend and they chat and Lewicki says to him, "That's the kind of stuff I can't stand. All the goddamn money they get paid today and they pull a Mickey Mouse stunt like that." He hangs up. It turns out that Lewicki's friend was at a charity golf tournament and a prominent current hockey player didn't show up, although he'd promised to, really upsetting the sponsors. "That's crap to pull a stunt like that," Lewicki says. "He didn't even have the manners to phone. It was for charity, for God's sake."

Following the 1948 Memorial Cup, Lewicki went to Stratford in the Ontario Hockey Association Junior A. One of his teammates was called Pierre Cadieux. They lived in the same hotel. "I don't know if he didn't speak English, or whether it was a con, but he travelled with an interpreter from Quebec," Lewicki says. "Pierre was a hell of a nice guy, but I used to wonder about his heavy beard. I was only seventeen and hardly had fuzz and he probably shaved twice a day."

It turned out that "Lucky Pierre" was twenty-five or twenty-six and was using a younger brother's birth certificate. Stafford Smythe, who was running the Junior Marlboros, blew the whistle on him and Stratford had to forfeit a playoff series. (George Sayliss, who played for Stratford, remembers Pierre. "He wore a Tyrolean hat with a big long feather." Sayliss thinks that he played in England or Scotland after being banned by the Canadian Amateur Hockey Association.)

Danny Lewicki doesn't know if he could have lived up to Red Sullivan's opinion of him, but he does feel that he never reached his hockey potential, perhaps because of his attitude. "I played nine years — Toronto, Chicago, New York — and I think it should have been thirteen or fourteen given the ability I had," he says. "I'm not complaining, I'm not blaming anybody but myself, but as other players will tell you, there were a lot of politics in that old six-team league. If you talked back to a coach or manager you could be buried in the minors for life." Conn Smythe, the Maple Leafs owner, once called him "an impertinent brat," he says. "I had to go home and look up the word 'impertinent'." And Hap Day, as Leafs coach, told him, "The day you've arrived in the NHL is the day you carve someone up."

"That's got nothing to do with ability. You can't be that if it's not your nature," Lewicki says. One of his worst coaches was Rudy Pilous, in Chicago. "One time he was ripping into me after I said that I'd learned in bantam that you held on to the puck until you could make a play. He benched me for forty games. I'd dress, go through the pre-game skate, then sit — for forty games. Eddie Litzenberger finally went to Pilous and said we needed goal-scorers and Pilous said it wasn't him, it was Tommy Ivan, the general manager. So Litz goes to Ivan and Ivan says it's Pilous. They kept passing it back and forth. Just a load of crap."

Lewicki says that the best coach he ever had was Joe Primeau, when Toronto won the Stanley Cup in 1951. "Joe knew that everybody was different," he says. "He knew what made you tick. He didn't threaten you or bully you. He knew which guys needed a pat and which guys might need a kick. He understood his players."

The Thunder Bay Thunder Cats are in the United Hockey League, which used to be the Colonial Hockey League. The UHL and the East Coast Hockey League and the Central Hockey League are about the same standard. They have a good mix of ex-major junior and top-flight ex-university players who are good, but not quite good enough for the American Hockey League or the International Hockey League.

Tonight the Thunder Cats are playing the Saginaw Lumber Kings, who used to be the Chatham Maroons. (Some years ago Saginaw had a team called the Gears, but it folded.) The teams played last night and Thunder Bay won, 4–3, and they'll play again tomorrow afternoon, a make-up game because of an earlier postponement. That'll be three games in less than thirty-six hours.

Two hours before the game is to start, the Lumber Kings' bus arrives at the Fort William Gardens from the Airlane Hotel, one of the Thunder Cats' sponsors, which gives visiting teams a deal. The players file into the arena with little talk. They're probably still sleepy from their pre-game nap, or perhaps the grim weather has got them down. With them is Larry Coulouris. He's short, seventy-two, and is wearing a snappy, small-brimmed hat. He's with the Lumber Kings' general manager, George Maniss. Coulouris asks him if he's coming for a beer. "The Elks is just around the corner," he says. Maniss says no, that he's doing colour on the radio play-by-play. He chats for a moment about the team's new ownership — "strong" — then follows the players inside.

Coulouris comes from Thunder Bay but he has lived in Saginaw for more than forty years. He owns what he describes as a saloon and sandwich shop. "It's called Larry's Lounge," he says. "What the hell else am I going to call it?" Back home, Coulouris says that he does some off-ice officiating for the Lumber Kings. "I like working the penalty box best," he says. "At least you can see the game. Being a goal-judge, half the time you can't see a goddamn thing. It's one big scramble." This weekend, he's just a fan, but he's not happy with the Lumber Kings. "People aren't coming out because we're not putting a good product on the ice," he says. "They got to go out and get some players, spend some dough." He nods goodbye and heads off alone through the gloom to the Elks.

Gary Cook is the Thunder Bay Thunder Cats' general manager, and a part-owner. He's short, balding, and wears glasses and a frown. His voice is hoarse and he's passionate about hockey. He comes from Thunder Bay and says that he's never wanted to leave. He works for Union Gas. "They treat me well and let me do the hockey," he says. "I've had chances to move on in hockey but so far I've said no. I do everything with the team, the office work, recruiting, travel. I used to cut players. That's one thing I don't do now. I leave that to the coach. You pay a coach, let him coach."

The travel is by bus, and sometimes by plane, if they're playing in Brantford or Binghamton or Winston-Salem, which is in North Carolina. Their shortest bus trip is nine hours. And how does Cook sell Thunder Bay to potential players over cities in the balmy south? "We have a good hockey operation," he says. "Secondly, our winters aren't *that* bad. Thirdly, hockey players in Canada qualify for unemployment insurance. That's a big draw if you don't want to work in the summer."

But Cook is worried. The league has a team weekly salary cap of US$9,200, which is a lot of money if you're not attracting good crowds. The Thunder Cats average 2,200 or 2,300 people a game. "We got to draw more," he says. "We need more people to survive. Jesus, I can remember when we'd put nearly six thousand in here."

Cook's talking about the heyday of senior hockey, before the Colonial/United league, when the Thunder Bay Twins won five Allan Cups. Cook was trainer for the 1975 team and general manager for the four in the '80s. "One year we went all the way to Newfoundland and we were down 3–0 to Corner Brook in Corner Brook," he says, "and every night they had the champagne ready and then we took four straight, right in their own building. And once here we were down 3–1 to Spokane and we won the seventh game in the last minute."

Downstairs, the lobby is beginning to fill up. Two men come in the front door and the younger one says to the doorman, "I'm going to get my dad's ticket, I'll be right back," and walks towards the team's office. The doorman calls out, "Who are you?"

"I'm Ken Tasker."

"So what?"

"I've been playing here most of the season, for God's sake."

The doorman says, "I can't keep track of them all. They come and go." Tasker returns a moment later with the ticket.

Ken's father, Ron, lives in Mount Hope, near Hamilton, Ontario. This weekend is the first time he's seen his son play for the Thunder Cats. Ken Tasker is twenty-two. He's the team's new enforcer because two of last year's de-camped for the International Hockey League. Last year Tasker played for the East Hants Molson Penguins in the Nova Scotia junior league. He has also played with St. Mary's University, in Halifax. Early this season he had stops with the Hampton Roads Admirals of the East Coast Hockey League and then the Flint Generals of the United Hockey League. "Twice, he was about the last guy to be cut," his father says. "He came home and we went to a game in Brantford when Thunder Bay was playing and he gave his résumé to the Thunder Bay coach. It's turned out well. It's really encouraging because he works so hard and he was getting kind of down."

(As it turned out, it wasn't a great weekend for Tasker. He was in two fights, winning one, losing one, suffering a concussion.)

By the time the game begins, the rink is half full, about 2,400, just so-so for a Saturday night. Russ Poole is seventy-seven and goes to every game. "I wouldn't miss one," he says. "I don't know what the hell people want these days. This is the best entertainment in town." Poole always sits in the same seat, high up in a corner, on an aisle because he doesn't get around easily. His metal, orthopaedic cane is beside him. He's been a hockey player, coach, manager, and scout, and he's seen them all since the '30s. His favourite was Edgar Laprade, now a member of the Hockey Hall of Fame, who played ten years for the New York Rangers.

"He was in a class by himself," Poole says. "He was the best stickhandler I think I've ever seen. He'd shift out defencemen and they'd still be looking for him the next day. And I really liked Gaye Stewart.

You know why? Anyone that went after him had better watch out. He was pretty mild-mannered, but he didn't mind giving that little tick with the stick. He could look after himself. I always looked for that in a player."

He goes on, "And Benny Woit was a helluva bodychecker. He hit you, it hurt. Hey, and get Ab Cava to tell you about his fight with Bill Juzda. Ab wasn't afraid of anybody. He'd never back down. You got to like a guy like that."

Just then, Mike Figliomeni moves in alone on the Saginaw goal. He dekes the goalie out and scores. Not only is it a nice goal but Figliomeni is a hometown boy, so the crowd cheers wildly. The program lists Figliomeni at five foot five and 155 pounds. "I didn't know how much help he'd be because he's so goddamn small," Poole says. "But nobody pushes him around."

This is Figliomeni's first year with the team. Last season he was with the Waco Wizards of the Western Pro League. "A German team was after him two weeks ago so we had to do something to keep him," says Ab Cava, the team's president and majority owner. "He's a helluva hockey player and the crowds love him so we dug a little deeper for him, but it's tough."

Figliomeni and Jason Firth are the most exciting players on the team. They play on a line with Brant Blackned, from Weminji, in northern Quebec. Firth, a centre, is from Dartmouth, Nova Scotia, and played major junior hockey for the Ottawa 67's and the North Bay Centennials. He's been averaging over a hundred points a season for five seasons.

"I often wonder why he hasn't gone higher with all that talent," says John Nagy, a former junior who covers hockey for the Thunder Bay *Chronicle-Journal*.

He says that Firth has been up with the Manitoba Moose of the IHL and Charlottetown when it was in the AHL. "I don't know what it is, but he doesn't stick." If Firth himself knows, he's not saying. He's a very quiet young man.

Up in the press box someone points out that of the sixteen or so players on each team, not counting the goalies, only one is wearing a face mask. "Yeah," Nagy says, "good old northern Ontario hockey." He looks up to check the clock. There's less than two minutes left in the game. "I'd hate to jinx it," he says, "but you know, there hasn't been a penalty. Not one." Fifteen seconds later, at 18:37, there's a fight. Nagy chuckles. "I should have kept my mouth shut." Four seconds later, right after the faceoff, there's another one. Ken Tasker, the new enforcer, gets a major and a game misconduct.

Thunder Bay wins, 6–3. Figliomeni and Firth get two points apiece, as they did the night before. Blackned scores twice. The next day, in the afternoon game, Firth gets three points, including his fiftieth and fifty-first goals, as Thunder Bay sweeps the three games. Nagy, referring to Firth, Figliomeni, and Blackned, says, "I know it's only minor pro, but it's hard to imagine a better line in hockey."

Gus Bodnar, one the "Flying Forts" — the others were Bud Poile and Gaye Stewart — was born in Fort William. He won the Calder Trophy as rookie of the year with Toronto in 1944, one of four Thunder Bay players to win it between 1943 and 1949. The others were Gaye Stewart (Toronto, 1943), Edgard Laprade (New York, 1946), and Pentti Lund (New York, 1949).

Bodnar holds the record for the fastest first goal by a rookie. And it's hard to imagine it being beaten

— at fifteen seconds of the first period of his first game. It was in 1943 and the Leafs beat the Rangers 5–3. And Bodnar was with Chicago in 1952 and assisted on the record three goals scored by Billy Mosienko in twenty-one seconds, again against the Rangers. "Easiest three assists I ever got," Bodnar says. "I just won three faceoffs. After the third goal Ebbie Goodfellow sent on another line. Mosie was mad. He said he was so hot, he might score again."

Today, a trim and healthy-looking seventy-two, Bodnar splits his year between Florida and Oshawa. He still has the boyish face that he carried through twelve NHL seasons long before the era of helmets and face masks. Sitting in his Oshawa rec room, he opens a scrapbook. The Fort William *Times-Journal*, the newspaper of the day, tracked his career. Headlines included "Fort William has Corner on Rookie Award" when he won the 1944 Calder Trophy the year after Gaye Stewart did, and "Bodnar Fires Goal that Eliminates Canadiens". Even modest achievements were noted: "Bodnar Gets Assist as Leafs Beaten 8–5".

Bodnar has good memories of his early hockey in Thunder Bay. "It was all outdoors," he says. "Firemen would flood vacant lots. Then we'd have to look after them. And there was river skating. It was great when the wind would clear off a big space. The ice was so hard you had to have really sharp skates. Most of the time we sharpened our skates with a file.

"And when we were kids our games were outdoors. It was so darned cold. I'm talking twenty, thirty below. We didn't mind, but we didn't get many people watching us. I remember the butcher's meat came in brown wax paper so I'd put on a thin sock, wrap the paper around it, then put on a wool sock. That helped a bit."

Bodnar's first junior team was the Fort William Hurricane Rangers. "Bud Poile was on that team. Gaye Stewart wasn't. He played for Port Arthur. We lost a western junior final to the Portage Terriers. They had a super club. Twelve of them turned professional, including Bill Juzda. I look back and I think those were some of my best days in hockey. We played hard but it was lots of fun."

Bodnar signed a "C" form with Squib Walker that bound him to the Leafs. "Squib lived in Fort William but he was the Leafs' scout for western Canada. He also signed Juzda and Wally Stanowski and Johnny McCreedy," Bodnar says. "He was in the insurance business. You signed the form, and he sold you a policy." He looks away for a moment, thinking. Then he says, "That's right, I got a hundred dollars for signing and I gave it to my dad and he said, 'They don't pay you to play hockey, do they?'"

Bodnar's first training camp with the Leafs was in St. Catharines. "I was a smart rookie, at least I thought I was. I'd dipsy-doodle, put the puck between the defencemen's legs, deke around them, trying to impress everybody," he says. "In those days the older players didn't believe in getting into shape until almost Christmas. They treated the first half of the season almost like a camp. So Bucko McDonald calls me over. 'Son,' he says, 'you're making us look bad.' I had long hair then, over my eyes, and the next time I came down the ice I guess I couldn't see and Bucko hit me. Boy, did he hit me. He had to help me to the bench. He said, 'I told you, you were making us look bad. Now go get a haircut so you can see.' I went in, showered and dressed, and went right to the barbershop in the Welland Hotel, where we were staying, and got a brush cut. That was the best lesson I ever got in keeping my head up."

He says one of the things that made the Leaf teams of the '40s so strong was their camaraderie. They had team meetings once a week, just the players. "They'd be in some out-of-the-way, dingy bar because hanging out in bars was a no-no, particularly with Conn Smythe," Bodnar says. "We'd all get in there and then go around the room and either cut someone up, or praise them. But it was all constructive and it never, never got any further. The next day we'd practise what we'd talked about. From what I'm told, players don't do that now. They're too busy seeing their brokers. We never had that problem."

In 1967 Bodnar coached the Toronto Marlboros to the Memorial Cup, and he still has some definite opinions about hockey. "Don't make it too complicated, because it isn't," he says. "It's simple, it's up and down. Depending on what's called for, you send in one forward, the others stay back on their wings, the defence stand up, whatever. What drives me crazy is when a player just shoots the puck in. You work so hard to get possession of it, why throw it away? It's stupid hockey. There's too much stupid hockey."

Ab Cava, the Thunder Cats' president, like his friend and general manager, Gary Cook, is worried about costs. He's standing in the glassed-in booth beside the hockey office above the rink. The game is over and the rink is emptying. Cava is a colourful man in his fifties, a former player and coach. "We got 2,500 great fans in Thunder Bay, some of them were coming back when I played, and guys like Benny who never miss, but we're just short a few here," he says. "It's a big ticket for us to play in this league. If only they could get a team in Duluth or Minneapolis it would cut down on travel, because our travel is a killer."

Cava has his own construction materials business, but he says the Thunder Cats are a twelve-month operation. "We don't have a lot of staff because we can't afford it," he says. "Cookie puts a lot of time in. Just everyday operations. It's a constant battle for players, there are so many leagues. We lost four or five guys from last year, good players, to the East Coast league, or Texas. But hockey is in my blood. It always has been."

Cava is asked about the fight with Bill Juzda, the ex-New York Ranger and ex-Leaf who loved the heavy-going. "I was just a kid and he was playing with the Winnipeg Maroons then," he says. "It happened in this rink. We were being intimidated and I knew someone had to take him on. So, of all the fights I had in hockey, this was the only premeditated one. It started in this corner." Cava points through the glass. "And we ended up at the blue line. I was on top. Back then you sat in the same penalty box, nobody between you. I wanted to go again so I started trash-talking: 'You old bastard, you should have quit a long time ago.' Stuff like that, trying to get to him. We had our gloves off, so I'm watching his right hand. But I didn't know that he was left-handed and he came out of nowhere, boom! Boy, did I see stars. So we're at it again, and again I ended up on top.

"We lost the game and the series so we're feeling pretty low and he comes into our dressing room. Our trainer said it wasn't a good idea, but Juzda said, 'Hell, it's over. I just want to talk to the boys.' I heard him say, 'Where's that Cava?' He comes over, shakes my hand, and we have a couple of beers and bullshitted a bit.

"That August I got a call from a guy in Windsor, Nova Scotia. A senior team wanted a playing-coach, good money. I decided no, but I asked him how he'd heard of me. He said Juzda was a good friend and he'd recommended me. How's that, eh? Later, when I was coaching and taking junior teams to Winnipeg, Bill would be the first guy down to the rink to see me. He was one of the best people I ever met in hockey."

During another series against the Maroons Cava was working with the board of grain commissioners when he was sent to audit elevators in Quebec City. Russ Poole, the team's manager, decided to fly him home for the weekend games. But the flight was delayed and when it finally arrived it was too late for the first game, which Thunder Bay lost.

Cava says, "Lee Fogolin was the coach and the next day he says, 'Jesus Christ, Ab, they got some big guys and they kicked the shit out of us.' Now, Fogie would never send anyone out to get somebody, but he did say I'd have to play tough. Then he says, 'I got this helmet from Tumba Johansson and I want you to wear it.'" (Johansson was Sweden's best player in the '60s. He was trying to market a helmet in North America and had given one to Fogolin when Fogolin was on a tour of Sweden.)

"I said no goddamn way. Helmets are for sissies. But Fogie says one of our guys was chopped last night and he insists that I wear it. So I said okay, reluctant as hell, though. Sunday, I start the game. They get the puck and I run at the guy and get two minutes. I get out and I run at someone else. Another two minutes. It was like an instant replay. I'm really wired because I missed Friday's game and I felt I owed something for being flown home. So back on I go and run at another guy. Two more minutes. My third minor expired at 6:35.

"By this time Fogie's waving, and yelling at me to get off the frigging ice. I can just imagine the

Maroons thinking, 'What the hell's going on with this crazy bastard in the helmet? He must be nuts.' Fogie was really mad. He sat me out the rest of the game. When it was over I went to the airport and flew back to Quebec City." Cava laughs. "Jesus, Quebec City to Thunder Bay and back for thirty-five seconds of ice time!"

Returning to the Thunder Cats, Cava says, "It's getting harder all the time. It's because of guys like Cookie that we still have hockey like this in Thunder Bay, because they love the game. That's the reason. But it's a question of how long we can go on getting beaten up by travel and the box office."

20

Drummondville, Quebec

February 1998

HIGHWAY 239, AN HOUR AND a half east of Montreal, is banked by huge, misshapen chunks of ice and uprooted trees, the aftermath of last month's storm that threw a great swath of Quebec into darkness. In the village of St-Germain, within an area that's been without power for weeks, there's a tavern owned by Yvon Lambert, the former Canadien. Inside, six men are sitting around a table, quarts of Molson's in front of them. Although it's lunchtime, they're the only people in the room — the waiter is out back helping to unload a beer truck. The tavern is powered by a generator, and because the day is overcast and all unnecessary lights are off, it's gloomy. But the men, likely farmers, ranging in age from their forties to their seventies, are in a good mood, laughing and saying that they feel things will soon be back to normal. On the wall beside the table is a poster promoting an NHL Oldtimers game and featuring Guy Lafleur, Gilbert Perreault, and, of course, Lambert.

Lambert doesn't spend much time in his tavern. He's in Montreal, where he runs the restaurant in the new Molson Forum. One of the men mentions that Marcel Dionne, Gilbert Perreault, and Yvan Cournoyer are from the area as well.

A few miles east of St-Germain, just off the Trans-Canada Highway, is Drummondville, Dionne's birthplace. It also was hit by the storm. However, except for shorn trees, it doesn't look too bad and it has had its power back for a week.

Drummondville's major junior team, the Voltigeurs, is on a two-week road trip from Montreal to Cape Breton. The city's main arena, "Centre Marcel-Dionne", has been taken over by an international midget tournament. Forty-three teams are entered, from Quebec, Ontario, Nova Scotia, Michigan, and Illinois. There's one from the Czech Republic and one from Poland. In the first game of the day, Team Illinois, from Chicago, is leading the Dartmouth Subways, and they'll go on to beat them.

Given that it's around noon on a Tuesday afternoon, there's not a bad crowd, at least a couple of hundred if the dozen or so having a smoke on the front steps are counted. Unlike its neighbour, Victoriaville, they don't smoke inside the rink. "There'll be fifteen hundred or so by tonight," says a middle-aged woman, apparently in charge of the hot dogs in the sit-down snack bar; she has watched crowds come and go for years.

Among the scouts here is Al Wagar, head coach and owner of the Junior A Cornwall Colts. His big selling point in trying to get kids to play in Cornwall is scholarships to American universities after they're finished. He says that he's already sent a handful of ex-Colts that way. "Kids nowadays know how important an education is," he says.

One of Chicago's players, Kevin Murray, impresses him. Kevin's father is Bob Murray, who played for the Blackhawks and is now their GM. Wagar and Murray were teammates with the old Cornwall Royals juniors. "It'd be great if he turned out to be as good as his dad." Wagar goes to about six tournaments a year. Drummondville's, he says, is one of the best.

On the other side of the rink, in the first row behind the Dartmouth bench, sits Euclid Descoteaux, a farmer in his sixties. He is short, ruddy-faced, and relaxed, his feet up on the rail in front of him. Descoteaux is from the nearby village of Notre-Dame-du-Bon-Conseil. He says that growing up on a farm didn't leave him much time for hockey. "And there was only an outdoor rink," he says. But he likes to watch the youngsters, no matter who wins. "I don't like the NHL any more," he says. "I really liked it in the old days, before masks and helmets, with the Richards and Béliveau and all of them."

While he's speaking, a Chicago player gets a breakaway. He plays it perfectly. Moving in, head up, he draws out the goalie and scores. "See what I mean?" Descoteaux says, punching the air. "In the pros they'd have hauled him down from behind or hooked him and there probably wouldn't even be a penalty. This is hockey."

Another man says, "I don't like hockey on TV so I come to games as much as I can. It makes the winter go faster. I can't afford to go to Florida." He adds sourly. "This sure as hell would have been the winter to go, though."

One wall of the arena's lobby is devoted to Dionne. (A second rink in Drummondville is named after Cournoyer, the other illustrious native son.) There are pictures of Dionne in his three uniforms — Detroit's, Los Angeles', and the New York Rangers'.

There's also a copper- or bronze-looking relief of his head in profile, like the side of a big coin, and his scoring record, year by year.

On another wall are pictures of Rosaire Smith, who, until Dionne came along, appears to have been Drummondville's most famous athlete. Smith was a weightlifter. In 1947 he came third in his class at the world championships in Philadelphia and in 1948 he was on the Olympic team.

From the '40s there's a photo of a softball team made up of Montreal Canadiens. The caption says that a Drummondville team beat them, but it must have been fun because they're all smiling — Maurice Richard, Phil Watson, Buddy O'Connor, Elmer Lach, Leo Lamoureux, and Bill Durnan. Drummondville would have been pretty good because Durnan was one of the best softball pitchers in Canada.

There's also a photograph of a 1972 Drummondville peewee team. On it was Alan Haworth, who went on to play eight seasons in the NHL, for Buffalo, Washington, and Quebec, scoring nearly two hundred regular-season goals.

Alan's father, Gordie Haworth, a teammate of Béliveau's with the junior Quebec Citadels in the early '50s, played two games with the New York Rangers in the 1952–53 season. He got an assist, and that was it for him in the NHL. But, as a consummate minor league professional, he spent fifteen years in the American league, the old Quebec senior league, and the old Pacific Coast Hockey League.

"When my dad played, everybody seemed to know each other," Alan Haworth says. "No matter where I was it seemed that there'd be someone asking about him. I'd be in the penalty box in L.A. and it would be 'Say hi to your dad for me.' The same thing in Boston. One night in Washington, Gordie

Howe presented me with a trophy for the best plus-minus on the team and the first thing he says is, 'How's your dad?' It was the same with Bobby Hull. I found it really neat."

There have been at least four generations of Haworth athletes. Gordie Haworth's grandfather played professional soccer for Blackburn, in England. Gordie's father was a hockey player. "He had a tryout with the Canadiens during the time of Howie Morenz," Haworth says. "I'm too young to remember that but I did see him play senior. And I played, and the important thing is that my dad, Alan's grandfather, saw Alan play for Buffalo that first year. It was like a dream come true for him, one of the family in the NHL."

Gordie Haworth lives in Drummondville, the small, prosperous city where he grew up. Opposite his house is a school where kids are skating on an outdoor rink. He is sixty-six and, like many old players, looks well. Going back over his career he says, "When I was fifteen one of the priests from the French college asked me to play for them. I told him that I couldn't because I was going to high school. He said, 'Don't worry, Gord, I'll fix it.' So I ended up playing for the high school and the college. Then I'm asked to play for the city, probably intermediate hockey then, so I said okay. That's three teams. I was playing six games a week."

The next team he joined was Victoriaville in the provincial junior league. Béliveau was there, too. When the team collapsed after one season Haworth and Béliveau ended up in Quebec City with the Citadels. "We were playing in front of eleven thousand, even more, in the old Coliseum," he says.

Besides Béliveau, the Citadels had Marcel Paille, a goalie, Camille Henry, and Bruce Cline, all of whom went on to play for the Rangers. Gordie Hudson, once one of the most promising young players in the country, was also on the team. He belonged to Toronto but he never played a game in the NHL. He's been dead for years.

"He was big for the time, over six feet, two hundred pounds, and he was a great skater," Haworth says. "But his life away from the rink screwed him up, even in junior. He was totally irresponsible. Sometimes when we went on roadtrips the bus would have to drive around looking for him. We'd never know where he'd have spent the night. I saw him a few years later when he was playing for Vancouver in the old western league. He was fat and could hardly move. It was so sad." He pauses for a moment, thinking. Then he says, "You know, Béliveau, Cline, and I would never go near a tavern. In those days it was hard to stick with a club. It wasn't like today. There were no long-term contracts. Most of us had to go and make the team each year, and I didn't want to take any chances."

Haworth has an example to illustrate how careful players had to be not to offend their bosses in the days before agents and unions. "During my last year with the Citadels, the Canadiens asked me to go on an exhibition tour with them to the Maritimes in the Christmas break," he says. "Phil Watson was our coach and he calls me and he says no way was he allowing me to go. 'You belong to the Rangers,' he said. I said okay, I understand that. About a month later Phil had to be in Montreal and he asked me to run the practice in Quebec. Punch Imlach is coaching the senior Quebec Aces and he comes into the rink and asks me whether I'd play for the Aces the next year if the Rangers said it was all right. Béliveau was playing for them and I said sure.

"The next day, Phil is back in Quebec and he finds out I've been talking with Punch. He gets mad and starts cursing Imlach. No way, he says, are the Rangers ever going to let me play for the Aces. I told him that that wasn't helping my career. I said that there was no guarantee I'd make the Rangers and if I didn't, I'd like to play for the Aces. But Phil stays mad as hell. That fall I'm meant to play for a Ranger team in Indianapolis. But the Rangers didn't get the franchise and although I still belonged to New York, I ended up in Valleyfield. Toe Blake was coaching and he wanted me.

"My second year, I got twenty-nine or thirty goals and it's announced at the end of the season that Blake is going to coach the Canadiens. He says to me, 'Gord, I'll see you in the NHL.' He said that he'd been talking to Frank Boucher, the Ranger general manager, and that Boucher had said that I'd be playing with them.

"During the summer, I get a letter from Boucher telling me to report to the Ranger camp in Lake Placid, New York. A month later it's announced that Watson is the new Ranger coach, replacing Muzz Patrick. Right away I get another letter. It says don't come to camp and before I know it I'm sold to Eddie Shore. I know that was all Watson's doing just because I'd spoken to Imlach. But you know something, about fifteen years later Phil Watson is in this very room, right here, almost down on his knees, begging me to come to play for him in Chicoutimi. And you know, I went and played for him." He pauses for a moment, then he says, "Maybe I wanted to show him I was a bigger man than he was."

When Haworth went to Springfield to play for Shore, Shore was fifty-five but he could still outskate a lot of the team. "He'd just slip into his skates, hardly tighten them up at all, and he'd dance in them, heels and toes, heels and toes," Haworth says. "Eddie knew so much about hockey, but when you played for him you weren't thinking about the game. You'd be thinking of him watching you. You were scared stiff about making a mistake. Still, whatever they teach now in hockey schools, it'll be what Shore taught."

Like everyone who ever played for Shore, Haworth has his stories. "Ernie Roche played for us. He was very good. He'd been on a Memorial Cup winner, the Junior Canadiens, with Dickie Moore and Charlie Hodge, that bunch, but one day Shore got on him about his skating. 'Mr. Roche,' he said — he called everybody 'Mister' — 'Mr. Roche, you're horseshit.' He followed him into the dressing room, still saying it. Ernie's sitting there, saying nothing, taking off his skates. Suddenly he lets one go at Shore. He misses, and Shore says, 'Mr. Roche, you are suspended.' Ernie lets the other skate go. Shore says, 'Mr. Roche, I said you are suspended. This is it.' And it was. I don't think Ernie ever played professionally again."

Haworth moved around after Springfield. He played in Victoria, Portland, and Los Angeles. Then it was back east. He was with his hometown Drummondville Eagles when they won the Allan Cup in 1967, the year before it was won by the Eagles' rivals, the Victoriaville Tigres. What he's most proud of is the Pacific Coast Hockey League championship he won with the Portland Buckaroos in 1960–61. Recently he received a letter saying that the team is to be inducted into the Oregon Sports Hall of Fame.

"It took a while," Haworth says, "more than thirty years. But I'm happy as hell about it. It's nice to be recognized."

Years ago, when Haworth and his pal Bruce Cline realized that they weren't going to get rich playing hockey, they bought a fast-food ice cream franchise, Sweden Frosty Treat, that grew into a restaurant. It was open during the summer and that meant working fourteen hours a day, seven days a week. But it paid off. Haworth sold his piece of the place some years ago and lives comfortably.

"I guess the most money I ever made playing was nine or ten thousand dollars, including playoffs," Haworth says. "When you think of that now, it's like playing for practically nothing."

It's not cold, but it's an overcast, cheerless evening. People hurry along the narrow grey streets, collars up, heads down, against blowing sleet. The town seems eerily quiet. At Le Plus, a sports bar and restaurant behind the hockey arena, it's a different story. People are laughing and greeting each other warmly and there's a good smell of cooking. A game between the Victoriaville Tigres and the Rouyn-Noranda Huskies starts at seven o'clock, so around six Le Plus begins to fill up. The Quebec Major Junior Hockey League has two eight-team divisions, named after Quebec hockey men, Frank Dilio and Robert Lebel. The Tigres are in fourth place in the Lebel, or western division, but only two points behind the three teams ahead of them. Tigres games usually start at seven-thirty. But power is still in short supply because of the ice storm, so to reduce the hours of usage, game time has been advanced half an hour.

Christian Paquin covers hockey for *La Nouvelle*, the Victoriaville newspaper. At thirty years old, he's worked in New Brunswick and in France and he expects to move on again. "But I like it fine here for now," he says. After he's finished his dinner, he heads towards the back door, breaking step to say hello to people at several tables along the way.

L'Amphitheatre Gilbert-Perreault, with its capacity of just over two thousand, is almost full. One reason for this is that two marquee players will be out there — Victoriaville's Daniel Corso and Mike Ribeiro of Rouyn. Ribeiro is considered almost in the same class as Rimouski's Vincent Lécavalier, who is probably the best junior in Canada. As well, it's Corso's first game in more than a month. He has been out with a groin injury. The rumour is that he could have been back sooner but that his father, a well-to-do Montreal businessman, doesn't trust the team doctors and wouldn't let his son play until his own specialist gave him the okay.

The Tigres' GM, Pierre Roux, denies the rumour about Corso's father. Then he says, "The playoffs are coming and that's when goaltending takes over. If we get good goaltending, we'll be all right."

Like in rinks everywhere, the music is loud and incessant. One number sounds like a French version of Stompin' Tom Connors' "Sudbury Saturday Night". In the press box are four or five men, including one who is videotaping the game for the league in case anything has to be reviewed.

Victoriaville drops behind by two goals in the first period. They can't seem to get organized. In the last two minutes of the second period Ribeiro, takes a minor penalty. A stubby, red-faced man in his fifties sitting right behind the penalty box begins to scream at him. There's nothing between them but three feet and a low pane of glass. A couple of times Ribeiro turns and stares at the man. He doesn't say anything, but he has a slight smile. He's taken off his helmet and is wiping his face mask with a towel. When the period ends, and the man is still screaming, Ribeiro takes his time getting up and crossing the ice to the dressing room. His message seems clear: he won't be intimidated, on or off the ice.

While the ice is being cleaned scores of people leave their seats to stretch their legs and have a smoke. They light up cigarettes and wander around the rink the way people did twenty years ago, even though they are surrounded by big signs that say smoking is forbidden. Christian Paquin, who doesn't smoke, shrugs. "C'est normale ici." The man who was screaming at Ribeiro lights up, takes a big drag, and says, "They come into our town, they have to learn to take things. This isn't for children. It's hockey."

Rouyn score three times in the third period and win 7–3. So it's a good thing the playoffs haven't started, because Pierre Roux certainly didn't get the goaltending he said was so important. Mathieu Garon, who belongs to the Canadiens, was pulled after he let in three goals. Pierre-Luc Therrien replaced him, and after he let in three more, Garon was sent back in. Corso looked rusty. Twice he gave up the puck in his own end and twice Rouyn almost scored. Ribeiro lived up to his press clippings. He scored twice and was in command whenever he was on the ice. He's not very big, but he stood up to some heavy hitting.

Jean-Pierre Mallette, a fireman, played senior hockey for Victoriaville in the '60s. His son Carl is a sixteen-year-old defenceman with the Tigres. Jean-Pierre thinks that the dream youngsters have of making the NHL is likely the same as when he was young. "But it seems the motivation is different. In our day it was a matter of pride, how proud we'd be to play in the NHL. Today, it's salary." He says this without bitterness, but he adds that although coaching is more specialized now, "there's still a place for hard work, will, and discipline."

His son partly agrees. He says it's hard to imagine a coach today getting results from players using the "draconian" coaching methods his father has told him about. "But hockey is just as tough or tougher today, I think," he maintains. "Particularly if you're talking about physical conditioning."

Alain Rajotte is the Tigres' coach. He's a young, good-looking man, sharply dressed and glum. He tells Christian Paquin that the Tigres were unlucky in their own end. Sloppy clearing, he says, gave Rouyn an early lead and his team couldn't get back in the game. He leaves and a moment later Rouyn's coach, Jean Pronovost, who spent fourteen seasons in the NHL, appears. He's equally sharply dressed and also unsmiling. He says it was a good game and he's happy with the win; there's no gloating. It's what Paquin expected, nothing special. He heads back to his computer in the press box. In a moment the players themselves begin to leave, in twos and threes, without much talking. They look tired and drawn and a little older.

21

Brandon, Manitoba

February 1998

THE BIGGEST NEWS IN BRANDON since the Wheat Kings reached the Memorial Cup final in 1979, where they lost to Peterborough, came out two months ago. Maple Leaf Foods is going to build a pork-processing plant here. That should mean at least twelve hundred jobs, and perhaps as many as twenty-two hundred, a heck of a shot in the arm for a city of forty thousand. Not everybody is thrilled, though. Some people worry that sewage from the pig farms needed to supply the plant will sully this golden, wheat-growing land. But as this golden land is now frozen and covered in snow, the anti-pig lobbyists have eased off a bit. Like most Manitobans, they just want to get through the winter. So until the snow melts and the land becomes soft and fertile again, and ripe for sullying, Brandon is back with what it does best — curling, and hockey.

Before the Wheat Kings, of the Western Hockey League, there were the Native Sons and the Elks. A raft of players from all three teams made it to the NHL, including Turk Broda, Don Raleigh, Wally

Hergesheimer, Jack McIntyre, and, later, Bill Fairbairn and Larry Brown. Then came Glen Hanlon, and Bill Derlago, Ray Ferraro, and Ron Hextall, Dave Semenko and Wade Redden. The late Juha Widing, a Finn, was a Wheat King, the first European to play junior in Canada, before playing for eight years in the NHL, largely with Los Angeles.

At one time there were as many as eight or nine top-rated Manitoba junior hockey teams. Right now, the Wheat Kings are the only major junior team left in the province. Their closest road game is Regina, four hours away; the farthest is Prince George, B.C., half the country away. "Every trip for us is a venture," says Rick Dillabough, who handles PR and marketing for the Wheat Kings. "The first week in November the fall fair was in here so we went to Lethbridge, Portland, Seattle, Tri-City, Spokane. We came home, played three games in four nights. Then the Olympic curling trials started and we left again and played Kelowna, Kamloops, Prince George, Edmonton, Calgary, Red Deer. It would make things a lot easier if Winnipeg were back in the league."

This weekend the Wheat Kings are home. Friday night, they play the Swift Current Broncos. On Saturday, it's the annual Wheat Kings Sportsmen's Dinner to raise money for the players' education fund. Brad Park, friend and ex-teammate of Bill Fairbairn with the Rangers, is the guest speaker.

The Wheat Kings have been in the league since the mid-'40s, but have never won a Memorial Cup. "I find that amazing," says Richard Lapp, who's written a book on the Memorial Cup. Besides the loss to Peterborough, the Wheat Kings reached the final in 1949. They lost, in what ended up as an eight-game series because of an unresolved tie, to the Montreal Royals. Joe Crozier and Glen Sonmor, later coaches and GMs in the NHL, were with Brandon; the great Canadien Dickie Moore played for Montreal. Lapp says that the 1979 Brandon team was very strong. It included Brian Propp, Laurie Boschman, Brad McCrimmon, and Ray Allison, all of whom had fine NHL careers. "They should have won when you think of all that talent," he says.

The Keystone Centre, in the city's fairgrounds, was built originally as an agricultural complex. It's vast: five hockey rinks, including the 4,800-seat main arena, a curling rink, exhibition halls and conference rooms, offices, snack bars and souvenir stalls, and livestock sheds. The Wheat Kings' small office is in there and it's made even smaller by boxes stacked with programs for the sportsmen's dinner — about six hundred tickets have been sold — and Wheat Kings mugs and caps and pucks. Rick Dillabough and Lyn Shannon are busy: the phones keep ringing. Dillabough is on one, arranging to have the dinner videotaped. Then he takes a call from an out-of-town reporter and explains the state of the team; another reporter is waiting to see him; players are coming in to pick up their tickets for the dinner; Dillabough now is trying to write a radio spot promoting tomorrow's game. . . .

When he finally breaks for coffee, he's suprisingly calm. "Patience is part of the game," he says. "It's a good thing I love my job or I'd go goddamn nuts." Dillabough is thirty-six. Before joining the Wheat Kings he was a broadcaster in Alberta. He knows Nanton, home of the Palominos and Hutterite hockey fans. "I did my first play-by-play when they were playing Lacombe, or Leduc," he says, "I can't remember which. Seems like a lifetime ago."

On the ice of the smallest of the Keystone Centre's five rinks, which smells of cattle from the sheds next door, Morris Mott is coaching ten- and eleven-year-olds. Mott teaches Canadian history at Brandon University. He played in the NHL with the California Seals and in Sweden and with Canada's national team. He got his Ph.D. from Queen's. On the ice with him is Kelly McCrimmon, once a Wheat Kings captain, now their GM. He is the older brother of Brad McCrimmon, the veteran NHL defenceman. They have the kids working on their power play. "You should never stand still on a power play," Mott calls out. "Pass it or move it yourself, but never stand still. Come on now, keep it moving." It's the final drill of the day. When the youngsters are finished they skate hard around the rink a couple of times before going to the dressing room. Mott, a compact fifty-one-year-old in a dark sweatsuit, skates to the bench to collect the water bottles, then follows the kids. A few minutes later, over a Coke in the curling rink's snack bar, he says, "Between coaching and oldtimers I'm around the rink five days a week, but none of it is the type of hockey where you go home and have a sleepless night."

Mott grew up in Creelman, Saskatchewan, a community of two hundred. He says hockey isn't as important in places that size as it used to be. "There aren't as many kids," he says. "And like everywhere else, things are more centralized. They go away to bigger places to play. Even Neepawa, which has four thousand people, has trouble putting teams together. Kids drop out earlier now. School sports take them away, snowboarding, what have you. It's an indication of the options they have. When I was young the rink was where everybody showed up. We'd be playing hockey and the adults would be curling on the rink beside us. Now, everybody in those small places is getting old and the younger people don't stay around."

Mott says he tries not to put pressure on his team because they are so young. "Some of them are starting to get emotional about wins and losses," he says, "and I think it's a little too early." He says they recently played four games in Regina, winning the first two, losing the second two. "After the two we lost, the kids sat around in the dressing room feeling bad for thirty seconds and then they were off to the swimming pool. I like that. It's good to see. I like kids who work hard on the ice but then don't worry too much about who won."

But Mott has his kids taking tae-kwon-do. They practise it for an hour a week to get ready for next season when they're allowed to bodycheck. "A lot of hockey is based on contact," he says. "You're confronting people close up. At our level, Atom, you're kicked out for fighting. But they won't be when they move up. It's a question of grappling techniques, how to sidestep, how to recognize where the blows are coming from, how to defend yourself. They're also learning techniques for controlling their temper. When they get to junior, the ones that do, they'll just let them fight. I've seen some guys get pretty badly beaten up. I want my kids to be ready."

Mott thinks that the players today are better than ever. "These Wheat Kings are light-years ahead of when we were playing," he says. "Shooting, God they can shoot, and take passes, backhand, forehand, going backwards. And they can skate. I'm sure glad I don't have to make a team today."

Bill Fairbairn lives in a big house in a Brandon subdivision that could belong to Toronto or Edmonton. He grew up in Brandon, played for the Wheat Kings, and spent eleven years in the NHL, mostly with the New York Rangers. But he has never got used to cities. On his lawn is a "For Sale" sign. "Now that the kids are grown up we want to move out to the country, maybe get some horses," he says. "I'm not comfortable in cities, even a place as small as Brandon."

Fairbairn is just back from New York, where he played in an alumni game. He mentions some of his ex-teammates who turned up: Rod Gilbert, Jim Neilson, Walt Tkaczuk, Brad Park, Pete Stemkowski, Rod Seiling, Marcel Dionne . . . Ed Giacomin, the great goalie, wasn't there. "He's still angry about that trade to Detroit," Fairbairn says. "He won't have anything to do with the Rangers. It's too bad. If he wants to take it out on them, fine, but not on the guys he played with."

Fairbairn says that he got his real start in hockey through the then Wheat King GM, Jake Milford, who later was GM in Los Angeles and Vancouver. "He brought me up from minor to play with the Wheat Kings when I was only fourteen," he says. "And I was up the next season for the playoffs against Edmonton when I was only fifteen. I was really lucky with him. He was like a father to me."

Bill Fairbairn was on some good Wheat Kings teams. "But Flin Flon always gave us trouble," he says. "Bobby Clarke, Reggie Leach, Gerry Hart. You knew every time you went up there there'd be brawls, every time. We didn't have any goons or fighters so they'd key on our best players. They'd try to get me or Juha Widing out of the game, but, luckily, I was never hurt."

Along with Milford, and Emile Francis in New York, Fairbairn says Eddie Dorohoy was great to play for. Dorohoy played a few games for the Canadiens in the '40s and then spent the rest of a long career in the minors. "He used to say, 'You want to know who I am, look me up under highest scorer in the (old) WHL,'" Fairbairn says. "Eddie and Milford made hockey around here. Eddie would take a couple of us to all the little towns for banquets, but he'd do all the talking. He could talk and talk and talk, that guy. One time in Moose Jaw we got a penalty for too many men on the ice. Eddie went wacko and starts yelling and his false teeth flew right out and you couldn't understand what he was saying. He's pointing at his teeth, trying to get them, and the refs are yelling at him. They tossed him out of the game. I don't think he ever did get the teeth back. But he was a heck of guy to play for. He'd back you all the way. Hustle was his thing. Skate, skate, skate. And God, he could handle the puck. He'd skate with us long after he'd retired, when he was coach and GM, and we couldn't get the puck away from him. He'd toy with us, like we were kids."

Fairbairn says he never saw any bitterness in Dorohoy over his abbreviated NHL career. "But he'd say that he should have played for Montreal, that he was better than anyone there. He'd say it, just like that, flat out."

Like other former players, Fairbairn is bothered by dangerously dirty play. He's talking about a cross-check that left Anaheim's Paul Kariya with a severe concussion just before the Olympics. "There's no reason for that. Apart from anything else, you're going to ruin the game by taking these guys out. If that keeps happening, hockey will really suffer. They're the ones people come to see. That's why I respect Bobby Orr. Once, in New York, when I had mono and I wasn't playing, Boston was in town. When I was watching the morning skate, Orr came up into the stands. He said, 'We need you, we want you back out there.'" Fairbairn gives a self-deprecating chuckle. "Maybe it was because he figured they could score against me. But it was nice of him to come and tell me. We didn't like to see other guys out of hockey. It hurt the game."

Andy Gurba is a sports buff with a vast collection of photos, old programs, pucks, baseballs, and books. He's a cheery, white-haired seventy-three, and a New York Yankees fan. He has the autographs of Joe DiMaggio and Whitey Ford and Hank Bauer, who was his favourite player, and Mickey Mantle and just about every Yankee who has counted in his lifetime. But his prize is a black-and-white photo of a young teenager, Turk Broda. "I'm not sure when it was taken," Gurba says. "I was very young, but it was in front of our house." It looks like winter, the trees are bare, but not a flake of snow or a sliver of ice is to be seen. Broda, in full equipment, including skates, is standing on the lawn. His jersey says simply 'HYDRO'. He has his characteristic broad smile.

Gurba worked for Canadian Pacific Railways. "I started as a call boy," he says. "There weren't many phones in those days so it was my job to ride my bike to the homes of the crews to tell them what time their trains were due." He has lived all his life in Brandon, apart from service in the Second World War. For twenty-five years he was an on-ice hockey official in senior and junior hockey in Canada and the United States. He refereed his first game when he was ten. "Nobody else would do it," he says. "I got twenty-five cents."

In the '50s the Canadian Amateur Hockey Association sent Gurba to a Memorial Cup eastern semifinal in Toronto. He says, "I was just to do one game. The regular ref was sick or something, I can't remember, but whoever replaced him had to be from the west, had to be neutral, so I was picked. It was the Marlies and I forget the other team, but Maple Leaf Gardens is full. I skate out and all of a sudden I hear, 'Hey, Andy, Andy,' and I look and it's Broda, shouting and waving to me. I'd forgotten he was coaching the Marlies. Christ, he calls me over, sticks out his hand. And here I am, the neutral ref, Jesus. Anyway, I said the hell with it and I skated over and we shook hands. The Marlies won the series, which was good, but they lost the game I refereed, which was also good."

What Andy Gurba wants is a hockey hall of fame in Brandon. "All the hockey players that have come out of here, all the hockey that's been played here, all the memories," he says. "Hockey put Brandon on the map and we don't have anything to show it off." He's trying to get the city to take over a hospital which is being closed down. He drives slowly past it. "This would be ideal," Andy says. "This is the spot where it should be."

It's hockey night in Brandon: the Wheat Kings against the Swift Current Broncos, who are in first place in the eastern division of the western league. It's drizzling and it's foggy. "This better be goddamn good," says a man in a Minnesota Vikings cap. "Christ, I could be at home." He pulls up the collar of his windbreaker and sprints from his car to the Keystone Centre. Inside, Rick Dillabough closes the door of the Wheat Kings' office behind him and goes to the press box with the lineups. By the time Brad Park, the visiting ex-Ranger and ex-Bruin, drops a ceremonial puck, the arena is about two-thirds full. People are still arriving, and it's close to capacity when the game starts. Many adults have kids in tow; it's a Friday, so there's no school tomorrow.

Bob Cornell, the Wheat Kings' owner, is wearing a Wheat Kings windbreaker; it's gold, the colour of wheat. Cornell is sitting in the press box with Kelly McCrimmon, the Wheat Kings' GM and the man who helps Morris Mott with his coaching. They watch the game in silence until a Wheat King breaks in alone on the Swift Current goal, is half-hooked down from behind, and there's no call.

"Jesus," Cornell says.

"I guess he's going to let that stuff go," McCrimmon says.

"Well then, he better let it go both goddamn ways," Cornell says. In the next few minutes the Broncos take three penalties in a row. McCrimmon is suddenly angry. According to him, the clock for one of the penalties was started too soon, reducing the total penalty time. "It's not right, it's not right," he says to Cornell. Just then, a Wheat King's clearing pass hits the linesman. A Bronco player pounces on it, moves in, and almost scores. It's Cornell's turn now. The press box is open and he leans out, yelling down at the official, "Jesus Christ, get the hell out of the way. You'll cost us the game."

Cornell is sixty. He played junior hockey in Edmonton and Winnipeg. The Red Wings were interested in him, but when that went nowhere he headed back to Brandon. "Hell, it's home," he says. "I was born and raised here, I know everybody in town." He's with his family's plumbing business.

McCrimmon is still incensed about the penalty clock. "We lost forty-six seconds of power play," he says. "Forty-six seconds."

"They should have called a hell of a lot more penalties," Cornell says. But one thing he is happy about is the Wheat Kings' goalie situation. Jamie Hodson and Jomar Cruz have great futures, he says.

"They're both young, only seventeen, and they're both big."

Cornell says that nowadays junior teams are recruiting the parents as much as the kids. "We have to assure them their kids will be okay with us." Since he's been involved, he says, no Wheat King has ever failed high school. Asked how they can study when they're on the road as much as they are, he replies, "They're on the semester system. And they know that if they miss a class when the team is in town the school will tell us and then they don't play the next game."

Down below, watching quietly and critically, is Richard Lapp, the author of the book on the Memorial Cup. Lapp is forty-one, tall, grey-haired. He says his book was long overdue. "I only played to the Junior B level but it seems that I've followed junior forever," he says. "And I'd see all these books and books on the Stanley Cup and nothing on junior. Do you know that they've been playing for the Memorial Cup since 1919? I worked on that book like hell, but I really wanted to do it." He pauses. "I hope it's selling in the east."

Of tonight's game, he says, sounding world-weary, "Because it's close and between two good teams, everybody's saying how good it is, but it isn't. There's no flow to it. It's both choppy and dull. No intensity." He says that he goes to about two hundred games a year. "I'm on the road all the time." He'll leave this game before it's over. He has at least a two-hour drive home to Winnipeg and he's worried about the fog. "I have to work tomorrow," he says. He's a security supervisor in a bingo hall.

A week ago, in Thunder Bay watching the Thunder Cats play the Saginaw Lumber Kings, Lapp was wearing a Philadelphia Flyers jacket. Tonight, he's wearing a Wheat Kings one. "I'm a fanatic about hockey jackets," he says. "I have about forty, every NHL team, and others, but I haven't bought one for four or five years. I hate to admit it, but I'm losing interest in the NHL. I still like junior, but the NHL is just going crazy with the salaries and the Americans taking over. It's not Canadian any more." He watches the game for a moment then he mutters, "So long," and takes off into the fog.

A few feet away, standing high over the Brandon goal, is Andy Gurba. He's wearing a Blue Jays cap. Swift Current gets a good scoring chance when a Brandon defenceman tries to be fancy at his own blue line. "That was really dumb, you see," Andy says. "All he had to do was flip it out. Simple as hell. I don't understand how a player can reach this level and make such a dumb play."

However, the whole time he's dumping on the Wheat King player, he's smiling. "I always have a good time at a rink," he says. And he doesn't agree with Lapp. "I think it's a helluva game," he says. "But look there, see him, the big guy, Number 4? He's a Boston draft and Don Cherry says he's so good he should be up playing for Boston now." Andy pauses, still smiling. "There's only one small problem: the guy can't skate. He's slow as hell. I really think Cherry is good, but he's wrong about this guy." After a moment he says, "You know, a few years ago at a game here I won six hundred dollars in a draw. I didn't need it. I gave it to the Red Cross." He watches the game without speaking for a couple of minutes. Then he says, "I'm tired." And, like Richard Lapp, he's off home.

The score remains 2–2 until, with only thirty-two seconds left, the Wheat Kings score. The crowd goes wild. This means they've closed the gap on Swift

Current. Only four points separate them now. They're still cheering when, with two seconds left, Swift Current scores to tie it again. "Two lousy seconds," says the man who moved into Andy Gurba's place. "Two lousy seconds." He's young and he's holding a sleeping infant on his shoulder.

Overtime is scoreless. The rink empties quickly. Outside the Wheat Kings' dressing room, Mike Sawatsky of the Brandon *Sun* waits to talk with Jamie Hodson, one of the young goalies. When Hodson appears in his sweat-soaked underwear and T-shirt, he says he's very disappointed, and he looks it. "This was kind of like a playoff game," he says. "It was that important. I guess we loosened up because we thought we had it won." Close by, the reporter for CKLQ, Brandon's main radio station, is doing his post-game wrap-up with another Wheat King.

Jimmy Mann, who is no relation to Jimmy Mann the old Winnipeg Jet enforcer, is pleased to hear that Andy McCallum, the Brandon native who played for Powell River, is well. "I was best man at his wedding," Mann says. "God, there are a lot of bonds in hockey."

Mann played junior in Brandon and then intermediate and senior in southern Manitoba. He was at a Providence Reds camp in the late '40s. "Allan Stanley was there," he says. "And Pete Kapusta, from Winnipeg." And Portland, Oregon, where Gordie Haworth played, was after him, but by that time he had a good job in Brandon. In his sixties, with his neatly trimmed white hair and clipped moustache, Mann looks more like a retired colonel from the British army than an ex-prairie hockey player with a rough past.

He says that he probably could have gone further if he'd been able to play more. He's in a restaurant having breakfast. He says, "My mother died in a fire and my dad died in the war, so I was raised by my grandmother and I just couldn't devote the time to hockey I'd have liked to." They were very poor, he says. "She'd take a sled down to the relief stores to bring us food and clothes."

He puts down his cup. "I've had some very bad things happen to me, and some very good things. I think my life could have gone either way. I remember playing ball at Stoney Mountain prison and I'm out in centre field and I hear this voice yelling my name. I look around and finally I look up and there's a guy I know calling down from his cell. That could have been me. Maybe growing up like that made me play hockey the way I did. I was a forward, but I liked the hitting."

Mann's coach in Dauphin was Roy Bentley, the brother of Doug and Max. "He'd send me out with one instruction: 'Hit everybody in sight.' The thing is, you don't see the open-ice checks now the way you used to. Lots of banging into the boards, but not real hitting. I played with Bryan Hextall after he came down from the Rangers and I asked him once what the difference was between the guy that makes it and the guy that doesn't quite. He said consistency. You've got to deliver every game. They have to be able to count on you. In my case, some coaches liked my style, and some didn't. But I never forgot what Hextall said."

Mann is retired from his senior management job with Simplot Canada, the large chemical fertilizer manufacturer, and lives well. "But I owe my grandmother a lot," he says. "I know that things could have gone either way if it hadn't been for her. It wasn't an easy time out here when I was growing up."

• • •

Barry Edgar, like Mann, was a hockey player. He's a small man, in glasses and a big parka. "Size was never an issue. I never thought of it," he says. "They'd try to intimidate you, that was the name of the game, but there were tricks to look after yourself. The end of the rink in those days was covered with wire mesh. You learned to jump when you went into the corner, to make sure your head was up so when you were hit you could keep your face out of it."

Edgar is sixty-four. He played and coached intermediate and senior hockey in Pierson, Killarney, Russell, and Mileta during the years when every farming community had a team and every boy wanted to play for the Wheat Kings or the Winnipeg Monarchs or the Portage Terriers. "Being farmers meant we didn't have too much to do in the winter and that left us a lot of time for practice." He says that as a youngster, when the roads were snowed in, he'd sometimes have to ride a horse to a highway to get a lift to a game. "I'd leave the horse at a neighbour's farm and pick it up on the way home," he says. "The team supplied the sticks but I'd carry the rest of my equipment." He tried out for the Wheat Kings. He didn't make them, but he impressed Jack Adams enough that Adams brought him to a Red Wings camp in Winnipeg. "For a young kid from the farm, that was a big deal even if nothing came of it," he says.

His favourite rink was Pierson, down near the Saskatchewan border, where he played for years. "It was so small it was called the matchbox," he says. "We won our share of away games but in our rink we hardly ever lost. We put together a team that suited that rink. The way it was built, people would climb up and in behind the beam supports. They'd be literally hanging from the rafters." One of his favourite hockey players was Jimmy McFadden, the Calder Trophy winner from Carman, south of Winnipeg. "I've never seen anyone skate the way he did," Edgar says. "He was simply he best I've ever seen. You can't teach skating like that."

Barry Edgar doesn't play oldtimers hockey. It bothers him too much, he says, not to be able to play the way he used to. He says that his only regret in hockey is that he wasn't as smart a player at sixteen as he was at thirty. "Then, things might have turned out differently," he says.

On Saturday night more than six hundred men meet in one of the huge rooms at the Keystone Centre, along from the main arena, for the Wheat Kings' Sportsmen's Dinner. Tickets cost sixty-four dollars apiece. Rick Dillabough says the dinner will raise about ten thousand dollars for the Wheat Kings' education fund for players going on to college or university. The Wheat Kings are in their team sweaters. The paying guests are in a mix of dress ranging from bankers' suits to jeans and sweatshirts. Harry's Ukrainian Kitchen catered the dinner. The main course is baron of beef, but it's the cabbage rolls, and the perogies and sour cream, that go first.

The first Brandon Sportsmen's Dinner was in 1959. The guests of honour that night were Bill Mosienko, "Lefty" Gomez, the great Yankee pitcher of the '30s, and Athol Murray, the hockey priest from Wilcox, Saskatchewan. Andy Gurba, in a blazer and flannels, remembers that first dinner. "I talked with Gomez," he says. "I told him I was a baseball man. What a gentleman he was."

When everyone is finished eating, Brad Park gets up and tells the hockey players that they've got to set their minds on what they want, then do their best to get it, because if they do anything less, they'll fail. "I like that message," Andy says. "That's what I tell my grandson. 'You may be good, but there's always someone better waiting to take your job, so never slack off.' That's what I tell him."

In another part of the Keystone Centre the arena, which last night held nearly five thousand shouting people, is empty and very still. It's hard to see the boards because of the shadows, so the ice, which glistens faintly through the half-light, looks as if it stretches out forever, that one could skate and skate and never have to stop. Jimmy McFadden and Danny Lewicki would have a hell of a time there, if only that were so.

22

Truro, Nova Scotia

April 1998

IT'S THE THURSDAY BEFORE Good Friday, or, as Michael MacDonald puts it, "Holy Thursday." He says, "We drove down from Mabou on Holy Thursday to watch Tommy Beaton play in the Allan Cup but he's been suspended." Mabou is on the west side of Cape Breton Island, about two hours from Truro. "Tommy's uncle and aunt came down, too," MacDonald says. He has a lean face and stiff, curly hair that sticks up at the front, making him look like the singer Lyle Lovett. He's drinking beer in the Bearcat Lounge at the Colchester Legion Stadium, Truro's hockey arena and the home of the Truro TSN Bearcats, Truro's senior team. The Bearcat Lounge is not really a lounge at all, but a big room that stretches across one end of the arena over the ice. Chairs run along the window that is over the ice and they are taken quickly by the early arrivals. Latecomers stand behind them or watch the game on closed-circuit on a big TV set. It's much warmer up there than in the seats below, and there's a bar at each end of the room selling beer and liquor. It's also the only place in the arena where smoking is allowed, and it seems nearly everyone is smoking, and that's got be more than a hundred people. A young man with MacDonald doesn't speak but nods slowly in agreement at everything MacDonald says, gripping his beer glass tightly as if he's worried that somebody might snatch it from him.

MacDonald goes on, "We never knew about the suspension until we bloody well got here. I'm glad we came, though, even if we have to drive all the way back tonight." Tommy Beaton, the man they came to watch, lives in Cape Breton and plays for the Bearcats, who are hosting the Allan Cup playoffs. In last night's game he butt-ended Larry Woo of the Ile des Chênes North Stars, and a butt-end means a match penalty and a two-game suspension. Larry Anthony, the Bearcats' co-general manager, says that Woo speared Beaton in the groin first, "but the ref only saw the butt-end. Tommy should have just dropped the gloves and belted him and he wouldn't have been suspended." Every time Woo has touched the puck since then, the crowd has chanted, "Woo, Woo, Woo."

Truro, in Colchester County, about an hour north of Halifax, is one of those old, graceful towns in a region that was first settled in the mid-1700s. It's a railway centre, which meant a lot when railways were more important — the first railway workers' union was formed here — and Truro still refers to itself as "The Hub of Nova Scotia". Stanfield underwear has its main plant in Truro; Polymer is here, too. The teachers' college closed a few years ago, but the agricultural school is still going. There are two shopping centres and seven Tim Hortons doughnut shops, but the streets in the older part of town are lined with trees and there are tall, gabled houses with the big porches and the long bay windows that are distinctive to the Maritimes. Many of them have widow's walks with wrought-iron railings.

About fourteen thousand people live in Truro proper, maybe thirty thousand if farming communities around it such as Bible Hill and Brookfield and Onslow are included. But even though they've been playing hockey here for nearly a hundred years, Nova Scotia has won just one Allan Cup. The Halifax Wolverines were victorious in 1935. Tommy Beaton was expected to be among the players to change that.

Under the present Allan Cup set-up, the host team qualifies automatically for the four-team tournament. The other qualifiers this year are B.C.'s Powell River Regals, who are the defending champions, the Ile des Chênes North Stars, from Manitoba, and the MacMaster Chev Admirals, from London, Ontario. The teams have a good mix of young and old players, with a smattering of ex-pros, some with NHL experience.

The Truro Bearcats play in New Brunswick's Northumberland Dairy League because there's no longer a Triple-A senior league in Nova Scotia. In fact, Nova Scotia doesn't even have another Triple-A senior team. "That's why this is it, our last year," says the team's owner, Stu Rath, the man who also owns the Junior Bearcats. "Without a league in Nova Scotia it's too hard to operate. Win, lose, or draw, this is our final season."

Jim Foley, Bearcats co-GM with Larry Anthony, is a burly, gruff man who works for Nova Scotia social services. He says, "Yeah, we got to face it, this is the last year for senior. It just doesn't make any sense to have only one senior team in all of Nova Scotia. A few years ago we had Port Hood, Bridgewater, the

Dartmouth Moosehead Mounties, and before that there was the great old Maritime senior league with Sydney and the rest, but interest has really fallen off. It's a question of money. People are spending it on other things. It's the same hockey story everywhere."

Stu Rath is wearing a windbreaker with the TSN logo. TSN bought the sweaters for the Bearcats, but that was all. The team has no actual sponsor. Rath is wealthy but even for someone like him there's a limit. Running hockey in Truro is expensive, getting on for $200,000 a year. "If we win the cup I know there'll be a lot of pressure to defend, but if we do it'll be without me," Rath says. "There's too much travel. And besides being expensive, our players have jobs. It's not like the old days when companies would make allowances for players to be away playing or practising. And on top of all that, it's too hard to build up rivalries and fan support when everybody you play is miles away, out of the province."

Foley says, "There's such a demand for players. It's funny to see minor pro hockey taking off in the States more than here. The standard isn't much higher. Hell, we cut a guy who'd played in the east coast league. Most of our players come from within a sixty-mile radius — Halifax-Dartmouth, maybe Antigonish, Port Hawkesbury. Any farther and they'd have trouble making practice. We don't pay them, but we give them gas money. Twenty dollars, say, for Halifax, twenty-five for Antigonish. Farther down the line, forty dollars."

He goes on, "We've won the Nova Scotia championship, the Maritimes senior championship. We've won the eastern Canadian championship twice, beating Ontario. Over the years we've played for the Allan Cup in Stony Plain, Alberta, in Unity, Saskatchewan, and in Powell River, B.C., but we've never won it. This time we're playing here and it'll be the last chance for most of these guys. They've sacrificed a lot over the years. They don't get paid a nickel. All they want is the Allan Cup. And it's the last chance for Nova Scotia, too. That'll be it. No matter what happens Saturday night, we're gone, and there'll be no more top-class senior hockey in Nova Scotia."

The four-team tournament began on Tuesday. By Holy Thursday the Powell River Regals, after two losses, have been eliminated. The team is sitting dispiritedly, some of the players hung over, in the lobby of Keddy's Inn. They are waiting for the van to take them to play their final game against Ile des Chênes. "We'll be playing for our pride, we'll play for that no matter how we feel," Tod English, the Regal veteran, says. "It hurt like hell to get knocked out so we got pretty shit-faced last night." The game is important for Ile des Chênes. A victory would send them directly to Saturday's final, giving them Good Friday to rest up. Instead, the Regals win 6–3.

"Yeah, we were really down," English, who scored a goal, says afterwards. "But we never quit. This is a hell of a team." English looks dead tired. There are dark circles under his eyes and a bruise on his cheek. His underwear is soaked in sweat. The dressing room is long and narrow with low overhead pipes that the players must duck under and there is barely room for their hockey bags, which they must step over. "I can't explain what happened to us here," English says. "We just came up flat in those first two games. I knew that we were a better team than that."

Because the Regals aren't in a league they played only twelve games — including the two in New Westminister in December when they had only half the team — before meeting Stony Plain in the western playoffs. "We figured we'd get more games in but we weren't able to," English says. "We beat Stony Plain okay, but the lack of games did hurt us." Then he adds hurriedly, "That's no excuse, though. We should have done better here."

"It's goddamn amazing that they're here at all," says Cliff Milne, an ex-player and one of a handful of supporters who came all the way from Powell River. "Running an amateur team takes a helluva lot of volunteers and they're harder to find now. Fewer and fewer people have the time. I mean, Jesus, our guys even buy their own sticks."

Erin Ginnell, a big forward who has played in Swift Current, Regina, and Seattle, says he's never been with a team as close as the Regals. Drafted by Washington, Erin is the son of Paddy Ginnell, who coached the old Flin Flon Bombers when they were a major junior team. "We'll be back next year, you'll see," Ginnell says. From the far end of the long room a player calls, "Sure we will. What the hell else are we going to do up there if we don't play hockey?"

Another Regal who says that he'll be back is Ken Clement, and he's thirty-four. Clement played junior in Victoria and Medicine Hat and in the old western pro league. One of his coaches was Paddy Ginnell. "He was a very emotional guy," Clement says. "That was the year he clocked a linesman and took a thirty-five-game suspension."

Clement hasn't been able to play since the first game, when he hurt his right knee. It turned out to be a cracked femur and it is so swollen and misshapen it looks like a couple of softballs. "It's tough with no league and no sponsor," he says. "We have to raise all the money ourselves." He touches his bad knee tenderly. "We're another good example of people playing for the love of the game."

Clement feels that the CHA, the Canadian Hockey Association ("Amateur" has been dropped), should help struggling senior teams. But Bob James, who oversees senior hockey for the CHA, and is in Truro for the cup, says there's not a chance of that. He'd like to find a sponsor for the Allan Cup — it's the only Canadian hockey trophy that isn't sponsored — but he says there's no way individual teams can be helped. "It's not our mandate," he says.

In the second game tonight, London's MacMaster Chev Admirals are playing Truro. The winner goes to the final, the loser will play off tomorrow against Ile des Chênes. The Colchester Legion Stadium can hold around 2,600 people if they're packed in, and they are. As the crowd gets to its feet for O Canada, a middle-aged man yells at an older man several rows ahead of him, "Take your goddamn hat off!" The second man takes it off without turning around. "I hate that," the first man says. His name is Robert Levine. "Jesus, at his age he should know better. This is a great country. The least you can do is take your hat off when they play the national anthem." Then he says, "This is terrific hockey. No floaters like in junior, no prima donnas. These guys are more mature and they give everything they have, otherwise they wouldn't bother to play."

Michael MacDonald, the man who drove from Cape Breton to see Tommy Beaton play, is still at his post in the Bearcat Lounge. He's sorry that Beaton won't be playing, but he's excited about the game. "There isn't anything in the world like hockey," he says, looking down from his corner. "The NHL is screwing it up so badly. It's all flash entertainment and the dollar to them, that's all. As a game, they don't give a shit about it. But here, this is real hockey, hockey's grassroots. It means something. I'd hate to lose this."

MacDonald is talking with Mike Allard. Allard comes from Sault Ste. Marie but he lives in Truro now. "I was weaned on junior hockey, the Greyhounds, Sudbury, North Bay . . . but I love senior hockey. It's their last hurrah. They give it everything they have." A woman sitting next to Allard gets up and asks him to save her chair. She comes back with a cardboard carton of french fries and ketchup. French fries outsell pizza and hot dogs two to one, according to a teenage girl ladling them out at one of the snack bars.

The Bearcats take a 4–3 lead late into the third period and then score an empty-netter, sealing their victory, 5–3. The room erupts with cheers and shouts and Cory O'Handley, one of the TV broadcasters, yells, "Truro's in the finals, the TSN Bearcats are in the Allan Cup final. They did it!" O'Handley is young, red-haired, and excitable, pacing around while he calls the game from a small space at the end of the lounge. "Wow," says Jim Foley, sitting back, "Wow, that feels good." He's been watching the game on the TV in the lounge. He lights another cigarette. "We're one step closer and we sure can use that day off." The crowd is happy as it files out into the spring-like night. Some of the young are wearing only short-sleeved shirts, it's that warm.

It's Good Friday and snow and freezing rain are falling and have been all day. A cold northeast wind is gusting in from the Atlantic. It's hard to believe that yesterday was like early summer. Inside the Colchester Legion Stadium, standing by the window in the Bearcat Lounge, watching the players warm up, is Cal Marvin. Marvin is seventy-four, a slim, white-haired man from Warroad, Minnesota. He's wearing a Warroad Lakers red, white, and blue windbreaker.

He owned the Lakers, who won Allan Cups three years in a row, 1994 to 1996. But that was it. He had to fold the team. "We couldn't keep going," Marvin says. "We couldn't get any competition. We didn't have anyone to play." He speaks softly but forcefully. He's seriously bothered by his team's fate. Marvin's son, Dave, and another former Laker play for Ile des Chênes. "They wanted to keep playing even though their old team is finished," he says.

It's less noisy up in the lounge tonight. For one thing, Truro isn't playing. For another, the bars are closed because it's Good Friday. Marvin moves a big cigar around in his mouth. "This is the first time in seven years Warroad hasn't been in the Allan Cup," he says wistfully. "You know one year we won thirty-five games and lost only one and the next year no one would play us? We tried to get into a league in Manitoba, but we couldn't do that either."

He goes on, "Warroad is a great hockey town. My brother built a state-of-the-art arena. Olympic size. Theatre seats. Just for hockey. Oh, maybe some figure skating, but no rock concerts, no car shows, no tractor pulls. Only hockey. High school and college now. I don't think you'll see senior there again. It won't be back." Marvin sucks on his cigar. "You know we only have sixteen hundred people in Warroad and we have six Olympic medals, three of them gold?" He names the brothers, Bill and Roger Christian, who won hockey golds in 1960, and Bill's son, Dave, who won a gold in 1980 and went on to the NHL. "You know," he says, not taking his eyes from the players below him, "I'm like an alcoholic with hockey. I can't get enough of it."

At rinkside, having a coffee, is Aubrey Rogers. He's eighty-three and has been around Truro all his life except for three years in the late '30s mining gold underground in Quebec. He's a small man with big glasses and he's wearing a natty tweed cap. He has no thumb or forefinger on his left hand. "That wasn't from mining," he says, holding up the hand. "I liked it underground. I only came back because of my family. I was working for CN here and something hanging off a moving car hit me. God, there was blood everywhere."

Rogers says that he began going to hockey games in 1927, "when the roads were mud, they didn't even have gravel, and they were so narrow that trees brushed the wagons taking us to the old arena . . . three games for fifteen cents with Onslow, North River, McClure's Mills, and Bible Hill . . ." and he has never stopped. "I saw a lot of hockey when I was in Quebec in the old mines league. The Carnegie brothers, Ozzie and Herbie, were there," Rogers says. "They could have played in the NHL but they wouldn't let them in because they were coloured, which was awful. Manny McIntyre was coloured, from New Brunswick. He went up there, too."

Rogers has a pass for all the Allan Cup games, season's tickets for the juniors, and tried to get to most of the seniors' games. When he's not at the rink, he's watching hockey on TV. Like many people of his age, he doesn't like some of today's play. "There's less skill now," he says. "I don't care what Don Cherry or anyone else says. It's dump it in and chase. The interference is dreadful. I'm really worried that the game is breaking down." In part, he blames the referees for inconsistent calls. Still, he'll likely be back next year for more, although he can't stand the music. "It's far too loud," he complains. "About eight out of ten people growl about it. They say they go to a hockey game, not a musical. You can't even talk to the person beside you, it's that bad."

On the ice, Ile des Chênes quickly take a 3–0 lead over London and Dennis Bean keeps insisting, "This isn't a 3–0 game, at least it shouldn't be." He's from North Bay, Ontario, and is wearing a Sturgeon Falls hockey windbreaker. His son Tim, who played junior for North Bay and then for four years with the Newmarket Saints when they were Toronto's AHL team, is with the MacMaster Chev Admirals. Dennis Bean is standing in a corner from where he can see the whole ice surface. He looks around at the crowd and says in near-awe, "This is great support. It reminds me of the old northern Ontario league, Sudbury, the Soo. These guys sure have a hard time quitting playing. But if they were up in Ontario now they'd be lucky to have a couple of hundred watching. It's too bad." This is the first time Bean and his wife, Sandy, have been to the Maritimes. "The people gave us a big welcome," he says. "Yesterday we went into Halifax and then to Peggy's Cove. I guess you get this far you got to see Peggy's Cove. Thank God for yesterday's weather."

An elderly man in the crowd collapses and, while the game goes on, paramedics slap an oxygen mask on him and take him out on a stretcher. An equally elderly man, in a Boston Red Sox cap, points to a spot across the rink. He says, "One night a woman died right there, right in the middle of a game. When that got around it sure quieted things down for a while."

Bean was right about it not being a 3–0 game. The MacMaster Chev Admirals tie it 4–4 late in the third period and then score the winning goal in the second overtime. It's almost midnight. In less than twenty-four hours they'll play the Truro Bearcats for the Allan Cup.

Outside, in the cold and wind, people are scraping the freezing rain from their windshields. They're in remarkably good humour, hardly a curse to be heard. "It's only April," a young man explains. "What do you expect, July? Anyway, if we win tomorrow, who cares?"

By early Saturday afternoon the weather has cleared partly, a milky sun is shining in fits and starts, and it's not quite so cold. About two o'clock, Bruce Campbell, a native of Cape Breton, has returned from the Bearcats' skate to his motel to rest until tonight's final game, the one that will decide the Allan Cup, Truro's last hurrah. At thirty-nine, Campbell is the oldest player on the team. He's listed at six feet and two hundred pounds, but he's clean-shaven and with his fair hair and in shorts and a T-shirt he seems smaller, and much younger. Campbell hasn't played competitive hockey for four years. He's an assistant coach with Cape Breton's major junior team, the Screaming Eagles, and he could only join the Bearcats a week ago when the Screaming Eagles were eliminated from the playoffs.

"There comes a time when you have to quit because of age, job, family, whatever," he says, "but I found I hadn't reached that yet. I beat out Brent Sutter for Junior A player of the year in 1980. I played senior and in the AHL and when I returned to university at thirty I played there. I've been to two NHL camps, the Jets and the Nordiques. It's hard when you don't make it. It hurts like hell when you're cut. But each time I thought of quitting, someone would call and I'd say, 'Okay, one more.' Jim Foley has been trying to get me for the Allan Cup for years so when he called again this year I said I'd play if I were free. He asked me what I wanted and I said room and gas money, that's all, and he said, 'That's good because that's all we got.'"

In 1984–85 Campbell was playing for Corner Brook in Newfoundland when they lost the Allan Cup four games to three to the Thunder Bay Twins after leading the series 3–0. "That's one of the reasons I came back, to get that Allan Cup," Campbell says. "You never forget losing a series like that, and now I've been given another chance. But this is it. I'm thirty-nine. Who knows, maybe I'll make the NHL through coaching as I couldn't as a player. I'll tell you, coaching is very demanding, very draining, but right now playing for the Allan Cup is what has me excited. And another great thing has happened. My dad still plays hockey twice a week and he's seventy-two and last week they retired his sweater and mine. They're hanging in our arena in New Waterford, on Cape Breton, my dad's sweater and mine, side by side."

This evening, about ten minutes past seven, twenty minutes before game time, there's a public appeal over the PA system at the Colchester Legion Stadium: "Could everybody shove together a bit, everybody please; we have more people trying to get in." At one end of the rink a security officer looks around: "She's busting at the seams tonight."

Up in the Bearcat Lounge the two bars, with Good Friday well behind them, are back in business. Close to two hundred men and women are there, many of them in the Bearcats black-and-yellow colours. They're standing three deep along the glass, the ones in the back on tip-toes, craning their necks to see. Others are watching the large TV, listening to the play-by-play from Cory O'Handley, who is pacing about with his mike on his headset, and his broadcast partner, Hoppy Dunn. It's like a big party and it begins to take off when Truro's Darren Welsh scores only a little more than a minute in. At thirty-five, Welsh is the oldest on the team after Bruce

Campbell. Like Campbell, he saw some action with the Cape Breton Oilers when they were in the AHL. There's another roar three minutes later when Sandy MacKenzie, a Truro native, scores a short-handed goal. MacKenzie, who played in Europe before joining the Bearcats two years ago, is one of the smallest players, weighing less than 170 pounds. The crowd takes up the chant: "Sandy, Sandy, Sandy . . ."

Jim Foley, in his Bearcats windbreaker, is in his place in front of the big TV screen. Someone claps him on the back and Foley says, without looking away from the screen, that the game is far from over. His face shows very little, but his right leg is moving up and down like a piston and he's smoking one cigarette after another. Not quite chainsmoking, but close to it. Truro score again before the period is over and the second period is less than two minutes old when Truro make it 4–0. London finally score and the second period ends 4–1.

Stan "Chook" Maxwell, whom many people say was the best hockey player ever to come out of Truro, is in the Bearcat Lounge. He's sixty-three and he was also a very good baseball player, sought by the old Milwaukee Braves. "I agreed to go south with them but each spring the hockey playoffs were on so I couldn't," he says. Maxwell played junior hockey in Quebec, Trois-Rivières, and for the Montreal Royals. "I left Truro pretty young, fifteen, sixteen years old, and I went up to Quebec, away from home, a change of language and atmosphere," he says. "You're kind of shy and all but it worked out fine for me although it was a bit hard at times. Anyway, they must have liked what I had because they kept me on."

Maxwell never made the NHL. He was at a couple of Boston Bruin camps and played in the Quebec senior league for Punch Imlach in Quebec City and in Chicoutimi for Gerry Plamondon, the ex-Canadien. "Gerry told me when you're in alone on the goalie, give him that split-second hesitation and go for the short side, always the short side. I learned to do that and I became a scorer because of him." Maxwell also played for Kingston and Ottawa–Hull in the old eastern league, for the Los Angeles Blades in the western league, and for Toledo in the international league. He was teammate of Willie O'Ree, the first black to play in the NHL. Like O'Ree, Maxwell is black, but he can't say whether that hurt his NHL chances. "For one thing, I'm quite fair-skinned," he says. "So I'm not sure how many people would even have noticed. Another thing, it was a six-team league, hard to make it anyway. The players were very close. It was a 'Buddy-Buddy' thing. They had their own jobs to protect. You can't blame them. They weren't about to make someone look good who was trying to take a job away from them or from a pal. And back then, if management didn't like you, for any reason, colour or not, they could bury you. But it definitely hurt Herb Carnegie. He should have been up there."

Maxwell says he met a lot of great hockey players on the way up and down. He mentions Marcel Bonin, Henri Richard, Eddie Johnston, and Leo Labine. Real Chevrefils, many people's pick as the most tragic example of the power of booze, was on his way down when Maxwell played with him in Los Angeles. "He had tremendous ability," Maxwell says. "It was awful what happened to him. You know, after a game we'd go for a beer and I'm not kidding when I say he would have twenty to my two. They brought his wife out to try to help him, but they had a real brawl in a bar and she nearly scratched his face off so they had to send her home. And, you know, sober, he was the nicest guy in the world."

Maxwell smiles. He says, "I've never regretted for a minute anything that happened to me in hockey. I figure I'm really lucky. For a guy like me, to come from a small town like Truro and do the things I did, meet the people I did, and see the things I've seen, well, it's hard to beat."

At the far end of the Bearcat Lounge, in his usual place, with a good view of the ice surface, is Mike Allard, the man from the Soo. He got there early and hasn't moved much. His seat is five feet from one of the bars. The window over the ice is open and he can lean out to cheer. "This is great, eh? They're going to do it. Jesus, the Bearcats, in their last year, and they're going to win the Allan Cup." He says that Michael MacDonald, the man who'd driven down from Cape Breton a couple of games ago, hasn't been around. "I guess he couldn't get back." He laughs. "After this I better get home myself. I have a fiancée and between the junior and senior playoffs she's hardly seen me the last month."

The third period is almost anticlimactic. The Bearcats score two more. They win 6–1 and Truro has its first Allan Cup, and in all likelihood its last. Jim Foley's leg stops jerking; he shakes a few hands, butts his cigarette, and heads down to see his team.

While the Bearcats mob each other, the London players stand along their blue line waiting for the ritual handshake, sweating, silent, and disconsolate. Most of them, leaning on their sticks, have their heads down. Around them, the crowd keeps up its yelling. Jim Foley and Larry Anthony, the associate GM, have joined the Truro players, hugging and slapping backs. Even the unassuming Stu Rath has appeared on the ice. On the London side of the rink, the equipment manager is moving the sticks and water bottles and first-aid kits into the Admirals' dressing room. "We did okay for a team cobbled together in less than a year," he says of London's return to senior hockey after more than twenty years. Back on the ice, the handshakes have finally begun. Jim Laing, the big Bearcat defenceman, is embraced by several of the London players whom he knows from his days playing senior in Ontario.

The corridor outside the Bearcat's steamy dressing room is jammed with fans. The players, when they're finally able to leave the ice, have a hard time pushing through them. Bruce Campbell calls out over the din. "I jump back into hockey for a week and get an Allan Cup."

"Jesus, it's just great," says Steve Gordon. Gordon is a twenty-nine-year-old forward who won the league scoring title three years ago. He played with a messy eight-stitch cut on his chin which is red and ugly against his white face.

After junior in Halifax, Gordon went to University College of Cape Breton. He's been with the Bearcats for five years. He travels for Maple Leaf Foods. "I think this is the hardest I've ever had to play, getting back from road trips at four-thirty in the morning and then having to go to work," he says. "A few years ago we got some money, but now it's just expenses. And practices all over the place, not only here, wherever we could get ice — Brookfield, New Glasgow, Halifax. We even had to play one game at nine in the morning on a Sunday. I can't understand these pros holding out for millions. Jesus, how much do they need? I'd think they'd feel so goddamn lucky just to be able to play. Like I said, we're playing for nothing and it's worth everything we have to put into it."

Jim Laing went shopping for the Allan Cup. He's an accountant in Toronto and signed with the Bearcats in January. He was flown down every weekend for games. According to the Allan Cup program, Laing comes from Dartmouth. "That's a mistake," he says. "I grew up in Seattle." After Junior B out there he played for Clarkson University in northern New York state. He was drafted by Calgary and played in the AHL for Moncton and the IHL for Salt Lake City. Then, figuring the NHL wasn't in the books, he returned to university, this time Concordia, in Montreal, where he got a master's degree in business. He was with the Chomedy Warriors, from outside Montreal, in 1989–90. Chomedy won the Allan Cup that spring, but Laing had had to quit the team to write exams and missed the playoffs. After another year with Chomedy, when it lost the eastern final, Laing moved to Ontario and played three years with the Oshwekan River Hawks in the South Western Ontario Senior Hockey League. Each year the Hawks were knocked out of Allan Cup play. Laing says last summer he got anxious. "I pointed out to the owners that we'd lost two good players, one to the western professional league and another to England, so we'd better recruit. Their attitude was, let's see what happens in training camp. They didn't do anything and we lost the first ten games of the season."

After some negotiations, and learning that Truro wanted him, Laing got his release. "I'd told them that Truro would be hosting the Allan Cup and that they had a good chance to win. Hell, I'm thirty-four. I'm not going to get many more opportunities. They said okay, and they let me go."

Laing says that he'll keep playing as long as he can. "I still have the talent to play at a highly competitive level," he says, "and it keeps you young. I've met so many good people in hockey. And the people in Truro have been wonderful. Another thing, everyone on this team was a team player. Nobody resented the guys like me who signed late. They were there to win and if they could pick someone up who could help, they would. It was worth it all, including the travel every weekend, worth it a thousand percent." Laing pauses. He pulls off his Bearcats sweater for probably the last time. "I've a couple of more years," he goes on, "So I'll begin looking for another Allan Cup contender. Maybe London if they stay in."

The hallway is still jammed outside the Bearcats' dressing room. Tommy Beaton, who was suspended for the final two games, says, "These guys have been playing hockey their whole lives, so to be able to go out with a national championship is incredible. This is our Stanley Cup."

Stu Rath is standing off by himself, accepting congratulations and watching his players push through the crowd. A man heading out a sidedoor calls, "Hey, you got to keep this team going. This is no time to fold it. You can afford it, for Christ's sakes, you're rich." Rath doesn't turn around. Bobby Gordon, Steve Gordon's father, is there, too. He's very excited. Steve is the Bearcat player with the badly cut chin. "Boy, I'm proud of him, proud of all of them," Gordon Sr. says. Then he spies "Chook" Maxwell. "Hey, Chookie, Chookie," he shouts over the noise. He gets through the crowd to Maxwell. "You don't remember me, do you? I used to hit more home runs off you than anybody." He sticks out his hand. "I'm Bobby Gordon." Maxwell, staring hard at him, smiles and says, "Yeah, I remember you now." They shake hands and talk for a few seconds about the old days and baseball.

Afterwards, Maxwell says. "I was an outfielder and played a little infield. When I retired from top-flight ball I went as playing-coach, a hundred dollars a week, to Cape Breton. It barely covered room and board but they treated me like royalty. Anyway, I was used to playing with guys from Triple-A and I had so many baseball smarts that in Cape Breton I even pitched a bit if I was needed. But I can tell you now, not too many guys hit home runs off me even though I wasn't really a pitcher."

For Jim Foley, the end of the team means that he'll look for a spot in Junior A. Some of the Bearcats, he says, such as Steve Gordon, will retire. "They all have young families and they've given up so much already," he says. Others, such as Tommy Beaton, may end up in New Brunswick. "He can get four hundred a game up in Miramichi," Foley says. "They love him up there. But maybe he'll stay at home, pick up 150 playing Senior B in Port Hawkesbury."

Beaton, a veteran of the East Coast Hockey League, is now settled in Port Hawkesbury and works with Stora, a forest industries company. He says, "I'm not sure what I'll do. Miramichi is a long drive, five and a half hours. Maybe playing weekends would be okay, but it's too soon to say."

Jim Foley says, "You got to understand one thing. These guys have won the Allan Cup. Now, if they play next year, they'll play for the buck. They've sacrificed themselves and haven't made any money. But what a feeling. I can't describe it. They won a national championship and that means they go to the Nova Scotia Sports Hall of Fame. Their pictures go up and will always be there. And then, when that Allan Cup goes back to the Hockey Hall of Fame, back to Toronto, the name 'Truro' will be on it, forever."

Afterword

Since the hardcover edition of *Hockey Towns* was published in November 1998, the Truro TSN Bearcats, who won the Allan Cup that spring, ceased operations, as they said they would. The league they played in, New Brunswick's Northumberland Dairy League, has also folded.

Another Cats team, the Thunder Bay Thunder Cats, were bought by a New York company and moved to Rockford, Illinois. They are still in the United Hockey League. Gary Cook, the Cats' former general manager, says that travel and the low Canadian dollar "was just way too much for us." Cook says that Thunder Bay's junior team, the Flyers, may also end up in the United States.

Timmins' Golden Bears of the junior Northern Ontario Hockey Association have gone to nearby Iroquois Falls. Trevor Morden, one of the players I talked with, didn't get his scholarship to a U.S. college. He's hoping to play in Europe.

To the west, things are brighter. In Manitoba, the Stonewall Flyers are thriving. Derek Arbez, their fractious defenceman, played last year with the Lundar Falcons, in the same league. He didn't become a fireman, after all; he's working for CP Rail.

In southeastern Saskatchewan, Frank Pastachak is still drumming up support for his beloved Bienfait Coalers. He says the league is in good shape. More than a thousand people showed up for the league's championship game in Carlyle where the Carlyle Cougars defeated the Carnduff Red Devils 6–5.

And in Nanton, Alberta, the Palominos are going strong, although Blair and Joan Martin are no longer involved. They have their hands full with their own children's hockey.

The Powell River Regals, who were the defending Allan Cup champions when they were ingloriously eliminated in the 1998 playdowns, reached the finals the next year in Stony Plain, Alberta. And in April 2000, in Lloydminster, Saskatchewan, playing five games in five days, they regained the Cup.

Lakefield, Ontario
May 2000

Index